Mathematics

YEAR 5

**David Hillard and
Serena Alexander**

401   1-3

GALORE
PARK

AN HACHETTE UK COMPANY

About the authors

During his long and distinguished career, David Hillard spent more than 45 years teaching mathematics in two preparatory schools. From 1980 to his retirement, he was associated with the Common Entrance Examination at 11+, 12+ and 13+ levels in the role of adviser, assessor or setter, playing a significant role in the revision of the syllabus in 2003 when the present format of the examination was introduced.

Serena Alexander has taught mathematics since 1987, originally in both maintained and independent senior schools. From 1999 she taught at St Paul's School for Boys, where she was Head of mathematics at their Preparatory School, Colet Court, before moving first to Newton Prep as Deputy Head and more recently to Devonshire House. She is an ISI inspector and helps to run regular mathematics conferences for prep school teachers. She has a passion for maths and expects her pupils to feel the same way. After a lesson or two with her, they normally do!

The publishers would like to thank the following for permission to reproduce copyright material:
Photo credits p13 (t) © Bettmann/CORBIS **p13 (b)** © S McTeir / Hodder Education **p14 (t)** © S McTeir / Hodder Education **p14 (b)** © S McTeir / Hodder Education **p16** © Cliff Hide Stock / Alamy **p20 (l)** © Stephen Barnes/ Religion / Alamy **p20 (r)** © bildagentur-online.com/th-foto / Alamy **p21 (tl)** © Todd Bannor / Alamy **p21 (ml)** © Artifex Lucis / Alamy **p21 (bl)** Courtesy of *ProhibitOnions* on Wikimedia Commons (http://en.wikipedia.org/wiki/ File:PapalAssassinationAttemptMarker.jpg). Released into the public domain **p21 (tr)** © CORNERSTONES of NY / Flickr (https://www.flickr.com/photos/28516908@N08/3336608877/sizes/m/in/photostream/) **p21 (mr)** Courtesy of WarpFlyght / Wikimedia Commons (http://commons.wikimedia.org/wiki/Commons:GNU_Free_Documentation_ License_1.2) **p21 (br)** © NPS Photo / Alamy **p23 (l)** © Chris Cooper-Smith / Alamy **p23 (r)** Courtesy of romaryka / Flickr (https://www.flickr.com/photos/romaryka/2557642907/) **p52** © Christian Musat – Fotolia.com **p53** © Topography Resources / Alamy **p162 (tl)** © Simon Morris / Alamy **p162 (tr)** © Robert Mora / Alamy **p162 (b)** © Art Kowalsky / Alamy **p176** © Artranq – Fotolia.com **p242 (t)** © Petro Feketa – Fotolia.com **p242 (b)** © leszekglasner – Fotolia.com **p273** © Steve Mann - Fotolia.com **p277** © cm studio / Alamy **p283 (1p, 2p, 5p, 20p, 50p, £2)** © claudiodivizia - iStockphoto - Thinkstock.com **p283 (10p, £1)** © asafta - iStockphoto - Thinkstock.com **p286** © Michael Flippo - Fotolia **p301** © VStock / Alamy **p324** © Ingram Publishing Limited / Ingram Image Library 500-Food **p327** © Olesia Sarycheva – Fotolia.com **p372** © Sergii Figurnyi – Fotolia.com **p373** Picture taken by Sharon McTeir

Acknowledgements This product includes mapping data licensed from Ordnance Survey ® reproduced by permission of Ordnance Survey on behalf of HMSO. © Crown copyright 2014. Ordnance Survey Licence number 150001477. Ordnance Survey and the OS symbol are registered trademarks and Explorer and Landranger are trademarks of the Ordnance Survey, the national mapping agency of Great Britain.

Every effort has been made to trace all copyright holders, but if any have been inadvertently overlooked the publishers will be pleased to make the necessary arrangements at the first opportunity.

Although every effort has been made to ensure that website addresses are correct at time of going to press, Galore Park cannot be held responsible for the content of any website mentioned in this book. It is sometimes possible to find a relocated web page by typing in the address of the home page for a website in the URL window of your browser.

Hachette UK's policy is to use papers that are natural, renewable and recyclable products and made from wood grown in sustainable forests. The logging and manufacturing processes are expected to conform to the environmental regulations of the country of origin.

Orders: please contact Bookpoint Ltd, 130 Milton Park, Abingdon, Oxon OX14 4SB. Telephone: +44 (0)1235 827827. Lines are open 9.00a.m.–5.00p.m., Monday to Saturday, with a 24-hour message answering service. Visit our website at www.galorepark.co.uk for details of other revision guides for Common Entrance, examination papers and Galore Park publications.

Published by Galore Park Publishing Ltd
An Hachette UK company
Carmelite House, 50 Victoria Embankment,
London EC4Y 0DZ
www.galorepark.co.uk

Text copyright © David Hillard and Serena Alexander 2014

The right of David Hillard and Serena Alexander to be identified as the authors of this Work has been asserted by them in accordance with sections 77 and 78 of the Copyright, Designs and Patents Act 1988.

Impression number 10 9 8 7 6 5
2022 2021 2020 2019 2018

All rights reserved. No part of this publication may be sold, reproduced, stored in a retrieval system, or transmitted, in any form or by any means, electronic, mechanical, photocopying, recording, or otherwise, without either the prior written permission of the copyright owner or a licence permitting restricted copying issued by the Copyright Licensing Agency, Saffron House, 6–10 Kirby Street, London EC1N 8TS.

Typeset in India
Printed in Dubai
Illustrations by Ian Moores and Aptara, Inc

A catalogue record for this title is available from the British Library.

ISBN: 978 1 471829 38 3

Contents

Introduction

This book is for pupils in Year 5. The authors aim to provide a sound and varied foundation on which pupils can build in the future. There is plenty of material to support this but, at the same time, there are possibilities for the more able to be extended.

The authors do not wish to dictate to either pupil or teacher. A combination of approaches, the more modern 'mental' and the more historical 'traditional', are both explored, so that the appropriate method for the individual can be adopted.

There is no prescribed teaching order. Topics may well be taught more than once during the year. The authors are convinced that it is the teacher who knows what is best for each individual pupil – and when each topic should be introduced.

⇨ Notes on features in this book

Words printed in blue and bold are keywords. All keywords are defined in the Glossary at the end of the book.

> Useful rules and reminders, looking like this, are scattered throughout the book.

Worked examples are given throughout to aid understanding of each part of a topic.

Activity

Mathematics is so often a question of patterns. Many chapters end with a freestanding activity, either numerical or spatial, to cover this aspect of the subject.

For some questions and activities, pupils are asked to copy diagrams from the book. They may find tracing paper helpful when doing this. Such activities are also supported by separate worksheets. These worksheets may be photocopied from the section at the back of the answers (available separately).

1 Introducing investigations

⇨ Investigating number patterns

Look at these two columns of numbers.

What do you need to do to each number in Column A, to arrive at the number in Column B?

Column A		Column B
1	→	2
2	→	3
3	→	4
4	→	5
5	→	6

Did you add 1? If so, you are correct because:

1 + **1**	=	2
2 + **1**	=	3
3 + **1**	=	4
4 + **1**	=	5
5 + **1**	=	6

If you add 1 to the number in Column A, you get the number in Column B.

Now look at these two columns.

What do you need to do this time, to turn the number in Column A into the number in Column B?

Column A		Column B
1	→	2
2	→	4
3	→	6
4	→	8
5	→	10

If your answer is 'double' or 'multiply by 2', you are correct because:

$1 \times \mathbf{2}$	=	2
$2 \times \mathbf{2}$	=	4
$3 \times \mathbf{2}$	=	6
$4 \times \mathbf{2}$	=	8
$5 \times \mathbf{2}$	=	10

The calculation you perform on the number in Column A, in order to make the new number in Column B, is called a function.

Some functions have more than one step.

What is happening here?

Column A		Column B
1	→	3
2	→	5
3	→	7
4	→	9
5	→	11

Look at the difference between consecutive numbers in Column B. It is always 2 ($5 - 3 = 2$, $7 - 5 = 2$, and so on). This suggests that the function may have something to do with the 2 times table.

Make a new column (C) and write down the 2 times table.

What can you do to the numbers in Column C to make them match those in Column B?

Column A		Column B	Column C
1	→	3	2
2	→	5	4
3	→	7	6
4	→	9	8
5	→	11	10

The answer is 'add 1'.

So, you have multiplied each number in Column A by 2 and then added 1 to the result, to make the number in Column B.

$$(1 \times \mathbf{2} = 2) + \mathbf{1} = 3$$
$$(2 \times \mathbf{2} = 4) + \mathbf{1} = 5$$
$$(3 \times \mathbf{2} = 6) + \mathbf{1} = 7$$
$$(4 \times \mathbf{2} = 8) + \mathbf{1} = 9$$
$$(5 \times \mathbf{2} = 10) + \mathbf{1} = 11$$

To help you find the function rule, look for the differences between consecutive numbers in Column B. If the differences are all the same, the function is based on a times table.

The function is 'multiply by 2 and add 1'.

Examples:

What functions have been used here?

(i)

Column A		Column B	
1	→	1	2
2	→	3	4
3	→	5	6
4	→	7	8
5	→	9	10

Look at the difference between the numbers in Column B first.

The differences are all 2

The function is 'multiply by 2 and subtract 1'

$$(1 \times \mathbf{2} = 2) - \mathbf{1} = 1$$
$$(2 \times \mathbf{2} = 4) - \mathbf{1} = 3, \text{ and so on.}$$

(ii)

Column A		Column B	
1	→	5	*3*
2	→	8	*6*
3	→	11	*9*
4	→	14	*12*
5	→	17	*15*

C

The difference between consecutive numbers in Column B is always 3. This suggests that the function rule may have something to do with the 3 times table.

The function is 'multiply by 3 and add 2'

$(1 \times 3 = 3) + 2 = 5$

$(2 \times 3 = 6) + 2 = 8$, and so on.

Once you know what the function is, you can find other pairs of numbers. For example, look again at Example (i) on the previous page. What number would you write in Column B, if the number in Column A was 6?

Column A		Column B
6	→	?

Use the function you discovered earlier: 'multiply by 2 and subtract 1'.

To find ? $6 \times 2 = 12$ then subtract 1, $12 - 1 = 11$

$? = 11$

The number in Column B is 11.

What number would you write in Column B, if the number in Column A was 25?

Column A		Column B
25	→	?

To find ? $25 \times 2 = 50$ then subtract 1, $50 - 1 = 49$

$? = 49$

Try the following example yourself.

Examples:

Look again at Example (ii) on the previous page.

(i) What number would you write in Column B, if the number in Column A was 6?

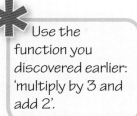

Use the function you discovered earlier: 'multiply by 3 and add 2'.

If the number in Column A is 6, the number in Column B is 20 because 6 × **3** = 18 and 18 + **2** = 20

(ii) What number would you write in Column B if the number in Column A was 20?

If the number in Column A is 20, the number in Column B is 62 because 20 × **3** = 60 and 60 + **2** = 62

Inverse of a function

In the previous section, you worked out the function that generated the numbers in Column B, when you knew the numbers in Column A. You can also do this in reverse. If you know the number in Column B, you can work out the corresponding number in Column A by using the inverse of the function. This means you reverse the calculation.

Function	Inverse function
×	÷
÷	×
+	−
−	+

Look at Example (i) on the page before last again. The function was 'multiply by 2 and subtract 1'.

The inverse of this function is 'add 1 and then divide by 2'

Notice that you **must** add the 1 first and **then** divide the result by 2

This is the complete reverse of the function.

Imagine that you are reversing through the commands of the original function.

Column A   **Column B**

   5   →   9   Function is 'multiply by 2 and subtract 1'

   6   →   11

Therefore, inverse function is 'add 1 and divide by 2'

   a ←   13 $13 + \mathbf{1} = 14$ and $14 \div \mathbf{2} = 7$
So $a = 7$

   b ←   41 $41 + \mathbf{1} = 42$ and $42 \div \mathbf{2} = 21$
So $b = 21$

Try the following example yourself.

Examples:

Look at Example (ii) on the page before last again. The function was 'multiply by 3 and then add 2', so the inverse function is 'subtract 2 and then divide by 3'

(i)   What number would you write in Column A, if the number in Column B was 23?

     If the number in Column B is 23, the number in Column A is 7 because $23 - \mathbf{2} = 21$ and then $21 \div \mathbf{3} = 7$

(ii)   What number would you write in Column A, if the number in Column B was 65?

     If the number in Column B is 65, the number in Column A is 21 because $65 - \mathbf{2} = 63$ and $63 \div \mathbf{3} = 21$

Exercise 1.1

For each of the patterns (a) to (f) below:

1 Write down, in words, what you do to change the numbers in Column A into the numbers in Column B.

2 Find the values of the letters in each pattern.

(a)
Column A		Column B
1	→	3
2	→	4
3	→	5
4	→	6
5	→	7
8	→	a
b	←	17

(b)
Column A		Column B
1	→	3
2	→	6
3	→	9
4	→	12
5	→	15
7	→	c
d	←	36

(c)
Column A		Column B
1	→	5
2	→	7
3	→	9
4	→	11
5	→	13
9	→	e
f	←	53

(d)
Column A		Column B
1	→	2
2	→	5
3	→	8
4	→	11
5	→	14
15	→	g
h	←	59

(e)
Column A		Column B
1	→	5
2	→	9
3	→	13
4	→	17
5	→	21
10	→	i
j	←	101

(f)
Column A		Column B
1	→	0
2	→	2
3	→	4
4	→	6
5	→	8
16	→	k
l	←	98

⇨ Investigating shape patterns

You can apply what you have learned about number patterns to patterns made from shapes.

These patterns of squares are made from lines and dots.

Look at these patterns. Can you work out what the next patterns in the sequence will look like?

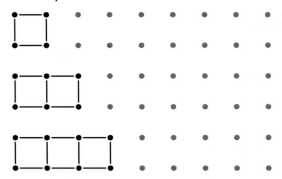

Example:

Draw the next two patterns in the sequence of lines and dots.

The next two patterns have 4 squares and 5 squares.

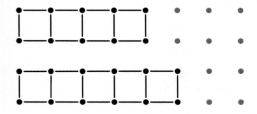

You can use a table like this one to record details of the patterns.

Number of squares	Number of lines	Number of dots
1	4	4
2	7	6
3	10	8
4	13	10
5	16	12

You now have a pattern of numbers like those you saw in the first part of this chapter.

You can use what you learned, there, to work out the functions that link:

- the number of squares to the number of lines
- the number of squares to the number of dots.

| squares | → | lines | 'multiply by 3 and add 1' |
| squares | → | dots | 'multiply by 2 and add 2' |

Now you can use these functions to answer questions.

Examples:

(i) How many lines are there in the pattern with 8 squares?

The function is 'multiply by 3 and add 1' (squares → lines).

$8 \times 3 = 24$ $24 + 1 = 25$

There are 25 lines in the pattern with 8 squares.

(ii) How many dots are there in the pattern with 25 squares?

The function is 'multiply by 2 and add 2' (squares → dots).

$25 \times 2 = 50$ $50 + 2 = 52$

There are 52 dots in the pattern with 25 squares.

(iii) How many squares are there, when the number of lines is 34?

This time you need to look at things in reverse by using the inverse function of squares → lines, which is 'subtract 1 and divide by 3'

$34 - 1 = 33$ $33 \div 3 = 11$

There are 11 squares when the number of lines is 34.

(iv) There are 202 dots. How many squares are there?

This time you need to look at the inverse function of squares → dots, which is 'subtract 2 and divide by 2'

$202 - 2 = 200$ $200 \div 2 = 100$

There are 100 squares when there are 202 dots.

Exercise 1.2

1 This pattern is made with vertical and horizontal lines.

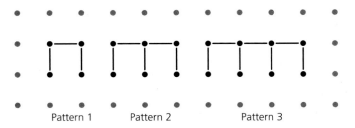

Pattern 1   Pattern 2   Pattern 3

(a) Draw patterns 4 and 5

(b) Copy and complete this table.

Pattern number	Number of horizontal lines	Number of vertical lines	Total number of lines
1	1	2	3
2	2	3	5
3			
4			
5			

First work out the functions for:

pattern number → horizontal lines

pattern number → vertical lines

pattern number → total number of lines

and the inverse functions of each of them.

(c) How many horizontal lines are there in pattern 19?

(d) How many vertical lines are there in pattern 38?

(e) What is the total number of lines in pattern 41?

(f) Which pattern number has 71 vertical lines?

(g) Which pattern number has a total of 101 lines?

(h) What is the largest pattern number that can be made with 145 lines?

2 This pattern is made with lines and dots.

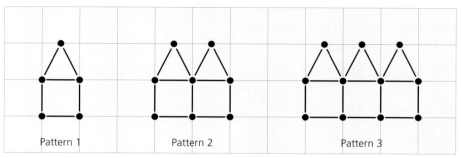

Pattern 1   Pattern 2   Pattern 3

(a) Draw patterns 4 and 5

(b) Copy and complete this table.

Pattern number	Number of lines	Number of dots
1	6	5
2	11	8
3		
4		
5		

(c) Work out the functions for the number of lines.

(d) Work out the function for the number of dots.

(e) How many lines are there in pattern 10?

(f) How many dots are there in pattern 12?

(g) Which pattern number has 101 lines?

(h) Which pattern number has 149 dots?

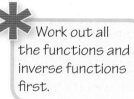

Work out all the functions and inverse functions first.

Activity – A mathematical magic trick

Try this mathematical magic trick. See if you can find out how it works.

There are some hints after the instructions!

1 Copy these grids onto card, and cut them out.

1	3	5
7	9	11
13	15	

2	3	6
7	10	11
14	15	

4	5	6
7	12	13
14	15	

8	9	10
11	12	13
14	15	

2 Ask a friend to look at the cards and pick any number, from 1 to 15, at random.

3 Ask your friend to give you back the cards that contain the chosen number.

You will always be able to tell what number your friend picked!

 Look at the numbers at the top left-hand corner of those cards with your friend's number on them. What do they add up to?

Roman numerals

If you had lived in Britain two thousand years ago, you would not be using the numerals that we use today. In Roman Britain, you would have used Roman numerals.

⇨ Introducing Roman numerals

Just as everyone does today, the Romans started counting with their fingers...

■ I 1

and when they got to five they had used a whole hand.

■ V 5

Look how the thumb and first finger make a letter V. When the Romans started to write numbers, they used V for 5

For ten, they needed all the fingers on both hands. Holding their hands this way made an X.

■ X 10

Exercise 2.1

Work with a partner, taking turns to make the numbers with your hands.

1 Use one hand to make a shape to represent three or four.
  Did your partner work out the right number?

2 Use two hands to make a shape to represent eight or nine.
  Did your partner work out the right number?

3 The Latin word for 'hundred' is *centum*. Make up a hand shape for C, *centum*.

4 The Latin word for 'thousand' is *mille*. Make a hand shape for M, *mille*.

5 Take turns with your partner to make up a hand shape for 50 Whose is better?

6 Take turns with your partner to make up a hand shape for 500 Whose is better?

7 Now you have some basic numbers, experiment and make up combinations such as 21. Using only your hands, demonstrate each number you choose.
Take turns to guess each other's numbers.

The Romans used L for 50 and D for 500. How close was your hand shape to that?

⇨ Reading and writing Roman numerals

Adding

Now you know that 1 is represented by I, 5 by V, 10 by X, 50 by L and 100 by C.

The Romans used a form of addition to make most of the other numbers.

Examples:

(i) What number does VII represent?

VII is V + I + I or 5 + 1 + 1, which is 7

(ii) What number does XXV represent?

XXV is X + X + V or 10 + 10 + 5, which is 25

Exercise 2.2

Write down the numbers that the Roman numerals represent.

1 II	**5** XII	**9** CLXIII
2 III	**6** XX	**10** CLXVI
3 VI	**7** LI	**11** CX
4 VIII	**8** LXI	**12** CLI

One number before another – taking away

All the numbers you found in Exercise 2.2 ended in 1, 2, 3, 6, 7, 8 or 0

You might expect that the Romans wrote 4 as IIII and 9 as VIIII and sometimes they did. But they also used subtracted forms such as IV for 4 (1 less 5) and IX for 9 (1 less than 10). This is how we write these Roman numerals today.

To make the numbers easier to write, they put a smaller number before the bigger number. For example, they wrote 4 as IV (one before five) and 40 as XL (10 before 50).

Examples:

(i) What number does IX represent?

IX is 1 before 10, so this represents 9

(ii) What number does XC represent?

XC is 10 before 100, so this represents 90

Exercise 2.3

Write down the numbers that the Roman numerals represent.

1 IV   5 XXIX   9 CLIX

2 XIV   6 XLV   10 XCIX

3 IX   7 XCVI   11 CXCV

4 LIX   8 CCXLVIII   12 CXLIX

Now that you have tried converting Roman numerals to ordinary numbers, try doing it the other way round.

Exercise 2.4

Write these numbers in Roman numerals.

1 3   6 56

2 7   7 38

3 22   8 49

4 15   9 62

5 29   10 84

11 92   16 72

12 164   17 69

13 94   18 35

14 47   19 190

15 89   20 194

D and M

The next two Roman numerals are D for five hundred and M for a thousand.

Larger numbers are made up in just the same way, by adding together the values.

MDCX = 1000 + 500 + 100 + 10 = 1610

You still need to take care with 4s, 9s, 40s and 90s.

MDXC = 1000 + 500 + 90 = 1590

Example:

What does this represent?

MDCCCLXXXVIII = 1000 + 500 + 100 + 100 + 100 + 50 + 10 + 10 + 10 +
5 + 1 + 1 + 1
= 1888

Exercise 2.5

Write down the numbers that the Roman numerals represent.

1 DC	**5** DCCCIV	**9** MDXCIV
2 MC	**6** MD	**10** CXC
3 MCC	**7** MDCIX	**11** MDCXCIX
4 DIX	**8** MXCIV	**12** MCMLXIV

Lower-case letters

Roman numerals can be written as lower case letters too, although we do not usually do this for numbers over 39, i.e. numbers using L, C, D or M.

Examples:

What do these Roman numerals represent?

(i) **iii** = 1 + 1 + 1 = 3

(ii) **iv** = 5 − 1 = 4

(iii) **ccv** = 100 + 100 + 5 = 205

Exercise 2.6

Write down the number that these Roman numerals represent.

1 xiii	**5** MI	**9** CLIX
2 xxiv	**6** xxxviii	**10** XCIX
3 DLIX	**7** XCVI	**11** xvii
4 CMXLIV	**8** CDXLVIII	**12** MDXLVI

To the left or to the right?

In question 10, you should have worked out that XCIX represents 90 + 9 = 99

You might think that you could write 99 as IC, because it is one less than a hundred, but that is not how the Romans did it.

When you are writing numerals before or to the left of another one, their value cannot be less than one-tenth of the value of the numeral to the right.

So you can write:

IV (4)   IX (9)   XL (40)   XC (90)

CD (400)   CM (900)

Traditionally, CD and CM were not used on buildings, so you may sometimes see CCCC (400) and DCCCC (900).

Exercise 2.7

Write these numbers as Roman numerals.

1	45	**6**	66
2	132	**7**	1066
3	501	**8**	849
4	1111	**9**	1965
5	424	**10**	2014
11	199	**16**	464
12	919	**17**	1812
13	444	**18**	969
14	949	**19**	1508
15	1745	**20**	1999

Although most of the numbers you see are likely to be the ones you use every day, there are still some places where you will find Roman numerals.

Exercise 2.8

Here are some Roman numerals from around the world.

For each picture, copy the Roman numerals, write down the number they represent and suggest what the signs represent, for example, a date on a building.

1

2

3

6

4

7

5

8

9 Which one of the numbers above is found on an ancient Roman building?

i or I = 1   v or V = 5   x or X = 10   L = 50
    C = 100   D = 500   M = 1000

With the exception of:

IV = 4   IX = 9   XL = 40   XC = 90
CD = 400   CM = 900

numbers are made by adding together the various numerals.
Always start with the largest, which is on the left.

Hence:

VI = 6   XI = 11   LX = 60   CX = 110
MC = 1100   CLX = 160

MDCCCIII = 1803

Exercise 2.9

For questions 1–10, write down the number that the Roman numerals represent.

1 viii

2 LXVI

3 xix

4 MDCV

5 DV

6 MMXV

7 MCLI

8 DIX

9 MXLIX

10 MCMLXXXIV

For questions 11–20, write the numbers in Roman numerals.

11 9

12 17

13 112

14 304

15 542

16 735

17 1114

18 1506

19 1939

20 2099

For questions 21–22, write down the numbers shown in the signs.

21

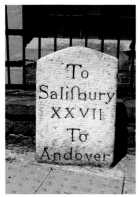

22

3 Place value

A **million** is a very large number.

- A million football fans would take up the seats in Wembley stadium more than 100 times over.

- A straight line between Land's End (the most south-westerly point in Great Britain) and John O'Groats (traditionally considered the most northerly point of Scotland) would be just less than a million metres long.

- Birmingham has a population of about a million.

⇨ Writing large numbers in words

You know how to write numbers with three digits, like this.

Hundreds	Tens	Units
9	4	7
nine hundred and	forty-	seven

The block for **thousands** has its own **hundreds**, **tens** and **units** positions.

Hundred thousands	Ten thousands	(Units) thousand	Hundreds	Tens	Units
HTh	TTh	Th	H	T	U
4	3	2	1	5	9
four hundred and	thirty-	two thousand	one hundred and	fifty-	nine

When a number has five or more digits, you leave a small space after the thousands block.

In your maths exercise book you can write one number in each square, leaving a blank square after the thousands block. The number above is written as:

Thousands				HTU		
HTh	TTh	Th		H	T	U
4	3	2		1	5	9

When you write a large number in words, follow these steps.

- Split the number into groups of three, from the right.
- Write the thousands block in words.
- Write the word 'thousand' instead of the space.
- Write the HTU block in words.

Written in words, 432 159 is four hundred and thirty-two thousand, one hundred and fifty-nine.

Consider the number 63 308

- This number has already been split into groups of three digits. Notice the small space after the thousands block.

Thou-sands			HTU		
TTh	Th		H	T	U
6	3		3	0	8

- For the thousands block: write 'sixty-three'.
- Write 'thousand' instead of the space.
- For the HTU block: write 'three hundred and eight'.

Written in words, 63 308 is sixty-three thousand, three hundred and eight.

Examples:

Write these numbers in words.

(i) **45 342**   forty-five thousand, three hundred and forty-two

(ii) **110 050**   one hundred and ten thousand and fifty

Exercise 3.1

Write these numbers in words.

1 4326

2 127 503

3 96 428

4 11 011

5 20 400

6 320 106

7 15 005

8 700 000

9 108 801

10 9050

For numbers with more than six digits, you need to use the **millions** block. This follows the same pattern as the thousands block.

Hundred millions	Ten millions	Millions	Hundred thousands	Ten thousands	Thousands	Hundreds	Tens	Units
HM	TM	M	HTh	TTh	Th	H	T	U
1	2	3	4	5	6	7	8	9
one hundred and	twenty-	three million,	four hundred and	fifty-	six thousand,	seven hundred and	eighty-	nine

In your maths exercise book you write one number in each square, leaving a blank square after the millions block and the thousands block.

Millions				Thousands				HTU		
HM	TM	M		HTh	TTh	Th		H	T	U
1	2	3		4	5	6		7	8	9

Follow these steps.

- Split the number into groups of three, from the right. The space on the left represents the word **million** and the space on the right represents the word **thousand**.
- Write the millions block in words.
- Write the word 'million' instead of the space.
- Write the thousands block.
- Write the word 'thousand' instead of the space.
- Write the **HTU** block.

Written in words, 123 456 789 is one hundred and twenty-three million, four hundred and fifty-six thousand, seven hundred and eighty-nine.

Example:

Write this number in words.

40 312 060   forty million, three hundred and twelve thousand and sixty

Exercise 3.2

Write each of these numbers in words.

1 1 206 450
2 2 450 070
3 20 525 000
4 13 013 103
5 125 080 007

6 4 600 000
7 46 000
8 460 000 000
9 460 000
10 46 000 000

⇨ Writing large numbers in figures

When you are writing a large number in figures, follow these steps.

- Look for the word 'thousand'.
- Write the number each side of it in blocks of three. The thousands block may have less than three figures.
- Leave a small space between the two blocks of numbers.

> The HTU block must have three figures in it.

Now think about the number fifty-two thousand, four hundred and sixty-four.

- Draw up the blocks for thousands and for HTU, leaving a space between them.
- Look for the word 'thousand'.
- Write fifty-two in the thousands block.
- Write four hundred and sixty-four in the HTU block.

The thousands block has its own hundreds, tens and units.

Thousands				HTU		
HTh	TTh	Th		H	T	U
	5	2		4	6	4

Fifty-two thousand, four hundred and sixty-four in figures is 52 464

Examples:

Write these numbers in figures.

(i)   Sixty-two thousand, two hundred and five   62 205

(ii) Four hundred and three thousand   403 000

Exercise 3.3

Write these numbers in figures.

1 One thousand, four hundred and fifty-six

2 Seventy-three thousand, two hundred and nineteen

3 One hundred and forty-eight thousand, six hundred and seven

4 Twelve thousand and two

5 Seven thousand and ten

6 Two hundred and eighty-four thousand, six hundred

7 Nine hundred thousand and nine

8 Six hundred thousand

9 Fifty-one thousand, five hundred and eleven

10 Twenty-seven thousand

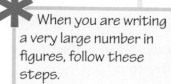 When you are writing a very large number in figures, follow these steps.

- Look for the words 'million' and 'thousand'.

- Write the numbers in blocks, leaving spaces between the blocks of numbers.

- After the first space, each block must have three digits in it.

Examples:

(i) Write three million, four hundred and one thousand and sixteen, in figures.

M		Thousands				HTU		
M		HTh	TTh	Th		H	T	U
3		4	0	1		0	1	6

(ii) Write twenty-seven million and nine thousand, in figures.

M			Thousands				HTU		
TM	M		HTh	TTh	Th		H	T	U
2	7		0	0	9		0	0	0

Write each of these numbers in figures.

1 Two million, one hundred and fifty-three thousand, five hundred and six

2 Sixty-seven million, one hundred and ten thousand, six hundred and fifty-four

3 Nine hundred and thirty-eight million, two hundred and seventy-four thousand, six hundred and fifty-one

4 Six million

5 Three hundred thousand and twenty

6 Thirty million, five hundred thousand

7 Four million and four

8 Sixty million, six thousand and sixty

9 One hundred and eighty million, eighteen thousand and eight

10 One million, one thousand and ten

⇨ Place value

You are using place value whenever you write down numbers. The value of each digit in a number depends on its place or **position** in the number.

Example:

Write down the real value of the underlined digit in this number.

23 4$\underline{7}$3 567   seventy thousand

Exercise 3.5

Write down the real value of the underlined digit in each number.

1 16 7̲28   6 4̲30 000 000

2 14̲3 269   7 6̲1 000 000

3 1̲ 432 657   8 6̲10 000

4 809̲ 528   9 6̲10 000 000

5 2̲4 350 075   10 6̲ 000 000

⇨ Counting in 10 000s, 100 000s and 1 000 000s

Look at the number line.

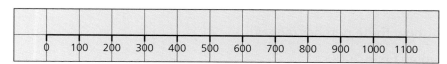

You know that, when you count in hundreds, the number that follows nine hundred is **one thousand**, not 10 hundred.

When you count in hundred thousands, the number that follows nine hundred thousand is **one million**. After this it is one million, one hundred thousand, and so on.

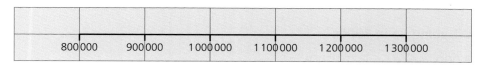

1 Work with a partner. Take turns to count aloud, following the instructions below. Correct each other if you make a mistake.

   (a) Starting at zero, count up in 100 000s until you get to two million.

   (b) Starting at three million, count down in 100 000s until you get to one million.

   (c) Starting at ninety thousand, count up in 10 000s until you get to one million and twenty thousand.

   (d) Starting at four million and thirty thousand, count down in 10 000s until you get to three million and fifty thousand.

   (e) Starting at nought, count up in millions until you get to twenty million.

   (f) Starting at three hundred million, count down in millions until you get to two hundred and eighty million.

2 Draw a number line to show these number ranges.

   (a) 17 000 to 21 000, going up in 1000s

   (b) 80 000 to 120 000, going up in 10 000s

   (c) 700 000 to 1 100 000, going up in 100 000s

   (d) 2 800 000 to 3 200 000, going up in 100 000s

3 Write down these numbers. Make sure you put the spaces in the right places.

   (a) 9000 to 15 000, going up in 1000s

   (b) 95 000 to 145 000, going up in 10 000s

   (c) 720 000 to 1 220 000, going up in 100 000s

⇨ Ordering

You can use the place values of the digits in two or more numbers to put them in order, from smallest to biggest or from biggest to smallest.

Think about the two numbers, 3 100 050 and 999 999

3 100 050 is three million, one hundred thousand and fifty.

999 999 is nine hundred and ninety-nine thousand, nine hundred and ninety-nine.

You can see straight away that 3 100 050 is bigger than 999 999 because three million is a bigger number than nine hundred thousand, even though nine is bigger than three.

The value of the first digit in 3 100 050 is three million, because of its place value.

The value of the first digit in 999 999 is nine hundred thousand.

When you are ordering numbers, follow these steps.

● Look at the first digit of each number and work out its value.

● If the first digits in both numbers have the same value, look at the second digits and work out their value.

● If the second digits also have the same value, look at the third digits and work out their values.

● Continue until you have worked out which is the largest number.

Examples:

Write the numbers in each set in order, starting with the smallest.

(i)   3000, 303 000, 33 000

    3000, 33 000, 303 000

(ii)   5 571 765, 1 575 675, 5 157 765

    1 575 675, 5 157 765, 5 571 765

Exercise 3.7

Write these numbers in order, starting with the smallest.

1 30 000, 500, 2000

2 75 000, 1 000 000, 900 000

3 2 000 000, 99 000, 300 000

4 200 000, 4000, 31 000

5 170, 17, 17 000, 1700

6 60 000, 63 150, 61 333, 62 500

7 1 300 000, 1 303 030, 1 030 003, 1 300 300

8 2 560 000, 2 565 000, 2 550 000, 2 556 000

9 4 060 000, 4 090 000, 4 070 000, 4 010 000

10 505 050, 505 000, 550 000, 505 500

⇨ Rounding very large numbers

You already know how to round numbers to the nearest 10, 100 and 1000

Look at the digit in the tens, hundreds or thousands column. Now look at the digit to the right.

If that digit is 0, 1, 2, 3 or 4   round down

If that digit is 5, 6, 7, 8 or 9   round up

924 is 920 to the nearest ten.

1375 is 1400 to the nearest hundred.

1504 is 2000 to the nearest thousand.

You can round to the nearest ten thousand, hundred thousand or a million in exactly the same way.

Rounding to the nearest ten thousand

Example:

Write: (a) 32 000   (b) 37 000   (c) 35 000
correct to the nearest ten thousand.

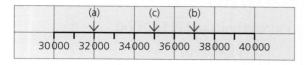

All three numbers are between 30 000 and 40 000 and 35 000 is the
halfway point.
From the diagram you can see that:

(a)   32 000 is less than 35 000 and therefore nearer to 30 000 than 40 000

so 32 000 correct to the nearest ten thousand is 30 000

(b)   37 000 is more than 35 000 and therefore nearer to 40 000 than 30 000

so 37 000 correct to the nearest ten thousand is 40 000

(c)   35 000 is exactly halfway between 30 000 and 40 000 and you always
round up if a number is exactly at the halfway point

so 35 000 correct to the nearest ten thousand is 40 000

Rounding to the nearest hundred thousand and to the nearest million

Examples:

(i)   Write: (a) 440 000   (b) 480 000   (c) 450 000
correct to the nearest hundred thousand.

(i)   All three numbers are between 400 000 and 500 000 and 450 000 is the
halfway point.

(a)   440 000 is less than 450 000 and therefore nearer to 400 000 than
500 000

so 440 000 correct to the nearest hundred thousand is 400 000

(b)   480 000 is more than 450 000 and therefore nearer to 500 000 than 400 000

so 480 000 correct to the nearest hundred thousand is 500 000

(c)   450 000 is exactly halfway between 400 000 and 500 000 and you always round up if a number is exactly at the halfway point

so 450 000 correct to the nearest hundred thousand is 500 000

(ii)   Write: (a) 5 450 000   (b) 6 875 000   (c) 1 500 000
correct to the nearest million.

(a)   5 450 000 is between 5 000 000 and 6 000 000 and nearer to 5 000 000

so 5 450 000 correct to the nearest million is 5 000 000

(b)   6 875 000 is between 6 000 000 and 7 000 000 and nearer to 7 000 000

so 6 875 000 correct to the nearest million is 7 000 000

(c)   1 500 000 is exactly halfway between 1 000 000 and 2 000 000 and you always round up if a number is exactly at the halfway point

so 1 500 000 correct to the nearest million is 2 000 000

Exercise 3.8

1 Round these numbers to the nearest ten thousand.

(a) 22 000   (b) 56 000   (c) 65 000   (d) 98 000

2 Round these numbers to the nearest hundred thousand.

(a) 372 000   (b) 450 000   (c) 820 000   (d) 960 000

3 Round these numbers to the nearest million.

(a) 1 240 000   (b) 13 690 000   (c) 5 490 000   (d) 135 500 000

4 The population of England in the 2011 census was 53 012 456
What is this, correct to the nearest million?

5 The population of Northern Ireland in the 2011 census was 1 810 863
What is this, correct to the nearest million?

6 The house next door was sold for £247 000
What is this, correct to the nearest £10 000?

7 The length of the equator is 24 901 miles. Write this number correct to the nearest ten thousand.

8 The speed of light is 299 792 458 metres per second. Write this number correct to the nearest million.

9 The population of Denmark is 5 571 345

Write this number correct to:

(a) the nearest million

(b) the nearest hundred thousand

(c) the nearest ten thousand.

10 The population of Birmingham is 1 075 000

Write this number correct to:

(a) the nearest million

(b) the nearest hundred thousand

(c) the nearest ten thousand.

⇨ **Problem solving**

Exercise 3.9

1 By counting up in 10 000s, find the number that is exactly 50 000 more than 72 300

2 By counting down in 100 000s, find the number that is exactly 400 000 less than 1 250 000

3 The population in Britain in 1951 was 50 225 000

It is now 63 100 000

By counting up in millions, find out by how much the population has grown.

4 Millie has rounded a number to 40 000, to the nearest ten thousand.

(a) What is the largest possible value of the number she started with?

(b) What is the smallest possible value of the number she started with?

5 Max has rounded a number to 3 400 000, to the nearest hundred thousand.

(a) What is the largest possible value of the number he started with?

(b) What is the smallest possible value of the number he started with?

6 If you started at 100 000 and counted up in 10 000s one hundred times, would your answer be bigger or smaller than if you had started at 100 000 and counted up in 100 000s ten times?

7 The Moon does not orbit Earth in a perfect circle, but instead travels in an orbit that is like an oval. Its distance from Earth varies between 363 300 kilometres and 405 500 kilometres.

(a) Round both numbers to the nearest 100 000 and find the difference between them.

(b) Is your answer the same if you round both numbers to the nearest 10 000?

Activity – Arithmagons

1 Copy the diagram. Write the numbers 1 to 6 in the circles, so that the total along each side of the triangle is 9

2 Now repeat the task, making the totals:

(a) 10   (b) 11   (c) 12

3 Did you find any pattern that helped you?

If so, explain what you found.

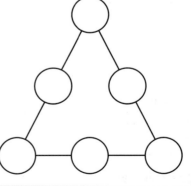

4 Adding and subtracting

⇨ Mental arithmetic

Even though you may be able to use a calculator for addition and subtraction, you still need to be able to do basic arithmetic in your head.

One useful technique is to break calculations down into manageable stages using basic number bonds.

Example:

Calculate 14 + 29 in your head.

Remember that 14 + 6 = 20

Break down 29 into 6 + 23

So, 14 + 29 = 14 + 6 + 23

$\qquad\qquad$ = 20 + 23

$\qquad\qquad$ = 43

Another method is to imagine a number line.

14 + 29 = ?

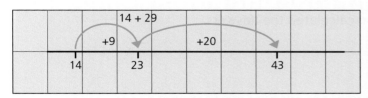

This time, the calculation looks like this:

14 + 29 = 14 + 9 + 20

$\qquad$ = 23 + 20

$\qquad$ = 43

There is never just one correct way of calculating mentally. If the method works then it is right. You do not need to write down all the stages. Just follow them through in your head.

1 Copy and complete these calculation squares.

+	12	35	14	43
28				
11				
33				
22				

+	54	27	53	37
34				
47				
65				
57				

2 Explain to your partner how you calculated the answers to each row, then to each column.

3 Copy and complete these subtraction or difference squares. Write the difference between the two numbers in the squares.

−	49	37	84	86
18				
23				
15				
32				

−	73	68	53	97
34				
17				
43				
68				

4 Explain to your partner how you calculated the answers.

Inverse operations

When you first learned your basic number bonds, you quickly found that once you knew one number bond you had actually learned four bonds in all. This is because subtraction is the inverse of addition.

The same idea works for large numbers as well.

4 Adding and subtracting

If you know that:

54 + 39 = 93

you also know that:

39 + 54 = 93

93 − 54 = 39

93 − 39 = 54

You can use inverse operations to complete the calculation squares in the next exercise.

Example:

Work out 48 − 25

$$48 - 25 = \underline{23}$$

$$\text{Check: } \underline{23} + 25 = 48$$

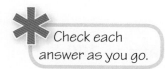

Check each answer as you go.

Exercise 4.2

1 Copy and complete each calculation square. Find all the outside numbers first.

+	15	37		36	
26					
	33	79			
45					72
	54				
23					

−	38	45		34	
	23				
28					
32			20		
		16			
17					2

2 Compare your answers with your partner's. Do you have the same answers for the difference square? Explain why your answers could be different.

3 Copy and complete these calculations squares.

+	34		36		57
29					
37				83	
		72			
	89				
42		61			

−	39	47		18	
	23				
27					
55			20		
		16			
62					2

Number pairs to 100

When you are working with larger numbers, it helps if you know the number pairs up to 100

You can spot them quickly by looking first at the units digit and then the tens.

Exercise 4.3

Use the inverse operation to check your answers to this exercise.

1 Copy and complete these additions.

(a) $16 + \square = 100$

(b) $11 + \square = 100$

(c) $18 + \square = 100$

(d) $12 + \square = 100$

(e) $17 + \square = 100$

(f) $19 + \square = 100$

2 You saw in question 1 that the units add up to 10 but the tens add up to 9. Use this fact to help you copy and complete these additions.

(a) $15 + \square = 100$

(b) $59 + \square = 100$

(c) $21 + \square = 100$

(d) $32 + \square = 100$

(e) $26 + \square = 100$

(f) $43 + \square = 100$

3 Now take it further. Copy and complete these additions.

(a) $41 + \boxed{} = 200$

(b) $108 + \boxed{} = 300$

(c) $305 + \boxed{} = 500$

(d) $199 + \boxed{} = 300$

(e) $94 + \boxed{} = 200$

(f) $27 + \boxed{} = 400$

4 Copy and complete these subtractions.

(a) $100 - 23 = \boxed{}$

(b) $200 - 49 = \boxed{}$

(c) $300 - 82 = \boxed{}$

(d) $600 - 73 = \boxed{}$

(e) $500 - 253 = \boxed{}$

(f) $600 - 482 = \boxed{}$

(g) $400 - 162 = \boxed{}$

(h) $100 - 71 = \boxed{}$

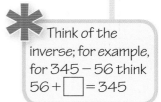
Think of the inverse; for example, for $345 - 56$ think $56 + \boxed{} = 345$

5 Copy and complete these subtractions.

(a) $345 - 56 = \boxed{}$

(b) $1200 - 115 = \boxed{}$

(c) $1090 - 109 = \boxed{}$

(d) $646 - 218 = \boxed{}$

(e) $501 - 289 = \boxed{}$

(f) $1660 - 725 = \boxed{}$

(g) $4500 - 1162 = \boxed{}$

(h) $1001 - 715 = \boxed{}$

6 Write some simple instructions to explain how to calculate the answer when subtracting from a multiple of one hundred.

7 (a) Try subtracting some numbers from multiples of thousands.

(b) Write some simple instructions to explain how to calculate the answer when subtracting from a multiple of one thousand.

⇨ Written calculations

For some calculations it is helpful help to write down the stages, rather than keeping all the numbers in your head. Some people think that it is more clever to work out the answers without writing anything down but this is not true. Clever people get the right answers and writing down the working helps them to do it.

Example:

Calculate $1300 - 925$

$$1300 - 900 = 400$$
$$400 - 20 = 380$$
$$380 - 5 = 375$$

 For the calculation above, never write:

$1300 - 900 = 400 - 20 = 380 - 5 = 375$

The equals sign (=) means 'exactly the same as' and $1300 - 900$ is **not** exactly the same as $400 - 20$

Incorrect use of the equals sign is bad mathematical 'grammar' and, just like incorrect grammar in English, it will be marked as incorrect.

Estimating

A useful variation of the equals sign is ≈, which means 'is approximately the same as'. You can use it when you check an answer by rounding the original numbers to the nearest ten or a hundred.

$$1300 - 925 \approx 1300 - 900$$

so $1300 - 925 \approx 400$

Using rounding in this way is called **approximating**.

Example:

In this solution to $3568 + 3569$, the equals sign has been used incorrectly.

$$3568 + 3000 = 6568 + 500 = 7068 + 60 = 7128 + 9 = 7137$$

Rewrite the calculation, using the equals sign correctly.

Then estimate the answer to check that the calculation looks correct.

$$3568 + 3000 = 6568$$

$$6568 + 500 = 7068$$

$$7068 + 60 = 7128$$

$$7128 + 9 = 7137$$

Check: $3568 + 3569 \approx 3600 + 3600$

so $3568 + 3569 \approx 7200$

Exercise 4.4

1 In each of these solutions to calculations, the equals sign has been used incorrectly. Rewrite each calculation, using the equals sign correctly.

(a) $1585 + 3537$

$1585 + 3000 = 4585 + 500 = 5085 + 30 = 5115 + 7 = 5122$

(b) $4313 - 2639$

$4313 - 2000 = 2313 - 600 = 1713 - 30 = 1683 - 9 = 1674$

(c) $3768 + 2563$

$3768 + 2000 = 5768 + 500 = 6268 + 60 = 6328 + 3 = 6331$

(d) $6341 - 4994$

$6341 - 4000 = 2341 - 900 = 1441 - 90 = 1351 - 4 = 1347$

2 Copy and complete these by breaking the calculation into stages. Use the equals sign correctly and check each answer by approximating.

(a) $4327 + 368$

(b) $6918 - 476$

(c) $3784 + 1475$

(d) $6719 - 4582$

(e) $5723 + 2948$

(f) $6452 - 3895$

(g) $5619 + 4728$

(h) $9324 - 8487$

Adding with four or more digits

When adding two numbers, it can be useful to break up calculations into stages. When you need to add more than two numbers, it is generally easier if you write your numbers in a frame. Mathematics exercise books have squares to help you with this. Treat the squares as **rows** and **columns**, to help you line up the thousands, hundreds, tens and units digits properly.

Example:

Add 14 007 + 5135 + 107 + 42

	TTh	Th		H	T	U
	1	4		0	0	7
		5		1	3	5
				1	0	7
+					4	2
	1	9		2	9	1
					2	

$7 + 5 + 7 + 2 = 21$

When the total in any column is 10 or more, use a small carried number, as in the example. Write your carried number under the line, in the column to the left of the one you are adding, to make sure that you write the correct whole number. In this case it is 21.

Exercise 4.5

Copy and complete each calculation, by writing the numbers in a frame. Make sure the digits are in the correct columns. Show all your working, including carried numbers.

1 1337 + 451
2 5146 + 520
3 1345 + 381
4 4307 + 2434
5 2534 + 5623

6 2345 + 4326
7 190 + 24 532
8 346 + 35 291
9 12 345 + 3283 + 11
10 25 543 + 4606 + 9

46

11 27 + 14 451 + 1089

12 32 477 + 1910 + 46

13 33 503 + 1570 + 305

14 51 965 + 14 852 + 167

15 23 + 564 + 1789 + 52 642

16 78 995 + 8 + 2193 + 387 + 8645

Subtraction with four or more digits

Just as with addition, when you have to subtract with large numbers it is helpful to write them into a frame and calculate, column by column.

Always put the larger number in the first row and the smaller number in the second.

Example:

Calculate 47 458 – 13 895

	TTh	Th		H	T	U
	4	7		4	5	8
−	1	3		8	9	5

Now work from the units column, subtracting each time. If the top number is smaller than the bottom number, take 1 from the column on the left and add it to the top number. This is called changing or **decomposition**.

	TTh	Th		H	T	U
	4	7		³4̶	¹5	8
−	1	3		8	9	5
					6	3

In the **units** column, 8 − 5 = 3

In the **tens** column, you cannot take 9 from 5, so take 1 from the 4 in the **hundreds** column, to leave 3, and add it to the **tens** column to make 15

15 − 9 = 6

	TTh	Th		H	T	U
	4	$^6\not7$		$^{13}\not{\cancel{8}}$	^{1}5	8
−	1	3		8	9	5
				5	6	3

In the **hundreds** column you cannot take 8 from 3, so take 1 from the 7 in the **thousands** column, to leave 6, and add it to the **hundreds** column, to make 13

$13 - 8 = 5$

	TTh	Th		H	T	U
	4	$^6\not7$		$^{13}\not{\cancel{8}}$	^{1}5	8
−	1	3		8	9	5
	3	3		5	6	3

Now subtract in the **thousands** column:

$6 - 3 = 3$

and in the **ten thousands** column:

$4 - 1 = 3$

Finally, use the inverse principle to check the answer mentally.

If $47\,458 - 13\,895 = 33\,563$ then $13\,895 + 33\,563 = 47\,458$

Mentally, add the answer to the number that was subtracted.

	TTh	Th		H	T	U
	1	3		8	9	5
+	3	3		5	6	3
	4	7		4	5	8

The answer is correct.

Exercise 4.6

Copy and complete each calculation, by writing the numbers in a frame. Make sure the digits are in the correct columns. Show all your working, including changed numbers. Check your answer mentally each time.

1 3548 − 317

2 5463 − 211

3 9352 − 8125

4 5474 − 3665

5 5358 − 4137

6 65 235 − 47 367

7 87 515 − 53 816

8 621 229 − 191 454

9 745 335 − 15 852

10 356 489 − 197 734

Subtraction with zeros

When the number in the top row is smaller than the number in the second row, you need to change the number in the column to the left. When that number is zero, it can be difficult to see what to change – you cannot take 1 away from zero. So look at the number in the next column to the left, and the next, until you find a number that is not zero. Then you can take 1 from that number. These examples will show you what to do.

Examples:

(i) Calculate 3403 − 1117

Th	H	T	U
3	³4̶	⁹0̶	¹3
− 1	1	1	7

In the units column, you cannot take 7 from 3

You need to take 1 from the tens column, but the number is 0, there are no tens.

Moving to the next column on the left, there are 4 hundreds.

400 − 10 = 390, add the 10 into the units, writing the small numbers as shown here.

Th	H	T	U
3	³4̶	⁹0̶	¹3
− 1	1	1	7
2	2	8	6

Now subtract, column by column, from right to left and mentally check the answer.

(ii) Calculate 600 005 − 4567

HTh	TTh	Th		H	T	U
⁵6̶	⁹0̶	⁹0̶		⁹0̶	⁹0̶	¹5
−		4		5	6	7

In the units column, you have 5 − 7 and you cannot take 7 from 5

You need to take 1 from the tens column, but there is a 0

Keep going to the left until you find a number that is not nought.

In the HTh column, you have 600 000

Taking 10 from that gives 599 990, add the 10 back into the units.

HTh	TTh	Th		H	T	U
⁵6̶	⁹0̶	⁹0̶		⁹0̶	⁹0̶	¹5
−		4		5	6	7
5	9	5		4	3	8

Now subtract, column by column, from right to left and mentally check the answer.

Exercise 4.7

Calculate the answer to each of these subtractions. Show all the working, including changed numbers.

1 4605 − 167

2 3052 − 188

3 7903 − 3345

4 60 007 − 2420

5 50 004 − 24 458

6 42 506 − 16 788

7 800 064 − 307 086

8 700 601 − 405 758

9 8 005 005 − 308 708

10 7 000 704 − 4 999 999

4 Adding and subtracting

⇨ Problem solving

Exercise 4.8

Calculate the answers to these problems. You may use any methods of calculation that you choose, but you must write down all of your working.

If you are doing a calculation in your head, write it down like this:

$54 + 63 = 117$

That shows that you have used the **correct** calculation in your head.

You can also break a calculation into stages, using the equals sign correctly, or you can write your calculations in a frame.

Whichever method you use, check your answers by estimating or by using the inverse.

1 A school has been collecting tokens from a supermarket to win some free software. Year 3 have 412 tokens, Year 4 have 596, Year 5 have only 98 and Year 6 have just 9

   How many tokens does the school have altogether?

2 The school has four houses, Ash, Beech, Oak and Thorn. When the headmaster added up the house points, Ash had 4275 more than Oak. If Oak had 9412, how many did Ash have?

3 Thorn had 2189 fewer house points than Beech. If Beech had 9404, how many did Thorn have?

4 The library has 4006 books this year. This is 468 more than last year. How many books did it have last year?

5 This table shows the lengths of some rivers.

River	Length (miles)
Nile	4132
Amazon	3976
Thames	346

   (a) How much longer is the river Nile than the Amazon river?

   (b) How much longer is the river Nile than the river Thames?

6 This table shows the areas and populations of some European countries in 2010.

Name of country	Area (km²)	Population (1 July 2010, estimated)
Andorra	468	8240
France	551 695	65 460 000
Iceland	103 000	304 261
Ireland	70 280	4 588 252
Malta	316	408 009
Portugal	91 568	10 607 995
Spain	504 851	47 150 800
United Kingdom	244 820	62 041 708

(a) What is the total area of Spain and Portugal together?

(b) What is the total population of France and Andorra together?

(c) How much larger is the area of Iceland than the area of Ireland?

(d) How any more people are there in Malta than in Iceland?

(e) How much larger in area is France than the United Kingdom?

Each of the remaining questions needs more than one calculation. Write each addition and subtraction down carefully, even if you are calculating mentally.

7 The rhinoceros is an endangered species. There are an estimated 1000 fewer Indian rhinoceroses than black rhinoceroses, but 13 500 more white rhinoceroses than black.

Given that there are 2500 Indian rhinoceroses, how many white rhinoceroses are there?

8 In our road, house number 4 has just been sold for £347 500 but number 6 sold for £125 700 more.

Number 7 has just been put up for sale for £79 000 less than number 6.

What is the price of number 7?

9 Mr McKay earns £45 600 per year.

Mrs Patel is paid £17 200 more than Mr McKay and Miss Jones is paid £2300 less than Mrs Patel. How much does Miss Jones earn?

10 Ben Nevis is the UK's highest mountain. It is 259 m taller than Mount Snowdon, in Wales, which is 97 m taller than Scafell Pike in England. If the height of Scafell Pike is 978 m, what is the height of Ben Nevis?

11 The area of Finland is 12 373 km² greater than the area of Norway and the area of Norway is 125 744 km² smaller than the area of Sweden. If the area of Sweden is 449 964 km², what is the area of Finland?

12 The three most densely populated Channel Islands are Jersey, Guernsey and Alderney. The population of Jersey is 90 800 and this is 25 227 greater than the population of Guernsey.

The population of Guernsey is 63 670 greater than the population of Alderney.

What is the population of Alderney?

Missing numbers

These questions are just like those you have been answering in this chapter, but some of the numbers are missing.

Exercise 4.9

Copy and complete each question, putting the correct numbers in the boxes to make the calculation correct.

1

H	T	U
2	□	3
+ □	5	□
5	8	7

2

H	T	U
4	□	8
+ 1	7	□
□	1	5

3

Th	H	T	U
4	□	7	5
− □	4	□	2
3	2	5	□

4

Th	H	T	U
6	□	5	□
− □	3	□	1
4	4	8	4

5

Th	H	T	U
5	□	3	8
− 3	4	□	□
□	6	5	3

6

H	T	U
4	□	6
+ □	7	□
5	8	3

7

Th	H	T	U
2	5	4	3
− 1	□	6	□
□	2	□	8

8

Th	H	T	U
4	□	4	□
−		4	4
3	9	□	8

9

TTh	Th	H	T	U
1	□	4	0	5
3	9	8	3	□
		□	4	4
+ □	0	7	□	6
9	4	0	3	1

Exercise 4.10: Summary exercise

Use an appropriate method to complete each calculation.

1 47 + 120

2 136 + 450

3 13 000 + 4356

4 12 500 + 2500

5 3620 + 13 000

6 100 − 49

7 12 000 − 350

8 1600 − 560

9 35 000 − 15 100

10 1 000 000 − 750 000

11 4557 + 129 + 17

12 1536 + 5701 + 346

13 8324 − 4356

14 12 503 − 2559

15 3620 + 13 005 + 175

16 17 009 − 4999

17 12 006 − 3507

18 100 008 + 56 019 + 456

19 30 070 − 15 180

20 3 004 000 − 700 909

21 Take one thousand, four hundred and twelve from five thousand, six hundred and two.

22 St Aeldric's Academy has 2004 pupils and St Clementine's Academy has 975 pupils. How many more pupils go to St Aeldric's than to St Clementine's Academy?

23 Mr Brown earns £45 700 more than Mr Green and £17 350 less than Miss Lemon. If Miss Lemon earns £70 650, how much does Mr Green earn?

24 Lithuania is 611 km² larger than Latvia and 19 974 km² larger than Estonia. If Estonia has an area of 45 226 km², what is the area of Latvia?

25 Fill in the missing numbers:

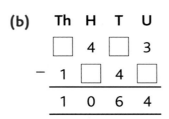

5 Multiplying and dividing

In Chapter 2 you learned about Roman numerals. Think how you might write down your nine times table as a Roman might have done. With their system of symbols they had to think of multiplying as adding on, so instead of knowing that 2 times 9 was 18 they would add IX to IX to make XVIII

⇨ Times tables

The counting system commonly used today is based on tens. It is easier than the Roman system for multiplying and dividing and for paper and pencil methods of calculation. However, to use our number system correctly, you must know your tables!

Exercise 5.1

1 Copy and complete this table square. Try to do it faster than anyone else in the room.

×	1	2	3	4	5	6	7	8	9	10	11	12
1												
2												
3												
4												
5												
6												
7												
8												
9												
10												
11												
12												

2 Copy and complete this table square.

×	7	5	2	11	9	8	3	6	10	4
2										
5										
8										
7										
9										
12										

⇨ Dividing

When you learnt your times tables, you discovered that – just as subtraction is the opposite of addition – division is the inverse of multiplication.

If you know that $8 \times 9 = 72$

you also know $9 \times 8 = 72$

and $72 \div 8 = 9$

and $72 \div 9 = 8$

You also learned that you can think of division as a fraction.

$\frac{1}{8}$ of $72 = 72 \div 8 = 9$

Sometimes a division works out exactly and sometimes there is something left over. This is called a remainder and you write it with a lower case 'r'.

Example:

Divide 77 by 8

$77 \div 8 = 9$ r5 (because $9 \times 8 = 72$ and $77 - 72 = 5$)

You can also write the remainder as a fraction.

Example:

Divide 19 by 2

$19 \div 2 = 9$ r1   or $19 \div 2 = 9\frac{1}{2}$

Exercise 5.2

1 Write down the answer to each division.

(a) $72 \div 9$

(b) $44 \div 11$

(c) $49 \div 7$

(d) $36 \div 12$

(e) $63 \div 9$

(f) $121 \div 11$

(g) $36 \div 9$

(h) $60 \div 12$

(i) $42 \div 6$

(j) $56 \div 7$

2 Work out these amounts.

(a) $\frac{1}{6}$ of 48

(b) a ninth of 108

(c) $\frac{1}{12}$ of 72

(d) one-seventh of 28

(e) one-eleventh of 110

(f) $\frac{1}{12}$ of 84

(g) an eighth of 56

(h) one-sixth of 72

(i) $\frac{1}{9}$ of 63

(j) $\frac{1}{8}$ of 64

3 Each of these divisions has a remainder. Calculate the answers and write the reminders as fractions.

(a) $78 \div 8$

(b) $19 \div 4$

(c) $52 \div 7$

(d) $36 \div 10$

(e) $68 \div 9$

(f) $26 \div 12$

(g) $37 \div 8$

(h) $63 \div 11$

(i) $47 \div 6$

(j) $59 \div 9$

4 Work out these divisions. Some have remainders and some do not. Write any reminders as fractions.

(a) $63 \div 8$

(b) $48 \div 5$

(c) $24 \div 11$

(d) $48 \div 8$

(e) $56 \div 7$

(f) $27 \div 4$

(g) $84 \div 12$

(h) $49 \div 11$

(i) $35 \div 7$

(j) $54 \div 8$

⇨ Multiplying and dividing by 10, 100 and 1000

You already know that, when you multiply a whole number by 10, 100 or 1000, the digits in the number you are multiplying move to the left and spaces at the end of the number are filled with 0s. The number of places the digits move depends on the number of 0s in the number you are multiplying by.

- When you multiply by 10, the digits move one place left.

- When you multiply by 100 they move two places left.

- When you multiply by 1000 they move three places left.

Example:

HTh	TTh	Th		H	T	U	
					6	5	
				6	5	0	
					2	7	
		2		7	0	0	
				4	6	0	
4	6	0		0	0	0	

65 × 10

     = 650

27 × 100

     = 2700

460 × 1000

     = 460 000

When you divide by 10, 100 or 1000, the digits move to the right. The number of places they move depends on the number of 0s in the number you are dividing by.

- When you divide by 10 the digits move one place right.

- When you divide by 100 they move two places right.

- When you divide by 1000 they move three places right.

Example:

HTh	TTh	Th		H	T	U	
				⌢→			
				3	7	0	
					3	7	
			⌢⌢→				
	2	7		0	0	0	
					2	7	

$370 \div 10$

$= 37$

$27\,000 \quad\quad \div \quad 1000$

$= 27$

Exercise 5.3

Copy and complete these calculations. Remember to put spaces in the correct places in the answer.

1 9×100

2 $500 \div 100$

3 17×1000

4 $350\,000 \div 100$

5 $108\,000 \times 10$

6 9500×1000

7 $507\,000 \div 100$

8 $46\,000\,000 \div 1000$

9 4030×1000

10 $2\,500\,000 \div 100$

11 950×1000

12 $56\,000 \div 100$

13 9400×1000

14 $9\,300\,000 \div 100$

15 4500×10

16 $75\,000 \div 1000$

17 $50\,700 \times 100$

18 $6\,050\,000 \div 1000$

19 5007×1000

20 $70\,070\,000 \div 100$

⇨ Using factors to multiply

Sometimes it is easier to break a multiplication down into steps by using factors.

Multiplying by 8, for example, is the same as multiplying by 4 and then by 2.

This is because 2 and 4 are a factor pair of 8

$$25 \times 8 = 25 \times 2 \times 4$$

This calculation can be broken down into two parts.

Step 1: $25 \times 2 = 50$

Step 2: $50 \times 4 = 200$

This method can be very helpful when you are multiplying by numbers larger than 12 – as long as you know your times tables up to 12. You can use more than two factors with this method, as shown in the third example below.

Examples:

(i)   Multiply 7 by 15

$$15 = 3 \times 5$$
$$7 \times 15 = 7 \times 3 \times 5$$
$$= 21 \times 5$$
$$= 105$$

The order in which you do the multiplication does not matter. In the example above, you could have worked out $7 \times 5 = 35$ and then $35 \times 3 = 105$

(ii)   Multiply 15 by 40

There are several factor pairs of 40 but the most useful is 4×10

$$15 \times 40 = 15 \times 4 \times 10$$
$$= 60 \times 10$$
$$= 600$$

5 Multiplying and dividing

(iii) Multiply 8 by 24

You can use more than two factors.

$24 = 2 \times 3 \times 4$ so the factors are 2, 3 and 4

$$8 \times 24 = 8 \times 2 \times 3 \times 4$$
$$= 16 \times 3 \times 4$$
$$= 48 \times 4$$
$$= 192$$

The examples above show the stages of the calculation you can do in your head. Sometimes you will be able to do all the stages in your head and write down just the calculation and the answer. At other times, writing down some of the stages helps you to find the right answer. If you need to write stages, then make sure you use the equals sign correctly.

You should not write:

$12 \times 15 = 12 \times 3 = 36 \times 5 = 180$

because 12×3 does **not** equal 36×5

Exercise 5.4

Calculate these mentally. Use factors or any other method.

1 8×15

2 9×16

3 14×12

4 5×24

5 7×18

6 6×32

7 24×25

8 8×14

9 5×35

10 5×16

11 5×48

12 6×54

13 15×72

14 25×60

15 19×40

16 6×56

17 8×42

18 5×36

19 25×64

20 12×45

21 17×12	**26** 17×56
22 24×35	**27** 25×32
23 35×42	**28** 30×36
24 15×27	**29** 45×24
25 24×18	**30** 15×72

⇨ Problem solving

You need to be good at mental arithmetic to be able to solve simple, everyday problems quickly. You also need to understand the language. There are some words that mean that you have to add and others that mean you have to subtract. There are also some that suggest you should multiply and some that suggest you should divide.

> You find the **sum** of two numbers by adding them together, so 5 is the sum of 2 and 3
>
> You find the **product** of two numbers by multiplying them together, so 6 is the product of 2 and 3

Exercise 5.5

1 Divide your page into four sections. Put a different sign, $+$, $-$, $\times$ or $\div$, at the top of each section. The words in the box tell you whether you should add, subtract, multiply or divide. Put each of the words into the correct section on your page.

plus	sum	away	greater	addition
more	rose	product	share	another
increased	subtract	total	each	less
down	lower	at	difference	
of	between	decreased	up	

2 Add some more words of your own to your lists.

3 **(a)** Find the sum of 4 and 6   **(c)** Find the sum of 7 and 8

   (b) Find the product of 4 and 6   **(d)** Find the product of 7 and 8

4 What is the smallest number that is greater than 100 and is also a product of 12?

5 Two numbers have a sum of 18 and a product of 72
   What are the numbers?

6 Find two numbers for which the product is less than the sum.

7 Two numbers have a difference of 2 and a product of 24.
   What are the numbers?

8 A bag of 100 sweets is shared among 8 children.

   (a) How many sweets does each child have?

   The teacher ate the sweets that were left over.

   (b) How many sweets did the teacher eat?

9 A group of seven children collected just fewer than a hundred shells on the beach. When they divided them equally among themselves, there were four left over.

   (a) How many shells did the children collect altogether?

   (b) How many shells did each child receive?

10 In our class, there are 21 children. Three-sevenths of them are girls. How many boys are there in our class?

⇨ Written multiplication calculations

It is useful to be able to calculate mentally, but when you are working with larger numbers you need to write them in a frame and work out the answer by multiplying each column.

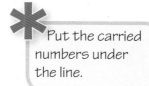

Put the carried numbers under the line.

Example:

Calculate 5327 × 4

Estimate first: 5000 × 4 = 20 000

This shows that there will need to be a TTh column in the grid.

Multiply the units:

TTh	Th		H	T	U
	5		3	2	7
				×	4
					8
				2	

$4 \times 7 = 28$

Write 8 in the **units** column and 2 under the line in the **tens** column.

Multiply the tens:

TTh	Th		H	T	U
	5		3	2	7
				×	4
				0	8
			1	2	

$4 \times 20 = 80$

$80 + 20 = 100$

Write 0 in the **tens** column and 1 under the line in the **hundreds** column.

Multiply the hundreds:

TTh	Th		H	T	U
	5		3	2	7
				×	4
			3	0	8
	1		1	2	

$4 \times 300 = 1200$

$1200 + 100 = 1300$

Write 3 in the **hundreds** column and 1 under the line in the **thousands** column.

Multiply the thousands:

TTh	Th		H	T	U
	5		3	2	7
				×	4
2	1		3	0	8
	1		1	2	

4 × 5000 = 20 000

20 000 + 1000 = 21 000

Write 21 in the thousands columns.

5327 × 4 = 21 308

* The answer is a large number, so an extra TTh column was needed. Always make sure that you leave space for extra columns to the left of your frame.

Exercise 5.6

Copy and complete these calculations. Show all your working, including the carried numbers.

1 132 × 3

2 234 × 2

3 427 × 3

4 236 × 5

5 152 × 4

6 2453 × 5

7 3436 × 7

8 3628 × 4

9 4352 × 6

10 8306 × 4

11 3451 × 9

12 3162 × 7

13 5423 × 11

14 2402 × 6

15 2016 × 8

16 3158 × 12

17 4025 × 7

18 6927 × 8

19 5705 × 9

20 8845 × 12

⇨ Multiplication by multiples of 10, 100, 1000

You know that you can think of 345 × 30 as:

$$345 \times 10 \times 3 = 3450 \times 3$$
$$= 10\,350$$

If the numbers are big you might find it useful to put them in a frame.

Example:

Calculate 7346 × 60

Estimate first: 7000 × 60 = 420 000

First write down the 0s as you multiply by 10

HTh	TTh	Th		H	T	U
		7		3	4	6
				×	6	0̸
						0

> Say, in your head: 'Cross out the naughty nought and write it here.'

Then multiply, column by column.

HTh	TTh	Th		H	T	U
		7		3	4	6
				×	6	0̸
4	4	0		7	6	0
	2	2		3		

7346 × 60 = 440 760

Exercise 5.7

Copy and complete these multiplications. Show all your working, including the carried numbers.

1 132 × 40

2 315 × 500

3 603 × 30

4 1241 × 600

5 5012 × 80

6 2351 × 900

7 3102 × 70

8 5023 × 600

9 4217 × 80

10 6321 × 90

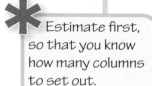

Estimate first, so that you know how many columns to set out.

11 7363 × 70

12 5378 × 80

13 5764 × 400

14 4352 × 600

15 8907 × 40

16 74358 × 120

17 53025 × 70

18 97927 × 1100

19 85025 × 90

20 67937 × 80

⇨ Using factors to divide

To be able to divide, you must make sure that you know your times tables really well. Just as with multiplication, it can be useful to use factors to divide.

Think how you would work out 288 ÷ 16

There are three factor pairs of 16, since 16 = 1 × 16, 16 = 2 × 8 and 16 = 4 × 4, but 4 × 4 seems to be the most useful.

Step 1: 288 ÷ 4 = 72

Step 2: 72 ÷ 4 = 18

288 ÷ 16 = 18

Examples:

(i) Calculate $450 \div 15$

The factors of 15 are 3 and 5

$450 \div 15 = 450 \div 3 \div 5$

$= 150 \div 5$

$= 30$

(ii) Calculate $1440 \div 40$

There are several factor pairs of 40 but 4×10 seems to be the most useful way of breaking up 40

$1440 \div 40 = 1440 \div 4 \div 10$

$= 360 \div 10$

$= 36$

In the examples, the stages were written down. Rather than writing them all down, try to do all the stages in your head and write down just the calculation and the answer. If you need to write stages, then make sure you use the equals sign correctly.

You should **not** write:

$240 \div 15 = 240 \div 3 = 80 \div 5 = 16$

because $240 \div 3$ does not equal $80 \div 5$

Exercise 5.8

Complete these calculations mentally, using factors or another method. All the answers are exact – there are no remainders.

1 $180 \div 20$

2 $64 \div 16$

3 $135 \div 15$

4 $175 \div 25$

5 $216 \div 24$

6 $98 \div 14$

7 $160 \div 32$

8 $189 \div 21$

9 $252 \div 36$

10 $210 \div 42$

11 360 ÷ 24	**16** 336 ÷ 28
12 180 ÷ 15	**17** 720 ÷ 45
13 575 ÷ 25	**18** 280 ÷ 56
14 384 ÷ 16	**19** 945 ÷ 63
15 405 ÷ 27	**20** 441 ÷ 49
21 357 ÷ 21	**26** 819 ÷ 21
22 480 ÷ 32	**27** 798 ÷ 42
23 312 ÷ 24	**28** 720 ÷ 48
24 490 ÷ 35	**29** 1400 ÷ 56
25 700 ÷ 28	**30** 1224 ÷ 72

⇨ Written division calculations

As with multiplication, with larger numbers it is best to work out division calculations by writing them one column at a time.

Division is the only calculation for which you work from the largest place value down to the smallest.

The number columns are still important in division. You must make sure that your answer is in the correct place.

The first example is worked out step by step and the second example is done all in one frame, as you would normally do it.

The answer to a division calculation may be exact or may have a number left over.

For example 13 ÷ 2 = 6 with 1 left over   or   13 ÷ 2 = 6 r1

In this calculation

      6 is called the quotient

      1 is called the remainder

Examples:

(i)   Calculate $5357 \div 4$

Divide into the thousands:

	Th	H	T	U
	1			
4	5	^{1}3	5	7

$5 \div 4 = 1\ r1$

Write 1 in the **thousands** column and carry the 1 to the **hundreds** column.

Divide into the hundreds:

	Th	H	T	U
	1	3		
4	5	^{1}3	^{1}5	7

$13 \div 4 = 3\ r1$

Write 3 in the **hundreds** column and carry the 1 to the **tens** column.

Divide into the tens:

	Th	H	T	U
	1	3	3	
4	5	^{1}3	^{1}5	^{3}7

$15 \div 4 = 3\ r3$

Write 3 in the **tens** column and carry 3 to the **units** column.

Divide into the units:

	Th	H	T	U	
	1	3	3	9	r1
4	5	^{1}3	^{1}5	^{3}7	

$37 \div 4 = 9\ r1$

Write 9 in the **units** column and write r1 to the right.

$5357 \div 4 = 1339\ r1$

(ii) Calculate $7172 \div 7$

	Th	H	T	U	
	1	0	2	4	r4
7	7	1	^{1}7	^{3}2	

$7 \div 7 = 1$

Write 1 in the **Th** column.

$1 \div 7 = 0$ r1

Write 0 in the **H** column, carry 1 to the **T** column.

$17 \div 7 = 2$ r3

Write 2 in the **T** column, carry 3 to the **U** column.

$32 \div 7 = 4$ r4

Write 4 in the **U** column and write r4 to the right.

$7172 \div 7 = 1024$ r4

Exercise 5.9

Calculate the answers to these divisions. Show all your working, including the carried numbers.

The answers to questions 1 to 10 are exact. The answers to questions 11 to 20 may have remainders.

1 $639 \div 3$

2 $634 \div 2$

3 $864 \div 3$

4 $855 \div 5$

5 $3124 \div 4$

6 $2435 \div 5$

7 $4178 \div 2$

8 $8316 \div 4$

9 $5325 \div 5$

10 $9237 \div 3$

11 $8235 \div 6$

12 $8237 \div 7$

13 $2558 \div 11$

14 $6137 \div 9$

15 $8215 \div 6$

16 $61492 \div 8$

17 $83236 \div 7$

18 $94525 \div 12$

19 $29617 \div 9$

20 $81956 \div 7$

Division with gaps

Sometimes a division calculation may have a zero in it.

Think how you would work out $804 \div 4$

$8 \div 4 = 2$

$0 \div 4 = 0$

$4 \div 4 = 1$

The answer is 201

It is important to write the 0 down too!

Example:

Calculate $8466 \div 7$

	Th	H	T	U	
	1	2	0	9	r3
7	8	^{1}4	6	^{6}6	

$8 \div 7 = 1\, r1$

$14 \div 7 = 2$

$6 \div 7 = 0\, r6$

$66 \div 7 = 9\, r3$

Exercise 5.10

The questions in this exercise may have 0s in the answers. Some may have remainders.

1 $648 \div 6$

2 $764 \div 7$

3 $843 \div 8$

4 $9407 \div 9$

5 $2256 \div 11$

6 $9609 \div 8$

7 $7179 \div 7$

8 $7218 \div 8$

9 $4875 \div 12$

10 $1459 \div 7$

⇨ More problem solving

Rounding

It is not always appropriate to give a remainder in problem-solving questions.

Examples:

(i)   There are 35 children in Year 5 and they are going on a trip to the museum. On the trip, there must be one teacher for every eight children. How many teachers must go on the trip?

$$35 \div 8 = 4 \, r3 \quad \text{or} \quad 4\frac{3}{8}$$

You cannot have $\frac{3}{8}$ of a teacher, so you must **round up**. Therefore five teachers must go.

(ii) The farmer has collected 213 eggs and puts them into egg boxes that can each contain 12 eggs. How many egg boxes does he fill?

$$213 \div 12 = 17 \, r9 \quad \text{or} \quad 17\frac{9}{12} = 17\frac{3}{4}$$

The farmer can fill 17 egg boxes but he cannot use the remainder to fill another and so you will have to **round down**.

Exercise 5.11

Calculate the answer to each problem. Some questions will give inexact answers. Think carefully about whether to round up or round down.

You may use any methods of calculation that you like. If you are doing a calculation in your head, write it down like this:

$$54 + 63 = 117$$

Write down any working that you need.

1   The milkman delivers 108 pints of milk to the school each weekday. How many pints does he deliver each week?

2   Today, he also delivered six trays of eggs, with 24 eggs in each tray. How many eggs is that?

3 I am at school for a total of 199 days a year. If there are five days in a school week, how many full weeks is that?

4 The 350 children in the school have to go to matron for an eye test. They go in groups of eight.

How many groups does matron have to see?

5 Rulers arrive in a box of 144. These are shared equally among eight classes. How many does each class receive?

6 There are 14 weeks in this term and the school chef orders 18 loaves of bread each day. There are five school days each week.

How many loaves of bread does he order this term?

7 Christmas decorations are packed in boxes of 24

If there are 14 508 Christmas decorations, how many boxes will they fill?

8 Visitors to the London Eye fill up the pods in groups of 24

If there are 8500 visitors on one day, how many pods will they need?

9 A theatre seats 950 people. It is fully booked for all of its nine shows a week for 50 weeks of the year.

How many people will visit the theatre?

10 The seats in a church are arranged in rows of nine.

How many rows will the 437 children and teachers in a school need for their carol service?

Two-stage calculations

The questions in the last exercise could all be answered with one calculation. Real-life problems often need more than one calculation.

Example:

Glue sticks come in boxes of 16. The school has ordered 12 boxes to be shared among 8 classes. How many glue sticks does each class get?

16 × 12

	H	T	U
		1	6
×		1	2
	1	9	2
		7	

192 ÷ 8

			2	4
8	1	9	^{3}2	

Each class has 24 glue sticks.

Exercise 5.12

1 A school has been collecting tokens from a supermarket to win some free sports equipment. Year 3 collected 114 tokens, Year 4 collected 143, Year 5 collected 98 and Year 6 collected 205. The school decides to exchange their tokens for footballs. For 80 tokens, they receive one free football.

   How many footballs can the school receive in exchange for the tokens?

2 The milkman delivers 14 bottles of milk to the school each weekday. Each bottle contains four pints. One pint is enough for three children to have a glass of milk at break time. There are 253 children in the school.

   How many do not have a glass of milk at break time?

3 Four trays of eggs were delivered to a school today, with 24 eggs in each tray. The school cook needs six eggs to make a batch of 20 biscuits.

   How many biscuits can the cook bake today?

4 There are 354 books in the library. The headteacher has asked that every child gives three new books to the library. There are 134 children in the school.

How many books will the school then have in the library?

5 The whole of middle school is going on a trip to the local museum. There are 24 children in Year 3, 31 children in Year 4, 29 children in Year 5 and 33 children in Year 6. They are going in groups of 8, each with a teacher or a parent helper.

(a) If there are nine teachers going on the trip, how many parent helpers will the school need?

(b) All the children ask not to be in a group with anyone that is not in their own year.

How many extra parent helpers does the school need now?

6 A school has a new library. It has 25 bookcases, each with six shelves. One shelf can take 30 books.

(a) How many books can the new library hold?

(b) If the school already has 2837 books, how many new ones could they order?

7 A theme park has 150 000 visitors in one day. The park is open for 8 hours and sells 12 000 souvenir photographs every hour. If visitors can only buy one photograph, how many visitors do **not** buy a photograph?

8 A theatre has 650 seats. It is sold out for all 11 shows this week. It expects that one-eighth of the visitors will each buy a programme. How many programmes does the theatre expect to sell this week?

9 It is 838 miles from John O'Groats to Land's End. A cyclist can cover 70 miles a day and a hiker can cover 28 miles a day.

How many more days does it take the hiker to walk the distance than the cyclist to ride?

10 There are 62 seats in a standard railway carriage and 48 seats in a buffet carriage. A train has nine standard carriages and one buffet carriage.

(a) How many passengers can it take, if no one stands?

(b) If the train company runs three trains every hour for 15 hours a day, how many passengers can they take each day?

Missing numbers

Exercise 5.13

These questions are just like those you have been answering in this chapter, but some of the numbers are missing. Copy and complete them, writing the correct numbers in the boxes to make the calculation correct.

1 $7 \times \boxed{} = 28$

2 $36 \div \boxed{} = 4$

3 $65 \div \boxed{} = 7 \text{ r } 2$

4 $3\boxed{} \times 6 = 1\boxed{}2$

5 $49 \div \boxed{} = \boxed{}\frac{4}{5}$

6 $2\boxed{} \times 7 = 2\boxed{}3$

7 $7\boxed{} \times 2 = \boxed{}56$

8

	Th	H	T	U
		5	4	3
×				☐
		☐	6	☐ 9

9

	Th	H	T	U
		☐	4	☐
×				7
	3	7	☐	4

10

		2	4	☐
4		☐	6	8

11

	Th	H	T	U
	☐	1	5	☐
×				4
	8	6	☐	8

12

	☐	7	2	0	r3
☐	8	☐	0	☐	

79

Exercise 5.14: Summary exercise

1 (a) 8 × 9

(b) 64 ÷ 8

(c) 7 × 8

(d) 63 ÷ 9

(e) 12 × 9

(f) 132 ÷ 11

(g) 8 × 6

(h) 24 ÷ 3

2 Write any remainders as fractions.

(a) $\frac{1}{6}$ of 55

(b) Divide 75 by 9

(c) $\frac{1}{12}$ of 37

(d) Divide 100 by 7

(e) An eighth of 63

(f) $\frac{1}{7}$ of 50

3 (a) 1600 × 10 000

(b) 3 500 000 ÷ 10 000

(c) 201 × 1000

(d) 30 000 ÷ 100

4 Show all your working clearly.

(a) 25 × 16

(b) 192 ÷ 24

(c) 36 × 60

(d) 324 ÷ 27

(e) 45 × 36

(f) 816 ÷ 48

5 Show all your working clearly.

(a) 1040 × 9

(b) 4068 ÷ 9

(c) 3924 × 8

(d) 5142 ÷ 7

(e) 3125 × 7

(f) 8315 ÷ 4

6 There are 425 children in the school. They share one packet of biscuits among 12 pupils.

How many packets did the cook order?

7 There are 54 cards in a pack and every one of the 21 boys in Year 4 has a pack of cards. How many cards is that in all?

8 Lockers come in stacks of three. If there are 268 children needing lockers, how many stacks must the school buy?

Fill in the missing numbers in these calculations.

9

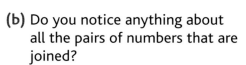

	Th	H	T	U
	☐	5	0	☐
×				6
	9	☐	4	8

10

		1	0	2	0	r1
5		☐	1	☐	☐	

Activity – Odds and evens

1 Copy and complete these calculations.

E stands for an **even** number. O stands for an **odd** number.

$6 - 4 = \ldots$ $E - E = \ldots$

$6 - 5 = \ldots$ $E - O = \ldots$

$5 - 2 = \ldots$ $O - E = \ldots$

$5 - 1 = \ldots$ $O - O = \ldots$

2 (a) Write the numbers 1 to 9 in the circles so that the difference between each pair of joined numbers is odd.

   (b) Do you notice anything about all the pairs of numbers that are joined?

   (c) Are there any other ways of arranging the numbers? If there are, draw them.

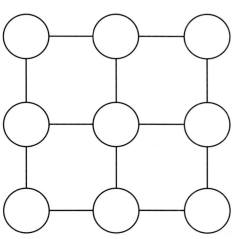

6 Factors and multiples

A **factor** is a number that divides exactly into another number without leaving a remainder. A **multiple** is a number that a factor divides into exactly.

- 2 is a factor of 12 because 12 ÷ 2 = 6 with no remainder.

- 12 is a multiple of 2 because 2 is one of its factors.

Every number has factors, since 1 divides exactly into any number.

There are clues that tell you whether a number is a factor of another number. They are called the rules of divisibility.

⇨ The rules of divisibility

Learning these rules can help you to develop your understanding of numbers.

Knowing your times tables will help you to understand and use these rules more easily.

Divisibility by 2, 4 and 8

- Numbers that can be **divided by 2** are called **even** numbers and end in 0, 2, 4, 6 or 8

- All even numbers have at least one even factor.

  For example, 30, 62, 74, 96, 138 are all divisible by 2

- A number can be **divided by 4** if the number formed by its last two digits can be divided by 4. This is because 100, and therefore any multiple of 4, is divisible by 4 (100 = 4 × 25)

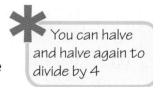

You can halve and halve again to divide by 4

Example:

Is 4 a factor of 136?

The number formed by the last two digits is 36, and 36 ÷ 4 = 9

So 136 is divisible by 4

This is the same as saying that 4 is a factor of 136 or that 136 is a multiple of 4

- A number can be **divided by 8** if the number formed by the last three digits is divisible by 8

 You can halve and halve and halve again to divide by 8

Example:

Is 8 a factor of 2120?

The number formed by the last three digits is 120, and $120 \div 8 = 15$

$(120 \div 2 = 60, 60 \div 2 = 30, 30 \div 2 = 15)$

So 8 is a factor of 2120

A multiple is a number that the factor divides into exactly.

The last example could have been written as: 'Is 2120 a multiple of 8?'

You would work the answer out in exactly the same way.

Exercise 6.1

1 List any number which has 2 as a factor.

(34)　　27　　(70)　　(116)

2 List any number which has 4 as a factor.

(56)　(68)　　74　　63

3 List any number which has 8 as a factor.

(96)　　116　　125　　160

4 List any number which is a multiple of 2

(128)　　4587　　(2302)　　(400)

5 List any number which is a multiple of 4

(264)　　2484　　3416　　2008

6 List any number which is a multiple of 8

680　　375　　2784　　3160

Divisibility by 5 and 10

- Numbers that can be **divided by 5** end in 5 or 0

  For example, 45 and 130 are divisible by 5

- Numbers that can be **divided by 10** end in 0

  For example, 270 and 20 are divisible by 10

Exercise 6.2

1 List any number which has 5 as a factor.

(10) (25) (15)   21

2 List any number which has 10 as a factor.

(30) (60)   75   (10)

3 List any number which is a multiple of 5

(65) (80)   58   (105)

4 List any number which is a multiple of 10

101   (120) (200)   145

Divisibility by 3, 6 and 9

- A number can be **divided by 3** if the sum of its digits is a multiple of 3

Example:

Is 3 a factor of 87?

Add the two digits, 8 and 7, together.

$$8 + 7 = 15$$

15 is a multiple of 3 (3×5)

So 3 is a factor of 87 and 87 is a multiple of 3

- A number can be **divided by 6** if it is even **and** the sum of its digits is divisible by 3

The rules of divisility

Example:

Is 6 a factor of 48?

48 is even.

4 + 8 = 12 and 12 is a multiple of 3

6 is a factor of 48 and 48 is a multiple of 6

- A number can be **divided by 9** if the sum of its digits is a multiple of 9

Example:

Is 9 a factor of 288?

2 + 8 + 8 = 18 and 18 is a multiple of 9

9 is a factor of 288 and 288 is a multiple of 9

Exercise 6.3

1 List any number which has 3 as a factor.

(6)   (30)   (33)   145

2 List any number which has 6 as a factor.

(12)   15   (30)   (300)

3 List any number which has 9 as a factor.

19   (405)   (36)   209

4 List any number which is a multiple of 3

(426)   571   7603   84 124

5 List any number which is a multiple of 6

721   (501)   (8613)   (10 200)

6 List any number which is a multiple of 9

107   (1701)   (2016)   30 612

Divisibility by 20, 25, 50 and 100

● Numbers that can be **divided by 20** end in multiples of 20, that is 20, 40, 60, 80 or 00

For example, 120, 340, 560, 680 and 900 are all divisible by 20

● Numbers that can be **divided by 25** end in multiples of 25, that is 25, 50, 75 or 00

For example, 225, 350, 475 and 600 are divisible by 25

● Numbers that can be **divided by 50** end in multiples of 50, that is 50 or 00

For example, 450 and 700 are divisible by 50

● Numbers that can be **divided by 100** end in multiples of 100, so the last two digits are 00

For example, 1200 is divisible by 100

Exercise 6.4

1 List any number which has 20 as a factor.

    40   85   60   100

2 List any number which has 25 as a factor.

    50   75   120   125

3 List any number which has 50 as a factor.

    100   150   1345   32 200

4 List any number which has 100 as a factor.

    100   250   4300   60 001

5 List any number which is a multiple of 20.

    80   110   2020   32 330

6 List any number which is a multiple of 25

    200   160   1175   13 125

7 List any number which is a multiple of 50

   400   180   5005   12 250

8 List any number which is a multiple of 100

   400   650   8050   201 000

Problem solving

Exercise 6.5

1 What is the largest number, less than 100, that is divisible by both 4 and 6?

2 What is the first three-digit number that has 4 and 10 as factors?

3 What is the largest number, less than 1000, that is divisible by 20, 25 and 50?

4 Which even number divisible by 9 is nearest to 200?

5 What is the first number that is a multiple of 3, 4 and 5?

6 Which number, between 120 and 130, is divisible by 3 and has a digit-sum divisible by 4?

7 A three-digit number is a multiple of 5 and the product (multiplication) of its digits is 35. What are the possible numbers?

8 Which number, closest to 100, has 8 and 9 as factors?

9 What is the first number that is a multiple of 2, 3, 4 and 6?

10 What is the smallest number that is divisible by all the numbers 2, 3, 4, 5, 6, 8, 10, 20, 25, 50 and 100?

11 What number less than 1000 has 3, 8 and 25 as factors?

12 What is the smallest number that has three odd numbers greater than 1 as factors?

⇨ Factor pairs

We looked at factor pairs in Chapter 5. A factor pair is a set of two whole numbers that, when multiplied together, give the required product.

Example:

What are the factor pairs of 6?

$6 = 1 \times 6$ 1 and 6 are a factor pair of 6, since their product is 6

$6 = 2 \times 3$ 2 and 3 are a factor pair of 6, since their product is 6

To find all the factor pairs of a number you need to work methodically, don't just guess.

● Start with 1 × 'the number'.

● Work through 2, 3, 4 and so on, remembering all the rules of divisibility you have learned.

● Stop when you reach a factor pair you already have in your list.

The next example shows how it is done.

Example:

Find all the factor pairs of 30

1 × 'the number'	1×30	1 and 30
Try 2: 2 is a factor because 30 is an even number	2×15	2 and 15
Try 3: 3 is a factor as $3 + 0 = 3$ which is a multiple of 3	3×10	3 and 10
Try 4: 30 cannot be divided by 4		
Try 5: 30 ends in 0	5×6	5 and 6

Try 6: 30 is even and the sum of its digits is divisible by 3, but the factor pair that includes 6 has already been found, so there is no need to write down 6×5 as well.

So the answer to the question 'Find all the factor pairs of 30' is:

1 and 30, 2 and 15, 3 and 10, 5 and 6

⁎ 5×6 is the same as 6×5

Exercise 6.6

List all the factor pairs of each number.

1 12		**6** 32	
2 16		**7** 36	
3 18		**8** 40	
4 20		**9** 42	
5 24		**10** 44	
11 45		**16** 64	
12 48		**17** 72	
13 50		**18** 80	
14 56		**19** 96	
15 60		**20** 100	

Follow the plan described above.

⇨ Common factors

Look at your answers to question 1 and question 2 in the last exercise.

12 has factors 1, 2, 3, 4, 6, 12

16 has factors 1, 2, 4, 8, 16

Both 12 and 16 have 1, 2 and 4 as factors.

We say that 1, 2 and 4 are **common factors** of 12 and 16

The **highest common factor** is 4

Again, to find all the common factors of two or more numbers you need to work methodically.

- Find all the factor pairs of each number. This will ensure that you find all of the factors.

- For each number, write a list of all its factors, in order.

- Highlight all the factors that are common to all the lists.

- The highest common factor is the largest number that appears in all of the lists.

Example:

Find the common factors of 30, 50 and 70 and write down the highest common factor (HCF).

30	50	70
1 × 30	1 × 50	1 × 70
2 × 15	2 × 25	2 × 35
3 × 10	5 × 10	5 × 14
5 × 6		7 × 10

List the factors of each number.

30:     1, 2, 3, 5, 6, 10, 15, 30

50:     1, 2, 5, 10, 25, 50

70:     1, 2, 5, 7, 10, 14, 35, 70

The common factors of 30, 50 and 70 are 1, 2, 5 and 10

The highest common factor is therefore 10

Exercise 6.7

Find the common factors of each group of numbers.

1 12 and 20

2 16 and 30

3 15 and 45

4 20 and 55

5 24 and 36

6 32, 36 and 40

7 25, 35 and 75

8 36, 48 and 72

9 24, 36 and 100

10 24, 25 and 37

11 Write down the highest common factor for each group of numbers in questions 1–10

⇨ Prime numbers

Look at these numbers. What happens when you try to find their factors?

2   3   17   23   31

Each number has only two factors, itself and 1

The factors of 2 are: 1 and 2

The factors of 3 are: 1 and 3

The factors of 17 are: 1 and 17

The factors of 23 are: 1 and 23

The factors of 31 are: 1 and 31

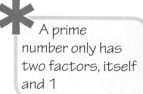

A prime number only has two factors, itself and 1

These numbers, which have only two factors, are called prime numbers.

A number that can be divided exactly by a number other than itself and 1 is called a composite number.

1 is not a prime number because it has only one factor, itself.

It is a square number.

Exercise 6.8

1 Write down all the prime numbers between 1 and 10
   (There are four of them.)

2 Write down all the composite numbers between 1 and 9
   (There are four of them.)

3 Write down the prime numbers from 10 to 20
   (There are four of these too!)

4 Write down all the composite numbers from 10 to 20

5 Copy the square below and use it to help you find all the prime numbers less than 100 (There are 25 of them.)
You might find it easier to cross out the numbers that are not prime (as in the first row of the square below). Use the rules of divisibility to help you.

~~1~~	2	3	~~4~~	5	~~6~~	7	~~8~~	~~9~~	~~10~~
11	12	13	14	15	16	17	18	19	20
21	22	23	24	25	26	27	28	29	30
31	32	33	34	35	36	37	38	39	40
41	42	43	44	45	46	47	48	49	50
51	52	53	54	55	56	57	58	59	60
61	62	63	64	65	66	67	68	69	70
71	72	73	74	75	76	77	78	79	80
81	82	83	84	85	86	87	88	89	90
91	92	93	94	95	96	97	98	99	100

6 Write down what you notice about the prime numbers that you have found. Check with your partner to see if you agree.
Can you identify a prime number that is the odd one out?

7 Use the rules of divisibility to decide whether each of these numbers is prime or composite.

111   414   1009   902   911   1005

8 Copy and complete each sentence.

All even numbers greater than 2 are ... numbers.

All numbers greater than 5 that end in 5 are ... numbers.

⇨ Prime factors

You know that a factor is a number that divides exactly into another number.

Now think about what prime factors could be.

A prime factor is a factor that is also a prime number.

Example:

What are the prime factors of 12?

Factors of 12: $12 = 2 \times 6$ but 6 is not prime.

$12 = 3 \times 4$ but 4 is not prime.

Both 6 and 4 can be written as multiples of prime numbers.

$6 = 3 \times 2$

$4 = 2 \times 2$

So you can write:

$12 = 2 \times 6 = 2 \times 3 \times 2$

$12 = 3 \times 4 = 3 \times 2 \times 2$

Since $12 = 2 \times 2 \times 3$, the prime factors of 12 are 2, 2, 3

> You should usually write the prime factors in order of size, smallest first.

The most common prime factors that you will meet are 2, 3, 5 and 7, but always check for larger prime numbers such as 11, 13, 17 and 19

Once again, working methodically, you should use a logical method to find the prime factors of a number. One method is a **factor tree**.

Factor trees

Example:

What are the prime factors of 12?

- Start with the number in the middle of the page.

- Write down a pair of factors as the first 'branches'.

Look at the numbers at the end of the 'branches'. If a number is prime, leave it alone (3 is prime).

Continue the process until all the numbers at the end of the 'branches' are prime. These are the prime factors of the number.

The prime factors of 12 are 2, 2 and 3

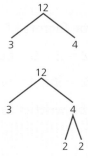

Sometimes there is more than one way of finding the answer.

Example:

Write 24 as the product of its prime factors.

Here are three different ways of arriving at the answer.

You can write 24 as a product (multiplication) of its prime factors like this:

$$24 = 2 \times 2 \times 2 \times 3$$

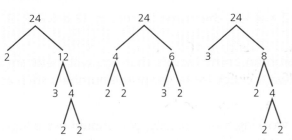

Exercise 6.9

Write each of these numbers as a product of its prime factors.

1 16

2 18

3 20

4 27

5 28

6 30

7 32

8 36

9 40

10 42

11	44
12	45
13	48
14	54
15	56

16	60
17	63
18	64
19	69
20	72

Ladder division

Ladder division is another method of finding the prime factors of a number.

Some people find this method easier with larger numbers, but you can use whichever method you prefer.

Example:

Write 300 as a product of its prime factors.

- Start dividing by the smallest prime that you can.

  Start with 2 because 300 is an even number.

- Continue dividing by 2 until you cannot divide by 2 any more.

- Then divide by 3, 5, 7 and so on, as necessary.

2	3	0	0
2	1	5	0
3		7	5
5		2	5
			5

- Stop when you reach a prime number.

  $300 = 2 \times 2 \times 3 \times 5 \times 5$

When using ladder division, you can divide by the prime numbers in any order, but it is usually best to work from smallest to largest.

Examples:

Write each number as a product of its prime factors.

(i) 280

2	2	8	0
2	1	4	0
2		7	0
5		3	5
			7

$280 = 2 \times 2 \times 2 \times 5 \times 7$

(ii) 588

2	5	8	8
2	2	9	4
3	1	4	7
7		4	9
			7

$588 = 2 \times 2 \times 3 \times 7 \times 7$

Exercise 6.10

Using whichever method you wish, write each of these numbers as a product of its prime factors.

1	80	6	120
2	84	7	132
3	90	8	140
4	96	9	144
5	100	10	160

11	180	16	576
12	196	17	729
13	225	18	850
14	360	19	1000
15	441	20	1225

⇨ Square numbers and square roots

Some of the pairs of factors you found in Exercise 6.6 included a number multiplied by itself. Numbers formed in this way are called square numbers because they can be drawn as square arrays of smaller squares or dots.

Example:

Is 16 a square number?

16 is a square number because $16 = 4 \times 4$

It can also be written as 4^2 (4 squared).

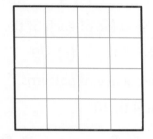

Every square number has a square root. This is the number that, when multiplied by itself, gives the square number. Finding a square root is the **inverse** of squaring a number.

Squares	Square roots
$1^2 = 1$	$\sqrt{1} = 1$
$2^2 = 4$	$\sqrt{4} = 2$
$3^2 = 9$	$\sqrt{9} = 3$
$4^2 = 16$	$\sqrt{16} = 4$
$5^2 = 25$	$\sqrt{25} = 5$
$6^2 = 36$	$\sqrt{36} = 6$
$7^2 = 49$	$\sqrt{49} = 7$
$8^2 = 64$	$\sqrt{64} = 8$
$9^2 = 81$	$\sqrt{81} = 9$
$10^2 = 100$	$\sqrt{100} = 10$

Exercise 6.11

1 Draw a square pattern, like the one above, to illustrate each of these square numbers.

Write down the total number of small squares under each pattern.

(a) 1^2 **(b)** 2^2 **(c)** 3^2 **(d)** 4^2 **(e)** 5^2

2 Write down the value of each of these square roots.

(a) $\sqrt{1}$ **(b)** $\sqrt{4}$ **(c)** $\sqrt{9}$ **(d)** $\sqrt{16}$ **(e)** $\sqrt{25}$

3 Look at this sequence of patterns.

Draw patterns 4 to 10

1

$2 \times 2 = 4$
$1 + 3 = 4$

$3 \times 3 = 9$
$1 + 3 + 5 = 9$

4 Make a classroom poster showing how the pattern of square numbers is built up. You could use sticky dots in different colours.

⇨ Cube numbers

Some of the numbers you worked with in Exercise 6.9 had one factor that occurred three times, such as $8 = 2 \times 2 \times 2$

These are called cube numbers because they can be drawn in the shape of a three-dimensional cube.

Example:

Is 8 a cube number?

8 is a cube number because $8 = 2 \times 2 \times 2$

It can also be written as 2^3 (2 cubed).

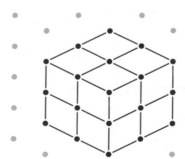

Exercise 6.12

1 With a partner, use small cubes to build larger cubes.

2 Write down the total number of small cubes in each of these numbers.

(a) 1^3 (b) 2^3 (c) 3^3 (d) 4^3 (e) 5^3 (f) 6^3

3 Calculate the value of each of these numbers.

(a) 10^3 (b) 8^3 (c) 7^3 (d) 12^3

4 Write each of these numbers as a product of its prime factors.

(a) 4^3 (b) 6^3 (c) 8^3 (d) 10^3

5 On isometric dotted paper, draw a family of cube shapes like the illustration in the example.

6 Make a classroom poster showing how the pattern of cube numbers is built up.

Exercise 6.13: Summary exercise

1 Choose all the factors of the given number, from the list in brackets.

(a) 138   (2, 3, 4, 6)   (c) 375   (3, 5, 20, 25)

(b) 234   (2, 3, 6, 9)   (d) 430   (5, 8, 10, 20)

2 Write down all the factor pairs of each number.

(a) 36   (b) 120

3 Write down all the prime numbers between 20 and 40

4 Write each of these numbers as a product of its prime factors.

(a) 60   (b) 96   (c) 189

5 Write down the first five square numbers.

6 What is the value of $\sqrt{64}$?

7 Calculate the value of 9^3

8 Which of these numbers has 3, 5 and 8 as factors?

115   150   240   265

9 Ramon's telephone number is made up of two of these numbers.

150   170   260   370

The first is a multiple of 20 and the second is a multiple of 25

What is Ramon's telephone number?

10 Use these numbers to answer the questions below.

4   8   9   10   12   17   21

Write down:

(a) a multiple of 6

(b) a number that has 7 as a factor

(c) a square number

(d) $\sqrt{16}$

(e) a prime number.

Activity – Square numbers investigation

Look at the dot pattern that you made earlier.

| 1 | 2 × 2 = 4 | 3 × 3 = 9 | 4 × 4 = 16 |

1 Copy and complete this table. Use your patterns to help you.

1	1
1 + 3	4
1 + 3 + 5	9
	16
	25
	36

2 Copy and complete this sentence.

Square numbers can be made by adding … numbers.

3 Write 10^2 as the sum of a sequence of numbers.

4 Copy and complete this table. Use your patterns to help you.

Pattern no.	Red dots	Black dots	Total
1	1	0	1
2	1	3	4
3	6	3	9
4	6		16
5		10	25

5 Continue your table up to pattern 10

6 Work out how many black dots and how many red dots you will need for pattern number 15

7 Number properties

⇨ Think about numbers

In this chapter you will answer questions that will make you think about numbers in various different ways.

If you think about all the things you have learned about numbers, you should find that you are able to answer these questions.

Sum means the result of adding two or more numbers.

Product means the result of multiplication (6 is the product of 2 × 3).

Difference means the result of subtraction (the difference between two numbers).

Consecutive means numbers that follow each other, such as 3 and 4, or 11, 12 and 13

Exercise 7.1

1 By giving several examples, show that these statements are true.

   (a) The sum of three odd numbers is odd.

   (b) Any odd number is double another number + 1

   (c) All multiples of 4 end in 0, 2, 4, 6 or 8

2 Find three consecutive numbers that add up to 39

3 What numbers, less than 50, can be made by adding three consecutive numbers?

4 Find two numbers that give:

(a) a sum of 11 and a product of 24

(b) a sum of 15 and a product of 54

(c) a sum of 7 and a product of 10

(d) a sum of 5 and a product of 6

(e) a sum of 19 and a product of 90

(f) a sum of 40 and a product of 400

5 Find a two-digit number with digits that have:

(a) a difference of 7 and a product of 18

(b) a difference of 1 and a product of 20

(c) a difference of 5 and a product of 14

(d) a difference of 2 and a product of 8

(e) a difference of 7 and a product of 8

(f) a difference of 6 and a product of 0

6 Replace each * with one of the digits 1, 3, 4 and 8 so that these statements are true. (* represents a digit.)

(a) * * − * = 38   (c) 4 * + * 9 = 82

(b) 3 * − * 9 = 19   (d) 3 * + * 7 = 120

7 Find as many ways as possible to complete this multiplication.

** × * = 252

8 Arrange the numbers 1 to 9 inclusive in three groups, so that each group has a sum of 15

Use each number only once.

9 Replace each * with a digit so that these statements are true.

(a) 1 * + * 7 = 32   (b) 3 * − * 4 = 4

10 How many groups of four odd numbers that add up to 20 can you find? The numbers within each group must all be different.

11 (a) What is the first odd multiple of 3 that is greater than 47?

(b) Write down a prime number between 29 and 35

(c) Write down a two-digit square number that is greater than 25 and the product of whose digits is 36

(d) Write down the number of which the square and the square root are the same.

12 Find as many as possible pairs of numbers with a product of 36

13 Find as many sets of three numbers as possible with a product of 24

14 Find a pair of consecutive numbers that add up to:

(a) 7   **(b)** 15   **(c)** 49   **(d)** 111   **(e)** 629

15 Each of these numbers is the result of adding three consecutive numbers.

$$15 = 4 + 5 + 6 \qquad 36 = 11 + 12 + 13$$
$$90 = 29 + 30 + 31 \qquad 123 = 40 + 41 + 42$$

(a) Do the four examples above have anything in common?

(b) Which of these numbers can be made by adding three consecutive numbers?

456   532   618   789   1234   3456

16 (a) I am a two-digit number between 30 and 60

I am a multiple of 4 and the sum of my digits is 4

What number am I?

(b) I am a two-digit odd number between 30 and 60

I am a multiple of 5 and the sum of my digits is 10

What number am I?

(c) I am a two-digit multiple of 3 but am less than 30

The difference between my digits is 5

What number am I?

(d) I am more than 20 but less than 30

There are 8 different numbers that are my factors.

What number am I?

17 Find a two-digit odd number that is a square number and the product of whose digits is 8

18 Which two-digit square number is four times another square number?

19 By thinking about square numbers, explain whether 1234^2 will be an even or an odd number.

20 Use some or all of the digits 1, 2, 3 and 4 (once only) and any operation to make the numbers 1 to 20

for example,

$$6 = 1 + 2 + 3$$

or $\quad 6 = 2 + 4$

or $\quad 6 = 2 \times 3$

or $\quad 6 = (3 \times 4) \div 2$

Activity – Similar sums

Find ways of arranging these numbers so that each row, column and diagonal has the same total.

1	1	1
2	2	2
3	3	3

Now try the same with the numbers 4, 5 and 6

Try to think of another three numbers you could use.

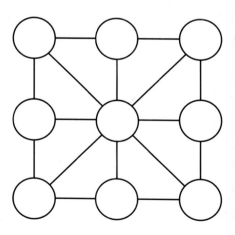

8 Angles

An angle is formed at the point at which two lines meet.

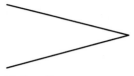

■ One line

■ Two lines

You need to know the words that describe different types of angle.

■ A **right angle** is exactly 90°.

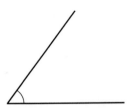

■ An **acute angle** is less than 90°.

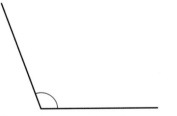

■ An **obtuse angle** is between 90° and 180°.

■ A straight line is an angle of 180°.

■ A full turn is an angle of 360°.

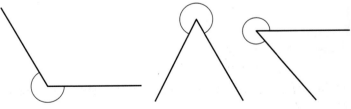

■ **Reflex angles** are between 180° and 360°.

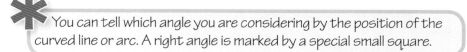

You can tell which angle you are considering by the position of the curved line or arc. A right angle is marked by a special small square.

⇨ Angles on a straight line

When a line is rotated about one end, through two right angles, it moves through 180° (90° × 2). Its position before and after the rotation together form one longer straight line.

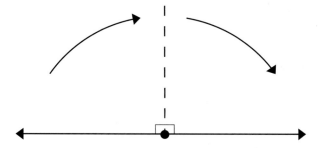

When a sloping line is drawn to meet a straight line, two angles are formed.

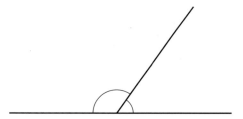

Because the original line was a straight line, it follows that the two angles formed must add up to 180°.

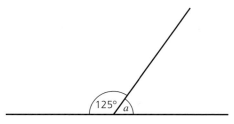

To find the size of the angle labelled a, subtract the given angle from 180°.

$a = 180° - 125°$

$\quad = 55°$

Calculate the size of the angles marked a.

1

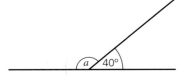

5

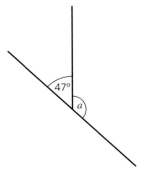

2

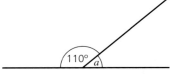

6

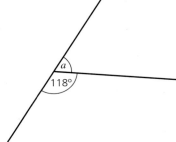

3

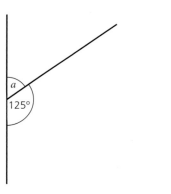

7

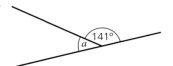

4

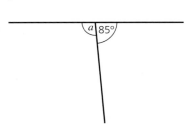

8

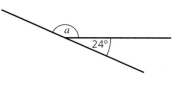

9

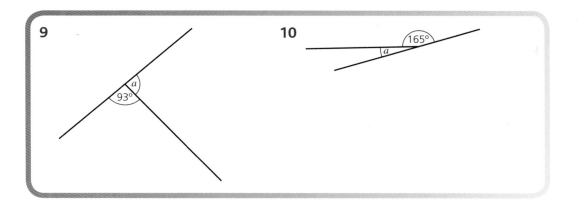

10

⇨ Angles round a point

When a line is rotated about one end, through a whole revolution, it has moved through 360° (4 right angles).

When two lines meet at a point, they form two angles.

As for angles on a straight line, if you know one of the angles around a point, you can work out the other one.

If one angle is 150°, the other is 210° (360° − 150°).

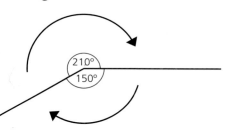

Exercise 8.2

Calculate the size of each of the angles marked a.

1

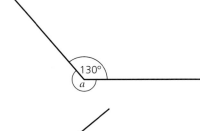

3

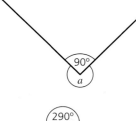

2

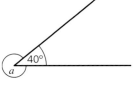

4

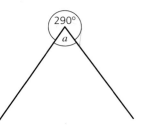

5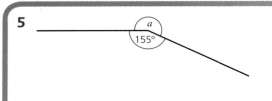

6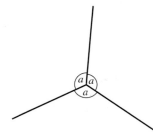

If more than one angle is marked a, it means that they are the same size.

7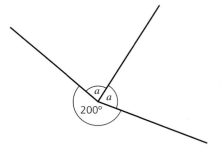

9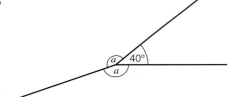

8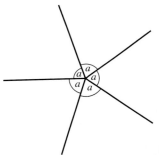

10

⇨ Measuring angles

To measure the size of an angle, you will need to use a protractor.
The angle being measured here is the acute angle of 50°.

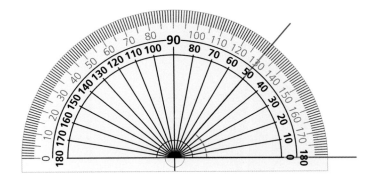

To use a 180° protractor to measure a reflex angle, you will have
to measure the other, smaller angle and subtract it from 360°, as
together the two angles make a full turn.

Example:

Measure this angle.

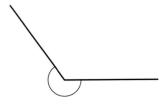

What type of angle is it?	Reflex
Estimate the size of the angle.	225°
Measure the obtuse angle.	125°

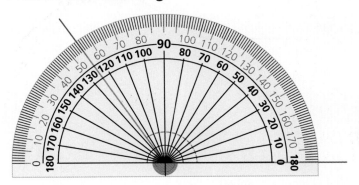

Calculate the reflex angle: 360° − 125° = 235°

For each angle:

(a) state whether it is acute, obtuse or reflex

(b) estimate the size of the angle

(c) measure the angle accurately.

1

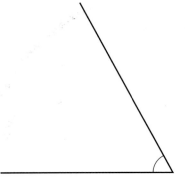

4

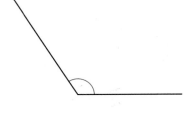

2

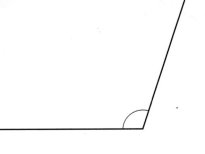

5

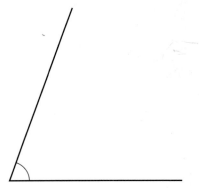

3

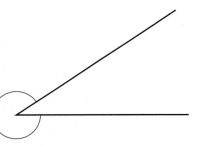

6

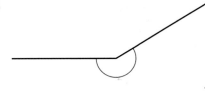

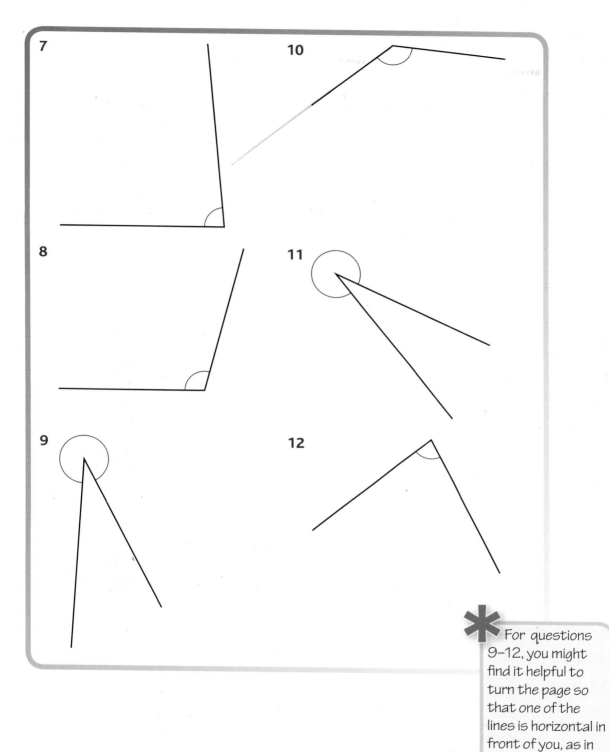

7

8

9

10

11

12

*For questions 9–12, you might find it helpful to turn the page so that one of the lines is horizontal in front of you, as in questions 1–8

⇨ Drawing angles

When drawing angles, follow these steps.

● Estimate the size of the angle by rotating your pencil.

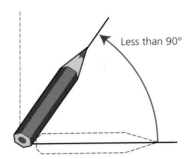

Less than 90°

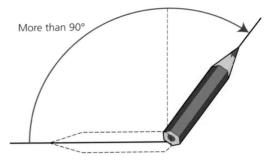

More than 90°

● Make sure you use the correct scale on the protractor (inside or outside).

Exercise 8.4

For each question, start by drawing a line about 6 centimetres long and label it AB.

Draw these angles.

1 angle A = 60°

2 angle B = 120°

3 angle A = 46°

4 angle A = 124°

5 angle B = 73°

6 angle B = 112°

7 angle A = 52°

8 angle B = 131°

9 angle B = 28°

10 angle A = 145°

Questions 11–20 are reflex angles. Calculate the complementary acute or obtuse angle first.

11 angle B = 190°

12 angle A = 260°

13 angle B = 300°

14 angle A = 293°

15 angle A = 327°

16 angle B = 283°

17 angle B = 255°

18 angle B = 204°

19 angle A = 269°

20 angle A = 333°

Exercise 8.5: Summary exercise

Calculate the sizes of the angles marked with the small letters.

1 AB is a straight line.

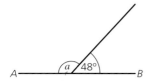

3

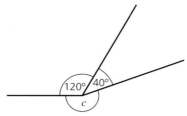

2 AB is a straight line.

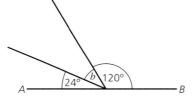

4

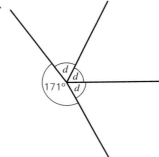

5 For each lettered angle:

    (a) state whether it is acute, obtuse or reflex

    (b) estimate the size of the angle

    (c) measure it accurately.

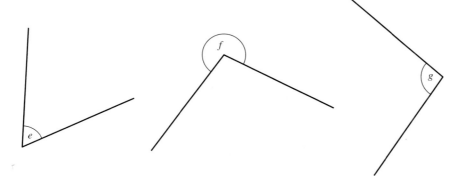

6 Draw these angles accurately.

    (a) 63°   **(b)** 235°   **(c)** 127°

Activity – Equilateral triangles

These triangles form a pattern. Each triangle is drawn with three lines and has a dot at each vertex.

1 Draw the pattern with five triangles.

2 Copy and complete the table.

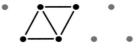
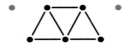

Number of triangles	Number of dots	Number of lines
1	3	3
2		5
3	5	7
4		
5		

3 (a) How many dots are there in the pattern with 12 triangles?

(b) If a pattern has 20 triangles, how many lines are there?

(c) How many triangles will you need to produce a pattern with 73 dots?

(d) How many triangles are there in the pattern made up of 121 lines?

 # Fractions

The bottom number of a fraction is called the denominator. It is very important because it tells you how many equal parts there are in the whole. The top number is the numerator. It tells you how many of these equal parts you have in the fraction.

Example:

What fraction of this circle is shaded?

$\frac{5}{6}$ ← 5 is the numerator
← 6 is the denominator

⇨ Simplifying fractions

Sometimes a fraction can be written more simply.

$\frac{4}{8} = \frac{1}{2}$

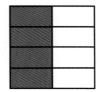

You can see that $\frac{4}{8}$ has been shaded and that this equals one half, $\frac{1}{2}$

This is called **simplifying** or writing a fraction in its **lowest terms**. You simplify a fraction by dividing the numerator and denominator by the same number.

Example:

Write $\frac{4}{8}$ in its lowest terms.

$\frac{4}{8} = \frac{4 \div 2}{8 \div 2} = \frac{2 \div 2}{4 \div 2} = \frac{1}{2}$

When you cannot simplify a fraction any more, it is in its lowest terms.

Exercise 9.1

1 Write down the fraction that is shaded in each shape.

(a)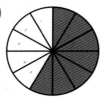

(c)

(b)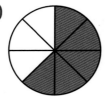

(d)

2 Write down the fraction that is shaded in each shape. Make sure you write the fraction in its lowest terms.

(a)

(d)

(b)

(e)

(c)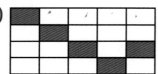

(f)

3 Draw four rectangles, each 4 cm by 9 cm. Shade them to show these fractions.

(a) $\frac{1}{4}$ (b) $\frac{5}{9}$ (c) $\frac{7}{12}$ (d) $\frac{11}{18}$

4 Simplify each fraction so that it is in its lowest terms.

(a) $\frac{8}{16}$ (d) $\frac{15}{20}$ (g) $\frac{12}{18}$ (j) $\frac{15}{18}$

(b) $\frac{2}{8}$ (e) $\frac{12}{20}$ (h) $\frac{9}{36}$ (k) $\frac{24}{56}$

(c) $\frac{5}{20}$ (f) $\frac{8}{24}$ (i) $\frac{10}{12}$ (l) $\frac{28}{49}$

⇨ Comparing fractions

Look at these fractions.

$$\frac{1}{2} \qquad \frac{1}{4} \qquad \frac{1}{8} \qquad \frac{1}{16} \qquad \frac{1}{32}$$

They are all part of the same family because all the denominators (the bottom numbers) are multiples of 2
You know that:

- one-half, $\frac{1}{2}$, is the largest, as it is one whole divided into two equal parts

- one-thirty-second, $\frac{1}{32}$, is the smallest as it is one whole divided into 32 equal parts.

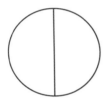 

- ■ Two $\frac{1}{2}$s   ■ Thirty-two $\frac{1}{32}$s

But which of these two fractions is larger: $\frac{3}{4}$ or $\frac{25}{32}$?

You can see that $\frac{25}{32}$ is larger than $\frac{3}{4}$

You can write $\frac{25}{32} > \frac{3}{4}$, which means that $\frac{25}{32}$ is greater than $\frac{3}{4}$

 > is the symbol for 'greater than' and < is the symbol for 'less than'.

Copy the fraction circles and colour them, to work out if the first
fraction is greater than or less than the second fraction.
Write > or < between the fractions.

1 $\frac{1}{4}$ $\frac{7}{32}$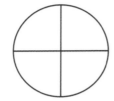

2 $\frac{3}{8}$ $\frac{7}{16}$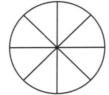

3 $\frac{3}{5}$ $\frac{9}{20}$

4 $\frac{3}{5}$ $\frac{16}{20}$

5 $\frac{2}{5}$ $\frac{7}{20}$

6 $\frac{4}{5}$ $\frac{17}{20}$

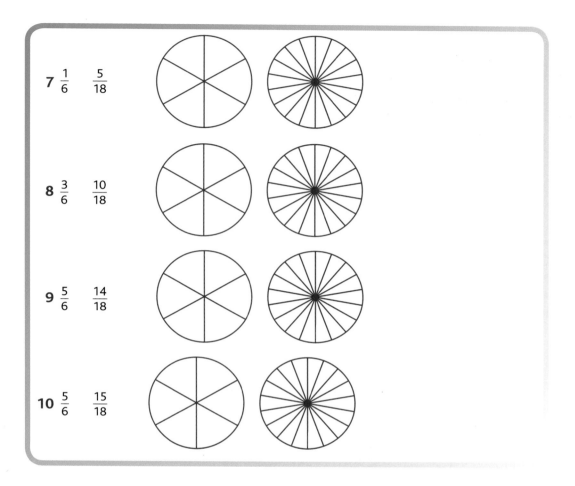

7 $\frac{1}{6}$ $\frac{5}{18}$

8 $\frac{3}{6}$ $\frac{10}{18}$

9 $\frac{5}{6}$ $\frac{14}{18}$

10 $\frac{5}{6}$ $\frac{15}{18}$

⇨ Equivalent fractions

Look at these two fractions.

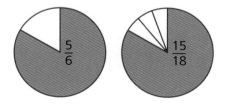

You can see from the shaded areas that these fractions are the same size, even though they have different denominators. Fractions that are the same size are called **equivalent fractions**.

You can find equivalent fractions by multiplying the numerator and denominator by the same number.

Example:

Use equivalence to find the missing number.

$$\frac{5}{6} = \frac{\square}{18}$$

$6 \times 3 = 18$, so you need to multiply numerator and denominator by 3

$$\frac{5}{6} = \frac{5 \times 3}{6 \times 3} = \frac{15}{18}$$

Exercise 9.3

1 Copy the fraction circles and colour them, to complete the equivalent fraction pairs.

(a) $\frac{1}{4} = \frac{\square}{32}$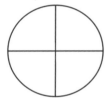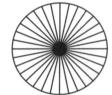

(b) $\frac{3}{8} = \frac{\square}{16}$

(c) $\frac{1}{5} = \frac{\square}{20}$

(d) $\frac{3}{5} = \frac{\square}{20}$

(e) $\dfrac{4}{5} = \dfrac{\square}{20}$

(f) $\dfrac{5}{8} = \dfrac{\square}{32}$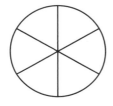

(g) $\dfrac{1}{6} = \dfrac{\square}{18}$

(h) $\dfrac{3}{6} = \dfrac{\square}{18}$

(i) $\dfrac{5}{6} = \dfrac{\square}{18}$

(j) $\dfrac{5}{8} = \dfrac{\square}{16}$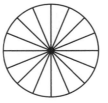

2 Copy each pair of rectangles into your book and shade them to
show each pair of equivalent fractions.

(a) $\dfrac{1}{5} = \dfrac{\square}{25}$

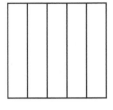
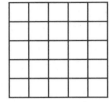

(b) $\dfrac{5}{8} = \dfrac{\square}{16}$

(c) $\dfrac{2}{5} = \dfrac{\square}{20}$

(d) $\dfrac{3}{10} = \dfrac{\square}{20}$

(e) $\dfrac{3}{4} = \dfrac{\square}{20}$

(f) $\dfrac{7}{10} = \dfrac{\square}{100}$

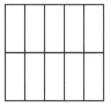
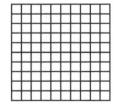

3 Work out these equivalent fractions by multiplying the numerator and denominator by the same number.

(a) $\frac{1}{4} = \frac{\square}{16}$

(f) $\frac{3}{10} = \frac{\square}{20}$

(b) $\frac{3}{8} = \frac{9}{\square}$

(g) $\frac{4}{11} = \frac{8}{\square}$

(c) $\frac{3}{5} = \frac{\square}{25}$

(h) $\frac{5}{6} = \frac{\square}{30}$

(d) $\frac{3}{5} = \frac{12}{\square}$

(i) $\frac{7}{10} = \frac{\square}{30}$

(e) $\frac{2}{5} = \frac{\square}{20}$

(j) $\frac{3}{4} = \frac{\square}{100}$

4 Work out these equivalent fractions by multiplying or dividing the numerator and denominator by the same number.

(a) $\frac{1}{4} = \frac{\square}{36}$

(f) $\frac{\square}{10} = \frac{8}{20}$

(b) $\frac{1}{\square} = \frac{25}{100}$

(g) $\frac{4}{\square} = \frac{8}{18}$

(c) $\frac{\square}{25} = \frac{24}{100}$

(h) $\frac{4}{6} = \frac{\square}{30}$

(d) $\frac{5}{\square} = \frac{10}{36}$

(i) $\frac{\square}{10} = \frac{18}{30}$

(e) $\frac{\square}{6} = \frac{16}{48}$

(j) $\frac{\square}{4} = \frac{9}{36}$

⇨ Ordering fractions

Now that you know how to work out equivalent fractions, you can use them to put fractions in order, when they have different denominators. You do this by finding the smallest number that all of the denominators will divide into, without leaving a remainder. This is the **lowest common denominator**.

> The lowest common denominator is the lowest common multiple of all the denominators.

Example:

Write $\frac{7}{10}, \frac{3}{5}$ and $\frac{19}{30}$ in order, starting with the smallest.

The denominators are 10, 5 and 30 and they will all divide exactly into 30

$$\frac{7}{10} = \frac{7 \times 3}{10 \times 3} = \frac{21}{30} \qquad \frac{3}{5} = \frac{3 \times 6}{5 \times 6} = \frac{18}{30}$$

In order, the fractions are:

$$\frac{3}{5} = \frac{18}{30}, \frac{19}{30}, \frac{7}{10} = \frac{21}{30}$$

A useful way of finding the lowest common denominator is to look at factors. In the last example, 10 and 5 are both factors of 30, so 30 was the lowest common denominator. In the next example the denominators are 3, 5 and 6. 3 is a factor of 6, but 5 is not. The lowest common denominator will be $5 \times 6 = 30$

Example:

Write $\frac{2}{3}, \frac{2}{5}$ and $\frac{5}{6}$ in order, starting with the smallest.

The denominators are 3, 5 and 6 ($6 = 3 \times 2$)

They will all divide into the number that is $3 \times 5 \times 2 = 30$

$$\frac{2}{3} = \frac{2 \times 10}{3 \times 10} = \frac{20}{30} \qquad \frac{2}{5} = \frac{2 \times 6}{5 \times 6} = \frac{12}{30} \qquad \frac{5}{6} = \frac{5 \times 5}{6 \times 5} = \frac{25}{30}$$

In order, the fractions are:

$$\frac{2}{5} = \frac{12}{30}, \frac{2}{3} = \frac{20}{30}, \frac{5}{6} = \frac{25}{30}$$

Exercise 9.4

1 Work out which is the larger in each pair of fractions. Then copy them and write > or < between them.

(a) $\frac{1}{4}$ and $\frac{1}{12}$

(b) $\frac{3}{4}$ and $\frac{7}{12}$

(c) $\frac{1}{3}$ and $\frac{5}{12}$

(d) $\frac{11}{15}$ and $\frac{4}{5}$

(e) $\frac{3}{7}$ and $\frac{8}{21}$

(h) $\frac{3}{10}$ and $\frac{9}{25}$

(f) $\frac{5}{12}$ and $\frac{3}{8}$

(i) $\frac{3}{10}$ and $\frac{5}{12}$

(g) $\frac{11}{15}$ and $\frac{5}{6}$

(j) $\frac{5}{12}$ and $\frac{3}{16}$

2 Write each set of fractions in order, starting with the smallest.

(a) $\frac{1}{4}, \frac{1}{3}, \frac{1}{12}$

(f) $\frac{7}{10}, \frac{3}{5}, \frac{9}{20}$

(b) $\frac{5}{6}, \frac{2}{3}, \frac{11}{12}$

(g) $\frac{4}{15}, \frac{1}{3}, \frac{2}{5}$

(c) $\frac{4}{15}, \frac{1}{3}, \frac{3}{10}$

(h) $\frac{3}{10}, \frac{2}{5}, \frac{1}{3}$

(d) $\frac{11}{30}, \frac{2}{3}, \frac{7}{10}$

(i) $\frac{3}{4}, \frac{2}{3}, \frac{5}{12}$

(e) $\frac{4}{7}, \frac{5}{14}, \frac{1}{2}$

(j) $\frac{7}{12}, \frac{3}{4}, \frac{2}{3}$

⇨ Proper and improper fractions

Look at these cakes.

$\frac{6}{6}$ $\qquad$ $\frac{6}{6}$ $\qquad$ $\frac{1}{6}$

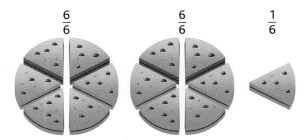

You can think of these cakes in two ways.

There are two whole cakes and one sixth, therefore you can write this as $2\frac{1}{6}$.

There are thirteen slices of cake and each slice is one sixth, so you can write this as $\frac{13}{6}$.

Therefore:

$2\frac{1}{6} = \frac{13}{6}$

Proper fractions are those in which the numerator (the number on the top) is smaller than the denominator (the number on the bottom). The value of a proper fraction is always between nought and one.

Improper fractions (sometimes called **top-heavy** fractions) are those in which the numerator (the number on the top) is bigger than the denominator (the number on the bottom). The value of an improper fraction is always greater than one.

Look at the family of fifths.

$$\frac{1}{5} \quad \frac{2}{5} \quad \frac{3}{5} \quad \frac{4}{5} \quad \frac{5}{5} \quad \frac{6}{5} \quad \frac{7}{5} \quad \frac{8}{5} \quad \frac{9}{5}$$

Proper fractions   1   Improper fractions

Thinking back to cakes, you should see that you can write an improper fraction as a mixture of a whole number and a proper fraction.

$$\frac{3}{5}$$

$$\frac{8}{5} = 1\frac{3}{5}$$

$1\frac{3}{5}$ is called a **mixed number**.

You will see and hear mixed numbers all the time, for example:

- It is a quarter past three.

- I am nine and a quarter years old.

- Platform $9\frac{3}{4}$

Examples:

(i)   Write $\frac{23}{7}$ as a mixed number.

    $\frac{23}{7} = 3\frac{2}{7}$ (as 23 ÷ 7 = 3 remainder 2)

(ii)   Write $3\frac{3}{5}$ as an improper fraction.

    $3\frac{3}{5} = \frac{18}{5}$ (as 5 × 3 + 3 = 18)

Exercise 9.5

1 Match these improper fractions and mixed numbers.

$\frac{10}{3}$	$\frac{15}{7}$	$\frac{13}{5}$	$\frac{7}{4}$	$\frac{5}{3}$
$2\frac{1}{7}$	$1\frac{3}{4}$	$1\frac{2}{3}$	$2\frac{3}{5}$	$3\frac{1}{3}$

2 Match these improper fractions and mixed numbers.

$\frac{11}{5}$	$\frac{22}{5}$	$\frac{13}{5}$	$\frac{7}{5}$	$\frac{17}{5}$
$4\frac{2}{5}$	$3\frac{2}{5}$	$1\frac{2}{5}$	$2\frac{1}{5}$	$2\frac{3}{5}$

3 Write these improper fractions as mixed numbers.

(a) $\frac{6}{5}$ (b) $\frac{9}{5}$ (c) $\frac{8}{5}$ (d) $\frac{5}{4}$ (e) $\frac{11}{6}$

4 Write these mixed numbers as improper fractions.

(a) $1\frac{1}{3}$ (b) $2\frac{3}{7}$ (c) $2\frac{5}{6}$ (d) $1\frac{3}{5}$ (e) $1\frac{5}{8}$

5 Write these improper fractions as mixed numbers.

(a) $\frac{18}{5}$ (b) $\frac{18}{7}$ (c) $\frac{21}{4}$ (d) $\frac{15}{2}$ (e) $\frac{27}{8}$

6 Write these mixed numbers as improper fractions.

(a) $3\frac{1}{5}$ (b) $2\frac{4}{9}$ (c) $4\frac{3}{11}$ (d) $5\frac{7}{10}$ (e) $4\frac{5}{12}$

7 Camembert cheese often comes in a circular pack divided into six individually packed cheese wedges. If a cheese factory produces 119 cheese wedges, how many whole packs of cheese can be filled and how many wedges are left over? Write your calculation as a number sentence, using improper fractions and mixed numbers.

8 Happy Cow cheese comes in small cubes. 12 small cubes make up one pack. If the Happy Cow factory produces 213 small cubes, how many whole packs of cheese can be filled and how many are left over?

9 Chocolates are packed in boxes of 12. If Ms Thornley makes 150 chocolates, how many boxes can she fill and what fraction of a box is left over?

10 What other examples can you think of where lots of items are packed into one box so each item is a fraction of the whole package? Write some story problems using improper fractions that have to be changed into mixed numbers.

⇨ Adding fractions

When adding fractions, you must remember what the numerator and the denominator mean.

$\frac{3}{6} + \frac{1}{6}$ means 'add 1 sixth to 3 sixths'.

Add the 1 and 3 to get 4 and the answer is 4 sixths:

$$\frac{3}{6} + \frac{1}{6} = \frac{3+1}{6} = \frac{4}{6}$$

Always give your answer in its lowest terms.

$$\frac{3}{6} + \frac{1}{6} = \frac{3+1}{6}$$
$$= \frac{4}{6}$$
$$= \frac{2}{3}$$

Sometimes when you add fractions you will get an answer that is greater than 1. You will need to turn it into a mixed number.

Example:

Add $\frac{3}{5} + \frac{4}{5}$

$$\frac{3}{5} + \frac{4}{5} = \frac{3+4}{5}$$
$$= \frac{7}{5}$$
$$= 1\frac{2}{5}$$

Exercise 9.6

Add these fractions. If your answer is greater than one, give it as a mixed number. Make sure all your fractions are in their lowest terms.

1 $\frac{1}{4} + \frac{3}{4}$

2 $\frac{5}{12} + \frac{2}{12}$

3 $\frac{1}{3} + \frac{1}{3}$

4 $\frac{11}{15} + \frac{2}{15}$

5 $\frac{3}{14} + \frac{5}{14}$

6 $\frac{3}{5} + \frac{2}{5}$

7 $\frac{7}{15} + \frac{4}{15}$

8 $\frac{3}{10} + \frac{3}{10} + \frac{1}{10}$

9 $\frac{7}{16} + \frac{5}{16} + \frac{3}{16}$

10 $\frac{7}{12} + \frac{1}{12} + \frac{4}{12}$

11 $\frac{3}{7} + \frac{5}{7}$

12 $\frac{7}{12} + \frac{7}{12}$

13 $\frac{2}{3} + \frac{2}{3}$

14 $\frac{11}{15} + \frac{13}{15}$

15 $\frac{9}{14} + \frac{11}{14}$

16 $\frac{3}{4} + \frac{3}{4}$

17 $\frac{7}{15} + \frac{13}{15}$

18 $\frac{9}{10} + \frac{7}{10} + \frac{7}{10}$

19 $\frac{9}{16} + \frac{15}{16} + \frac{13}{16}$

20 $\frac{7}{12} + \frac{11}{12} + \frac{7}{12}$

Adding fractions with different denominators

If you have to add fractions with different denominators, you need to write them as equivalent fractions with a common denominator first.

Example:

Add $\frac{3}{4} + \frac{5}{6}$

12 is the smallest multiple of both 4 and 6

$$\frac{3}{4} = \frac{9}{12} \qquad \frac{5}{6} = \frac{10}{12}$$

$$\frac{3}{4} + \frac{5}{6} = \frac{9}{12} + \frac{10}{12}$$

$$= \frac{19}{12}$$

$$= 1\frac{7}{12}$$

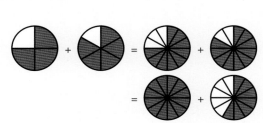

Exercise 9.7

Add these fractions.

1 $\frac{1}{4} + \frac{1}{12}$

2 $\frac{1}{6} + \frac{7}{12}$

3 $\frac{1}{3} + \frac{5}{12}$

4 $\frac{7}{15} + \frac{2}{5}$

5 $\frac{3}{7} + \frac{5}{14}$

6 $\frac{1}{4} + \frac{5}{12}$

7 $\frac{7}{15} + \frac{1}{3}$

8 $\frac{3}{10} + \frac{1}{5}$

9 $\frac{1}{8} + \frac{7}{16}$

10 $\frac{5}{12} + \frac{1}{4}$

11 $\frac{3}{4} + \frac{7}{12}$

12 $\frac{5}{6} + \frac{7}{12}$

13 $\frac{2}{3} + \frac{7}{15}$

14 $\frac{11}{15} + \frac{4}{5}$

15 $\frac{1}{2} + \frac{9}{14}$

16 $\frac{3}{4} + \frac{9}{16}$

17 $\frac{7}{15} + \frac{4}{5}$

18 $\frac{3}{7} + \frac{11}{14}$

19 $\frac{5}{8} + \frac{7}{12}$

20 $\frac{5}{12} + \frac{5}{9}$

21 $\frac{2}{3} + \frac{7}{12}$

22 $\frac{1}{6} + \frac{2}{3} + \frac{5}{12}$

23 $\frac{1}{15} + \frac{1}{3} + \frac{1}{5}$

24 $\frac{2}{15} + \frac{2}{3} + \frac{3}{5}$

25 $\frac{1}{7} + \frac{1}{14} + \frac{1}{2}$

26 $\frac{1}{10} + \frac{2}{5} + \frac{3}{20}$

27 $\frac{2}{15} + \frac{1}{3} + \frac{1}{5}$

28 $\frac{3}{10} + \frac{1}{5} + \frac{1}{2}$

29 $\frac{1}{8} + \frac{1}{2} + \frac{3}{4}$

30 $\frac{11}{12} + \frac{1}{4} + \frac{2}{3}$

Convert them to equivalent fractions first.

⇨ Subtracting fractions

The method for subtracting fractions is very similar to that for adding them.

Examples:

(i) Subtract $\frac{4}{5} - \frac{1}{5}$

Both fractions have the same denominator.

$$\frac{4}{5} - \frac{1}{5} = \frac{4-1}{5}$$
$$= \frac{3}{5}$$

(ii) Subtract $\frac{5}{6} - \frac{1}{6}$

Both fractions have the same denominator, proceed as before.

$$\frac{5}{6} - \frac{1}{6} = \frac{5-1}{6}$$
$$= \frac{4}{6}$$
$$= \frac{2}{3}$$

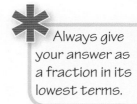

Always give your answer as a fraction in its lowest terms.

Sometimes you will need to turn a mixed number into an improper fraction before you subtract.

(iii) $1\frac{1}{6} - \frac{5}{6}$

Both fractions have the same denominator but $\frac{1}{6}$ is smaller than $\frac{5}{6}$

$$1\frac{1}{6} = \frac{7}{6}$$

$$1\frac{1}{6} - \frac{5}{6} = \frac{7}{6} - \frac{5}{6}$$
$$= \frac{7-5}{6}$$
$$= \frac{2}{6}$$
$$= \frac{1}{3}$$

Subtract these fractions. Make sure your answers are fractions in their lowest terms.

1 $\frac{3}{4} - \frac{1}{4}$

2 $\frac{11}{12} - \frac{5}{12}$

3 $\frac{5}{7} - \frac{2}{7}$

4 $\frac{11}{14} - \frac{3}{14}$

5 $\frac{8}{15} - \frac{2}{15}$

6 $\frac{9}{16} - \frac{3}{16}$

7 $\frac{11}{15} - \frac{4}{15}$

8 $\frac{9}{10} - \frac{3}{10}$

9 $\frac{7}{16} - \frac{5}{16}$

10 $\frac{11}{12} - \frac{5}{12}$

11 $1\frac{2}{7} - \frac{5}{7}$

12 $1\frac{1}{12} - \frac{7}{12}$

13 $1\frac{1}{4} - \frac{3}{4}$

14 $1\frac{3}{10} - \frac{7}{10}$

15 $1\frac{2}{15} - \frac{7}{15}$

16 $1\frac{3}{11} - \frac{4}{11}$

17 $1\frac{1}{12} - \frac{5}{12}$

18 $1\frac{1}{10} - \frac{3}{10}$

19 $1\frac{3}{8} - \frac{7}{8}$

20 $1\frac{7}{12} - \frac{11}{12}$

Subtracting fractions with different denominators

Just as when adding, if you have to subtract fractions with different denominators, you need to write them as equivalent fractions with a common denominator first.

Example:

Subtract $\frac{1}{2} - \frac{1}{6}$

6 is the smallest multiple of both 2 and 6

$$\frac{1}{2} = \frac{3}{6}$$

$$\frac{1}{2} - \frac{1}{6} = \frac{3}{6} - \frac{1}{6}$$

$$= \frac{3-1}{6}$$

$$= \frac{2}{6}$$

$$= \frac{1}{3}$$

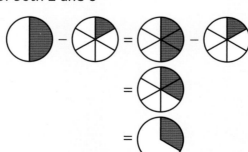

Exercise 9.9

Subtract these fractions.

1 $\frac{1}{7} - \frac{1}{14}$

2 $\frac{5}{6} - \frac{5}{12}$

3 $\frac{5}{12} - \frac{1}{3}$

4 $\frac{2}{5} - \frac{1}{10}$

5 $\frac{5}{8} - \frac{1}{4}$

6 $\frac{11}{12} - \frac{3}{4}$

7 $\frac{11}{15} - \frac{2}{3}$

8 $\frac{7}{10} - \frac{2}{5}$

9 $\frac{5}{12} - \frac{1}{6}$

10 $\frac{19}{20} - \frac{4}{5}$

 Convert the fractions to equivalent fractions with a common denominator first.

11 $1\frac{1}{5} - \frac{3}{10}$

12 $1\frac{1}{3} - \frac{5}{9}$

13 $1\frac{2}{3} - \frac{5}{6}$

14 $1\frac{1}{14} - \frac{1}{2}$

15 $1\frac{7}{15} - \frac{2}{3}$

16 $1\frac{3}{4} - \frac{11}{12}$

17 $1\frac{3}{10} - \frac{2}{5}$

18 $1\frac{9}{10} - \frac{1}{2}$

19 $1\frac{7}{9} - \frac{2}{3}$

20 $1\frac{7}{20} - \frac{4}{5}$

⇨ Multiplying fractions

Multiplying fractions by a whole number

You know that multiplying is the same as repeated adding.

$$3 \times \frac{3}{4} = \frac{3}{4} + \frac{3}{4} + \frac{3}{4}$$

You can write this more neatly as:

$$\frac{3 \times 3}{4} = \frac{9}{4} = 2\frac{1}{4}$$

Example:

Multiply $3 \times \frac{4}{5}$

$$3 \times \frac{4}{5} = \frac{3 \times 4}{5}$$
$$= \frac{12}{5}$$
$$= 2\frac{2}{5}$$

Copy and complete these multiplications. If the answer is an improper fraction, write it as a mixed number. Make sure that the fractions in your answers are in their lowest terms.

1 $3 \times \frac{1}{4}$

2 $5 \times \frac{1}{2}$

3 $4 \times \frac{2}{7}$

4 $3 \times \frac{3}{4}$

5 $2 \times \frac{4}{5}$

6 $5 \times \frac{3}{8}$

7 $4 \times \frac{3}{7}$

8 $3 \times \frac{4}{5}$

9 $4 \times \frac{7}{8}$

10 $3 \times \frac{5}{6}$

11 $3 \times \frac{5}{12}$

12 $4 \times \frac{8}{12}$

13 $3 \times \frac{5}{16}$

14 $5 \times \frac{4}{15}$

15 $3 \times \frac{5}{7}$

16 $2 \times \frac{5}{8}$

17 $3 \times \frac{5}{9}$

18 $5 \times \frac{3}{10}$

19 $3 \times \frac{7}{15}$

20 $4 \times \frac{5}{6}$

Multiplying mixed numbers

When you need to multiply a mixed number by a whole number, proceed in just the same way. First multiply the whole number, then the fraction.

$$3 \times 2\frac{3}{4} = 3 \times 2 + 3 \times \frac{3}{4}$$

Example:

Multiply $3 \times 2\frac{4}{5}$

$$3 \times 2\frac{4}{5} = 3 \times 2 + 3 \times \frac{4}{5}$$

$$= 6 + \frac{12}{5}$$

$$= 6 + 2\frac{2}{5}$$

$$= 8\frac{2}{5}$$

Exercise 9.11

Copy and complete these multiplications. Make sure that the fractions in your answers are in their lowest terms.

1 $3 \times 1\frac{1}{4}$

2 $5 \times 2\frac{1}{7}$

3 $4 \times 1\frac{2}{9}$

4 $3 \times 3\frac{1}{5}$

5 $3 \times 2\frac{3}{8}$

6 $4 \times 2\frac{1}{8}$

7 $4 \times 3\frac{1}{4}$

8 $2 \times 3\frac{1}{4}$

9 $4 \times 1\frac{1}{12}$

10 $5 \times 2\frac{3}{20}$

11 $2 \times 1\frac{2}{3}$

12 $2 \times 2\frac{5}{7}$

13 $3 \times 2\frac{3}{4}$

14 $2 \times 1\frac{4}{5}$

15 $3 \times 2\frac{2}{5}$

16 $4 \times 2\frac{5}{6}$

17 $3 \times 1\frac{4}{9}$

18 $5 \times 3\frac{7}{10}$

19 $4 \times 2\frac{7}{12}$

20 $2 \times 3\frac{5}{8}$

⇨ Fraction patterns

This number line shows the family of fifths.

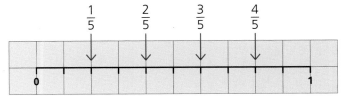

The fraction pattern is: $0, \frac{1}{5}, \frac{2}{5}, \frac{3}{5}, \frac{4}{5}, 1$

Now look at this fraction pattern.

$\frac{1}{5}, \frac{3}{5}, 1, 1\frac{2}{5}, 1\frac{4}{5}, \dots$

What comes next?

The pattern starts at $\frac{1}{5}$ and goes up by $\frac{2}{5}$ each time, so the next number is:

$$1\frac{4}{5} + \frac{2}{5} = 2\frac{1}{5}$$

To complete fraction patterns, follow these steps.

● Work out the difference between two adjacent terms in the pattern.

● Add or subtract the difference to find the missing term.

Examples:

Find the missing terms in these patterns.

(i)　$\frac{1}{7}, \frac{3}{7}, \frac{5}{7}, 1, 1\frac{2}{7}, ..., ...$

The difference between adjacent terms is $\frac{3}{7} - \frac{1}{7} = \frac{2}{7}$

The missing terms are $1\frac{4}{7}\left(1\frac{2}{7} + \frac{2}{7}\right)$ and $1\frac{6}{7}\left(1\frac{4}{7} + \frac{2}{7}\right)$

(ii)　$\frac{2}{5}, 1, 1\frac{3}{5}, ..., 2\frac{4}{5}, ...$

The difference between adjacent terms is $1 - \frac{2}{5} = \frac{3}{5}$

The missing terms are $1\frac{3}{5} + \frac{3}{5} = 1\frac{6}{5} = 2\frac{1}{5}$ and $2\frac{4}{5} + \frac{3}{5} = 2\frac{7}{5} = 3\frac{2}{5}$

Exercise 9.12

Find the missing terms in each of these patterns.

1 $\frac{1}{3}, \frac{2}{3}, 1, 1\frac{1}{3}, ..., ...$

2 $\frac{1}{3}, 1, 1\frac{2}{3}, 2\frac{1}{3}, ..., ...$

3 $\frac{1}{4}, \frac{1}{2}, \frac{3}{4}, 1, ..., ...$

4 $\frac{1}{7}, \frac{4}{7}, 1, 1\frac{3}{7}, ..., ...$

5 $\frac{1}{5}, \frac{4}{5}, 1\frac{2}{5}, 2, ..., ...$

6 $\frac{1}{6}, \frac{1}{2}, \frac{5}{6}, 1\frac{1}{6}, ..., ...$

7 $\frac{1}{8}, \frac{3}{8}, \frac{5}{8}, \frac{7}{8}, 1\frac{1}{8}, ..., ...$

8 $\frac{1}{8}, \frac{1}{2}, \frac{7}{8}, 1\frac{1}{4}, ..., ...$

9 $..., ..., 2\frac{1}{7}, 2\frac{4}{7}, 3, 3\frac{3}{7}$

10 $..., ..., 5\frac{2}{5}, 5\frac{4}{5}, 6\frac{1}{5}, 6\frac{3}{5}$

11 $4\frac{1}{2}$, $4\frac{3}{4}$, ..., $5\frac{1}{4}$, $5\frac{1}{2}$, ...

12 $2\frac{1}{3}$, ..., 3, $3\frac{1}{3}$, ..., 4

13 $1\frac{1}{6}$, ..., $1\frac{5}{6}$, $2\frac{1}{6}$, ..., $2\frac{5}{6}$

14 ..., 3, $3\frac{3}{7}$, ..., $4\frac{2}{7}$, $4\frac{5}{7}$

15 $5\frac{1}{8}$, ..., $5\frac{7}{8}$, $6\frac{1}{4}$, $6\frac{5}{8}$, ...

16 Explain to your partner how you can check that your answer to question 11 is correct. (Think how many steps you made, and how much you added to your first term.)

17 Explain to your partner how you can check that your answer to question 15 is correct. (Think how many steps you made, and how much you added to your first term.)

⇨ Problem solving

Exercise 9.13

Calculate the answers to these questions. Show all your working.

1 If I eat three-quarters of a packet of sweets, what fraction of the packet is left?

2 If $\frac{5}{9}$ of the class are boys, what fraction of the class are girls?

3 It is half past five. What time will it be in $\frac{3}{4}$ of an hour's time?

4 My dog eats $\frac{2}{3}$ of a tin of dog food a day.

How many tins will I need to buy to last him a week?

5 A snail crawls $\frac{7}{8}$ of a metre in an hour.

What is the furthest the snail can crawl in five hours?

6 A snail is crawling up a window. First it crawls up $\frac{5}{6}$ of a metre and then it slips down $\frac{1}{3}$ of a metre.

What is its total distance from the bottom of the window?

7 I have to run $1\frac{3}{4}$ miles, walk $1\frac{3}{4}$ miles and swim $1\frac{3}{4}$ miles. What total distance will I cover?

8 A jar weighs $2\frac{3}{8}$ kg. What is the mass of three jars?

9 I take $\frac{3}{8}$ kg of flour out of a bag holding $\frac{3}{4}$ kg.

   What fraction of a kilogram is left?

10 A farmer collects 86 eggs and packs them in boxes of 8
   How many full boxes will she pack and what fraction of a box
   is left?

11 A train journey lasts $2\frac{1}{4}$ hours. A train does five of these
   journeys in a day.
   For how many hours, in total, does the train travel?

12 At half term, one-third of my class went to the seaside, one-
   quarter went camping, one-sixth went to London and the rest
   stayed at home. What fraction of the class stayed at home?

Exercise 9.14: Summary exercise

Give your answers to these questions in their lowest terms.

1 What fraction of each shape is shaded?

(a)   (b)   (c)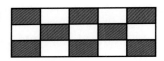

2 Write these improper fractions as mixed numbers.

(a) $\frac{6}{5}$ (b) $\frac{9}{4}$ (c) $\frac{25}{7}$

3 Write these mixed numbers as improper fractions.

(a) $1\frac{1}{8}$ (b) $2\frac{5}{8}$ (c) $4\frac{5}{9}$

4 Simplify these fractions to their lowest terms.

(a) $\frac{4}{6}$ (b) $\frac{15}{20}$ (c) $\frac{100}{15}$ (d) $\frac{115}{100}$

5 Fill in the missing numbers, in these pairs of equivalent
   fractions.

(a) $\frac{3}{4} = \frac{\square}{12}$ (b) $\frac{5}{8} = \frac{15}{\square}$ (c) $\frac{\square}{20} = \frac{25}{100}$

6 Copy these pairs of fractions and write < or > between them.

(a) $\frac{2}{3}$ and $\frac{5}{9}$ (b) $\frac{3}{4}$ and $\frac{7}{12}$ (c) $\frac{7}{9}$ and $\frac{5}{6}$

7 Write a fraction that is greater than $\frac{2}{3}$ but less than $\frac{5}{6}$

8 Copy and complete these calculations. If the answer is an improper fraction, write it as a mixed number.

(a) $\frac{3}{7} + \frac{2}{7}$ (c) $\frac{5}{6} - \frac{1}{6}$ (e) $\frac{5}{12} + \frac{5}{6} + \frac{1}{2}$

(b) $\frac{5}{6} + \frac{2}{3}$ (d) $\frac{7}{8} - \frac{5}{8}$ (f) $\frac{7}{15} - \frac{1}{5}$

9 Copy and complete these calculations. Give your answers as fractions in their lowest terms. If the answer is an improper fraction, write it as a mixed number.

(a) $2 \times \frac{2}{7}$ (b) $3 \times \frac{5}{6}$ (c) $3 \times 2\frac{3}{5}$

10 One-half of my class has brown eyes, one-third has blue eyes and the rest have green eyes. What fraction of the class has green eyes?

10 2D shapes

⇨ Triangles

The general term for a two-dimensional figure with three sides is a **triangle**.

A triangle has three corners (or points or **vertices**). At each corner there is an **angle**. In the triangle *ABC*, the three sides of the triangle are different lengths and the three angles are all different sizes and all less than 90°.

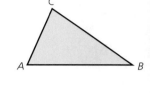

When a triangle has one angle which is equal to 90°, it is called a right-angled triangle. The right angle is marked with a small square.

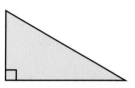

■ Right-angled triangle

When a triangle has one angle greater than 90°, it is called an obtuse-angled triangle.

There are three types of triangle: equilateral, isosceles and scalene.

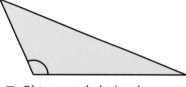

■ Obtuse-angled triangle

When a triangle has three sides of different lengths and three angles of different sizes it is called a scalene triangle. Scalene triangles may be right-angled or obtuse-angled.

When a triangle has two equal angles and two equal sides, it is called an isosceles triangle. Isosceles triangles may be right-angled or obtuse-angled.

When a triangle has all three angles equal to 60° and all three sides equal, it is an equilateral triangle.

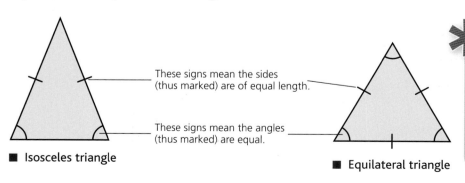

These signs mean the sides (thus marked) are of equal length.

These signs mean the angles (thus marked) are equal.

■ Isosceles triangle

■ Equilateral triangle

There are special marks to show that two or more lines are of equal length and two or more angles are of equal size.

Exercise 10.1

(a) Measure the lengths of the sides of each triangle.

(b) Measure the size of the angles of each triangle.

(c) Look at each triangle and write down whether it is scalene, right-angled, isosceles, obtuse-angled or equilateral.

1
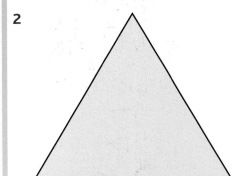

2

3
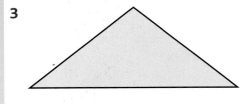

4

5
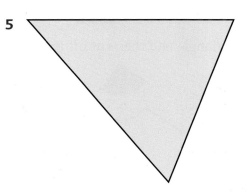

6
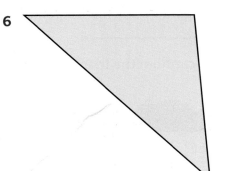

⇨ The sum of the angles in a triangle

Add up all the angles in each triangle from Exercise 10.1
What do you notice?

If you have measured correctly, you should find that all the angles add up to 180°.

Work through the next exercise, to learn about the sum of the angles of a triangle.

Exercise 10.2

1 Start by drawing any triangle and mark each of the angles with a different colour.

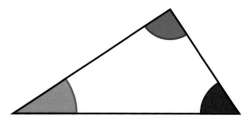

2 Cut out the triangle and then cut off the corners.

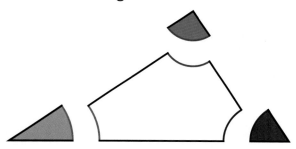

3 Next draw a straight line and mark a point on it.

4 Place the angles cut from the triangle together, at the point on the line.

What do you notice?

The three angles from a triangle can be arranged in a straight line. This shows that they add up to 180°.

Finding missing angles

You have learned that the sum of the angles in a triangle is 180°. This means that, if you know the size of two of the angles in a triangle, you can find the size of the third angle.

Example:

Find the value of c.

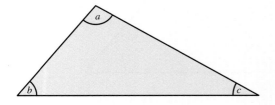 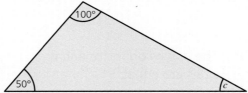

You know that $a + b + c = 180°$

If $a = 100°$ and $b = 50°$, then:

$100° + 50° + c = 180°$

$c = 180° - 100° - 50°$ or $180° - (100° + 50°)$

$c = 30°$

You already know something about the angles in right-angled, isosceles and equilateral triangles.

A right-angled triangle has one angle equal to 90°

Example:

Find the value of a.

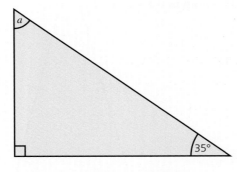

$90° + 35° + a = 180°$

$a = 180° - 90° - 35°$ or $180° - (90° + 35°)$

$a = 55°$

An isosceles triangle is symmetrical. It has a pair of equal sides.

The angles opposite the equal sides are equal to each other.

If you know the size of one angle, you can find the size of the other two.

Always start by marking the equal angles.

Examples:

(i) Calculate the size of the angle labelled a.

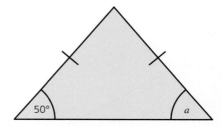

$a = 50°$ The angles opposite equal sides are equal.

(ii) Calculate the size of the angle labelled b.

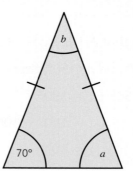

$a = 70°$ It is the other equal angle.

$b = 180° - 140°$ From the sum of the angles of the triangle, and $70 + 70 = 140$

   $= 40°$

(iii) Calculate the size of the angle labelled c.

Sum of the two unknown angles $= 180° - 30°$

$= 150°$

(From the sum of the angles of the triangle)

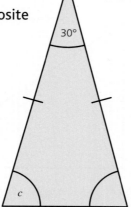

The angles are equal (angles opposite equal sides), so:

$c = 150° ÷ 2$

$= 75°$

10 2D shapes

An equilateral triangle has three equal sides and three equal angles (180 ÷ 3 = 60°).

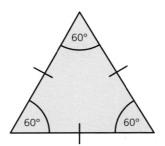

Exercise 10.3

Calculate the sizes of the angles marked with small letters.

1

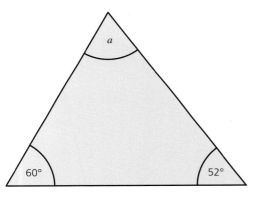

2

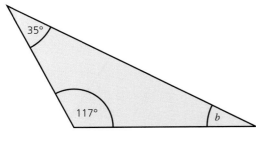

3

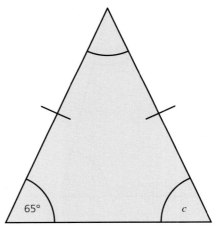

4

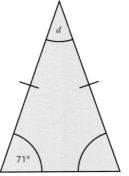

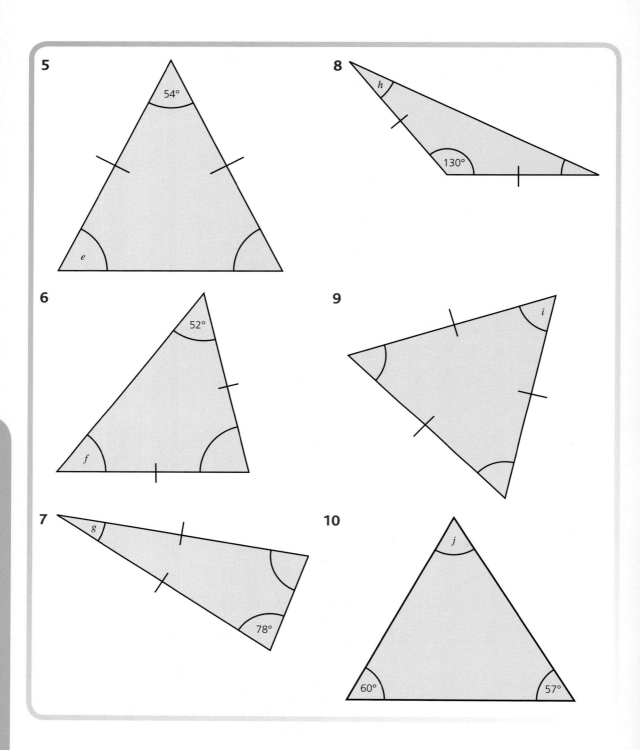

5 54°

e

8 h

130°

6 52°

f

9 i

7 g

78°

10 j

60°   57°

⇨ Drawing triangles

To draw a triangle accurately, follow these steps.

● Draw the base.

● Mark and label the ends with the correct letters.

● Draw any angles and mark off any distances carefully.

● Complete and label the triangle.

Examples:

Draw these triangles accurately.

(i)   **Two sides and one angle**

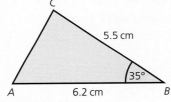

Step 1:   Use a ruler to draw the line *AB* accurately.

Step 2:   Use your protractor to measure and mark the angle at *B*, then draw a line through the mark and the point *B*.

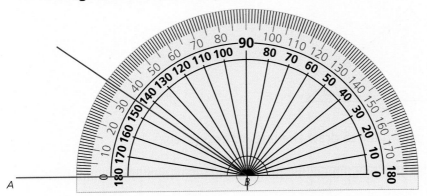

Step 3: Use your ruler to mark off the length *BC*.

Step 4: Join the points *A* and *C*, at the ends of the lines, label the measurements you were given.

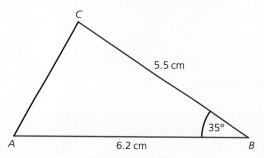

Step 5: Measure any unknown lines or angles as required.

(ii) One side and two angles

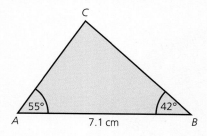

Step 1: Use your ruler to draw the line *AB* accurately.

Step 2: Use your protractor to measure and mark the angle at *A*, then draw a line through the mark and the point *A*.

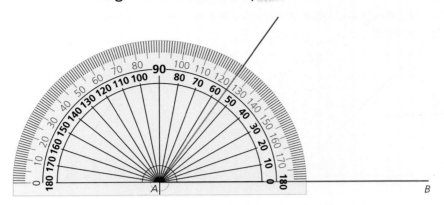

Step 3: Use your protractor to measure and mark the angle at *B*, then draw a line through the mark and the point *B*, to cross the first line. This is point *C*.

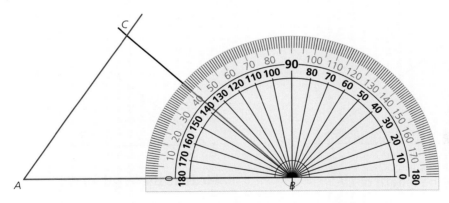

Step 4: Label your triangle with the given length and angles. Measure any lines or angles as required.

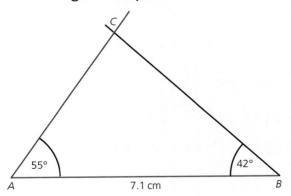

Exercise 10.4

Make accurate drawings of these triangles. Measure any lengths and angles as required.

1

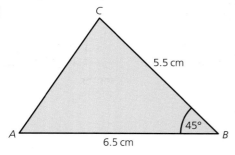

Measure the angles at *A* and *C*.
Measure the length of *AC*.

4

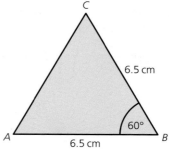

Measure the angle at *A* and the angle at *C*.

2

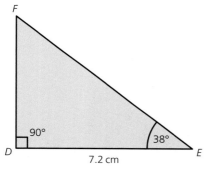

Measure the length of *DF*.

5

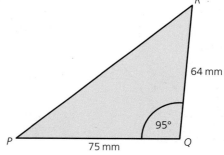

Measure the length of *PR*.

3

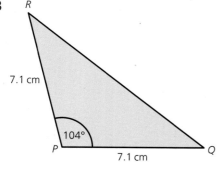

Measure the angle at *Q* and the angle at *R*.

6

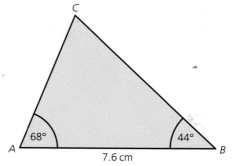

Measure the length of *BC*.

⇨ Four-sided shapes

The general term for a two-dimensional four-sided figure is a **quadrilateral**.

In a triangle, all the lines slope in different directions. In shapes with more than three lines, it is possible that some lines will slope in the same direction.

Parallel lines are lines that are a fixed distance apart and will never meet, however far they are extended.

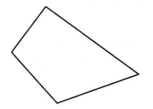

■ A quadrilateral with four sides of different lengths

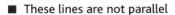

■ These lines are not parallel   ■ These lines are parallel

Arrows are used to mark parallel lines or sides of shapes.

Quadrilaterals may have two or more equal sides or angles, or one or more pairs of parallel sides. There are special marks to show these on drawings.

You have already seen how to use dashes to mark lines that are of equal length.

If two pairs of lines on the same figure are of equal length, use two dashes to mark the second pair.

If two pairs of lines on the same figure are parallel (as in a square), use two arrows to mark the second pair.

Special quadrilaterals

A **square** has four angles of 90° and four equal sides.

A **rectangle** has four angles of 90° and two pairs of equal sides.

They both have two pairs of parallel sides.

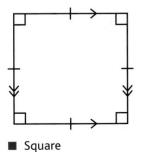

■ Square

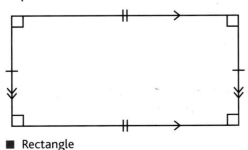

■ Rectangle

A **parallelogram** and a **rhombus** both have two pairs of parallel sides.

They both have two pairs of equal angles.

In a rhombus, all the sides are equal. In a parallelogram, there are two pairs of equal sides.

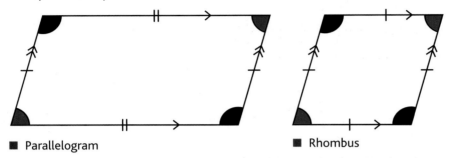

■ Parallelogram   ■ Rhombus

A **trapezium** has one pair of parallel sides.

An **isosceles trapezium** has one pair of parallel sides and its other two sides are equal in length. It has two pairs of equal angles.

A **kite** has no parallel sides, but it has two pairs of equal adjacent sides. It has one pair of equal angles.

The plural of trapezium is trapezia.

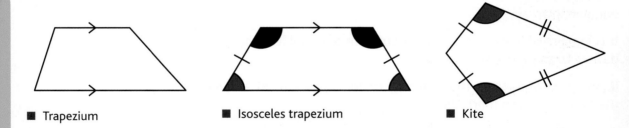

■ Trapezium   ■ Isosceles trapezium   ■ Kite

An **arrowhead** has one **interior** reflex angle.

An interior angle is one that is inside the shape.

An **isosceles arrowhead** has two pairs of equal adjacent sides and one pair of equal angles.

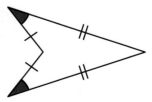

■ Isosceles arrowhead (or delta)

Exercise 10.5

1 Which special quadrilaterals have only one pair of equal angles?

2 Which special quadrilaterals have two pairs of equal angles?

3 Which special quadrilaterals have two pairs of equal sides?

4 Which special quadrilateral has one pair of equal sides?

5 Which special quadrilaterals have two pairs of parallel sides?

6 Which special quadrilaterals have one pair of parallel sides?

7 Which special quadrilaterals have no parallel sides?

8 Copy this table in your book and complete it.

	No equal sides	1 pair of equal sides	2 pairs of equal sides
No equal angles			
1 pair of equal angles			Kite
2 pairs of equal angles			
4 right angles			Rectangle

9 Copy this table in your book and complete it.

	No parallel sides	1 pair of parallel sides	2 pairs of parallel sides
No equal angles			
1 pair of equal angles	Kite		
2 pairs of equal angles			
4 right angles			Square

Diagonals in quadrilaterals

The lines that join non-adjacent sides or vertices in a shape are called diagonals.

Look at the diagonals in the rectangle.

Can you see that they cross at their halfway points?

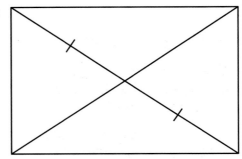

Each diagonal is divided in two by the other diagonal.

When a line or an angle is divided in two equal parts, it is **bisected**.

The diagonals in the rectangle **bisect** each other.

In the square, the diagonals bisect each other and also bisect the angles.

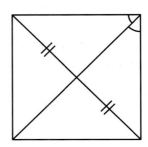

Exercise 10.6

For each shape below:

(a) draw an example of the shape in your exercise book and draw the two diagonals

(b) write down the properties that are true for that shape. Choose from the list below.

- The diagonals are equal.
- The diagonals meet at right angles.
- The diagonals bisect each other.
- The diagonals bisect the angles.

1 Square

2 Rectangle

3 Parallelogram

4 Rhombus

5 Kite

6 Trapezium

7 Isosceles trapezium

⇨ The sum of the angles in a quadrilateral

In a rectangle and a square all the angles are 90°.

Any quadrilateral can be divided into two triangles. As the angle sum of a triangle is 180°, then it follows that the angle sum of a quadrilateral is 360°.

You can use this fact, with what you know about special quadrilaterals, to find missing angles and lengths.

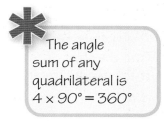

The angle sum of any quadrilateral is $4 \times 90° = 360°$

Example:

Find the sizes of the angles and sides labelled with small letters in this rhombus.

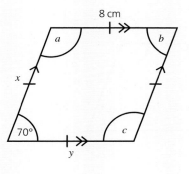

$b = 70°$ (Opposite angles in a rhombus are equal.)

$a = c$ (Opposite angles in a rhombus are equal.)

$a + c + 70° + 70° = 360°$ (The angle sum of a quadrilateral is 360°)

$a + c = 360° - (70° + 70°)$

$ = 220°$

$a = c = 110°$

$x = y = 8\,cm$ (All the sides of a rhombus are equal.)

Exercise 10.7

Find the sizes of the angles and sides labelled with small letters in these quadrilaterals.

1

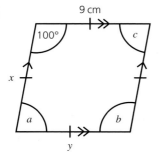

5

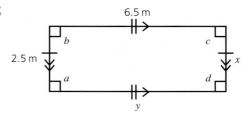

2

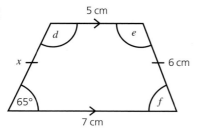

6

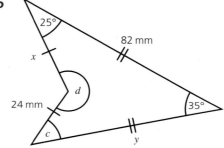

3

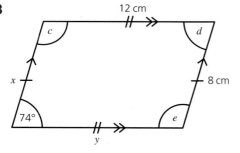

7

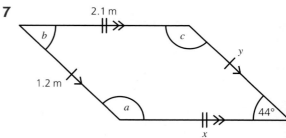

4

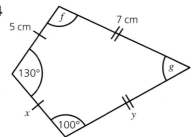

8

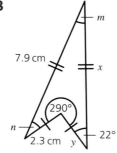

⇨ Polygons

A polygon is a two-dimensional shape with three or more sides. You have already learned about:

● triangles, which have three sides and three angles

● quadrilaterals, which have four sides and four angles.

Polygons can be either **regular** or **irregular**. In a **regular polygon**, all the sides are the same length and all the interior angles are equal.

Regular		Irregular
	3 sides 3 angles **Triangle**	
	4 sides 4 angles **Quadrilateral**	
	5 sides 5 angles **Pentagon**	
	6 sides 6 angles **Hexagon**	

Regular		Irregular
	7 sides 7 angles **Heptagon**	
	8 sides 8 angles **Octagon**	
	9 sides 9 angles **Nonagon**	
	10 sides 10 angles **Decagon**	
	12 sides 12 angles **Dodecagon**	

Exercise 10.8

1 Measure and write down the interior angles of each regular polygon on the previous two pages. As the sides are all equal, the angles will also be equal.

(a) Triangle   (f) Octagon

(b) Quadrilateral   (g) Nonagon

(c) Pentagon   (h) Decagon

(d) Hexagon   (i) Dodecagon

(e) Heptagon

2 Copy this table and then write down the name of each polygon and the size of the angle.

No. of sides	Name of polygon	Size of angle	No. of sides	Name of polygon	Size of angle
3			8		
4			9		
5			10		
6			12		

3 You know that the angles round a point add up to 360°

If you put four squares together, so that they meet round a point, the angles at the corners will add up to 360°

What other angles from your table can you put together, to make 360°? They do not all have to be the same size.

4 Draw some of your combinations of polygons. Then extend the pattern to see what designs you can make. Here are some regular polygons that fit round a point to get you started.

Use tracing paper to copy the patterns and extend them. Colour your resulting patterns to make them as beautiful as possible:

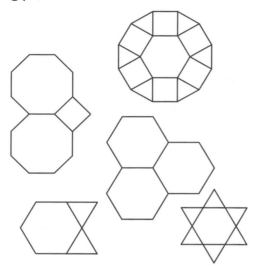

5 These pictures show how squares and right-angled triangles can be put together to make some exciting patterns. You could try this, too.

Activity – Tiling patterns

Use a computer to design some tiles and fit them together to make some beautiful patterns. This one is from the Topkapi Palace, Istanbul.

# Translation

Moving a point or shape in a straight line is called translation.

Always describe how to translate the point or shape in the same order:

1 horizontally (right or left)

2 vertically (up or down).

⇨ Using a co-ordinate grid

You can use a square or **co-ordinate** grid to make translations.

A point on a co-ordinate grid is identified by two numbers. The first is the **horizontal** distance from the axis and the second is the **vertical** distance from the axis. $P(3, 2)$ is 3 along and 2 up.

You should measure the **length of movement** in **units** (not squares). A unit is the distance between consecutive whole numbers on the axes.

Movement horizontally right or left is movement **parallel to the x-axis**.

Movement vertically up or down is movement **parallel to the y-axis**.

Always decide what a unit is before answering the question. Look at the scales of the axes carefully.

Examples:

(i) Write down the translation that moves $P(2, 3)$ to $Q(7, 7)$

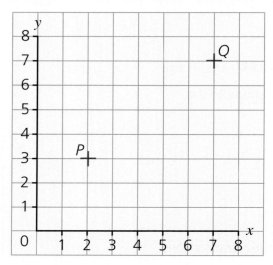

1 unit is 1 square.

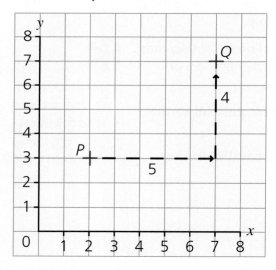

The translation is 5 units right followed by 4 units up.

(ii) Plot the position of the image of P (3, 3) after a translation of 1 unit left followed by 2 units down.

Label the image Q.

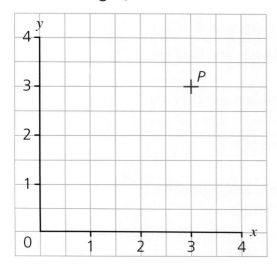

1 unit is 2 squares.

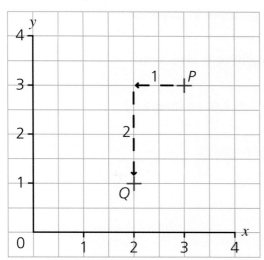

Positive and negative directions

Instead of describing the **direction** of movement in a translation as up or down, right or left, you can use the words **positive** and **negative**.

Think of a number line. Imagine that you are starting at 0

- If you move to the **right**, the numbers get **larger**, and they are **positive**.
- If you move to the **left**, the numbers get **smaller**, and they are **negative**.

Now imagine that the number line is the x-axis of a co-ordinate grid.

- Then movement to the **right**, parallel to the x-axis, is **positive** in direction. The numbers on the axis become **larger**.
- Movement to the **left**, parallel to the x-axis, is **negative** in direction. The numbers on the axis become **smaller**.

Now imagine that your number line is vertical, the y-axis of a grid.

- Then movement **up**, parallel to the y-axis, is **positive** in direction. The numbers on the axis become **larger**.
- Movement **down**, parallel to the y-axis, is **negative** in direction. The numbers on the axis become **smaller**.

This means that you can work out the co-ordinates of an image by adding or subtracting.

Look at the examples on the previous two pages again.

Examples:

(i) Describe the translation that moves $P(2, 3)$ to $Q(7, 7)$

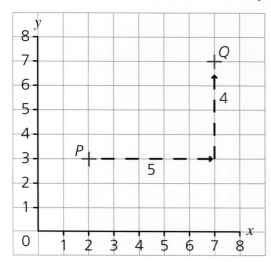

The translation is positive in both directions.

It adds 5 to the x-co-ordinate. $2 + 5 = 7$

It adds 4 to the y-co-ordinate. $3 + 4 = 7$

The translation that moves P to Q is +5, +4

(ii) Describe the translation that moves P(3, 3) to Q(2, 1)

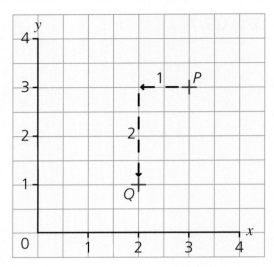

The translation is negative in both directions.

It subtracts 1 from the x-co-ordinate.   3 − 1 = 2

It subtracts 2 from the y-co-ordinate.   3 − 2 = 1

The translation that moves P to Q is −1, −2

Exercise 11.1

1

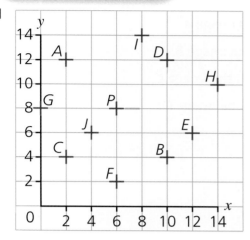

Write down the translation that moves *P* to:

(a) *A*   (f) *F*

(b) *B*   (g) *G*

(c) *C*   (h) *H*

(d) *D*   (i) *I*

(e) *E*   (j) *J*

2

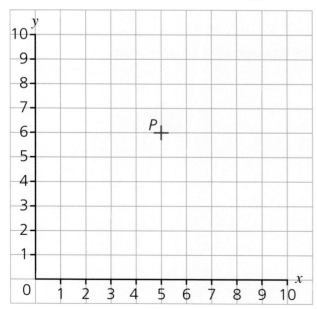

Copy the grid on the previous page, then plot the following translations of the point *P*.

(a) 3 units left followed by 4 units up. Label the image *A*.

(b) 4 units right followed by 2 units up. Label the image *B*.

(c) 3 units right followed by 6 units down. Label the image *C*.

(d) 4 units left followed by 5 units down. Label the image *D*.

(e) +3 followed by +1   Label the image *E*.

(f) −2 followed by +3   Label the image *F*.

(g) +2 followed by −4   Label the image *G*.

(h) −1 followed by −3   Label the image *H*.

(i) −5 followed by 0   Label the image *I*.

(j) 0 followed by −6   Label the image *J*.

⇨ Translating shapes

To translate a shape, move each **vertex** (corner) by the given translation.

Examples:

(i) Translate triangle *ABC* 7 squares right followed by 2 squares down.

Label the image *PQR*.

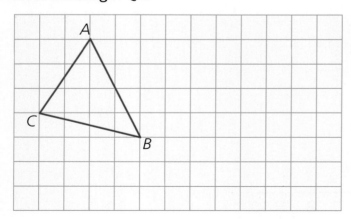

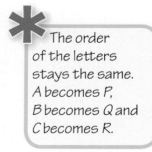

The order of the letters stays the same. *A* becomes *P*, *B* becomes *Q* and *C* becomes *R*.

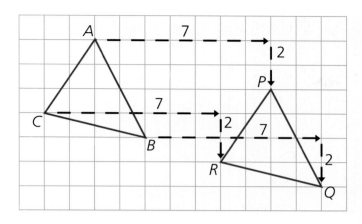

Notice that the shape stays the same way round. This is because each vertex moves the same distance in the same direction. This means that you can count units for just one vertex and then copy the rest of the shape.

(ii) Translate *ABCD* 5 units left followed by 3 units down.

Label the image *WXYZ*.

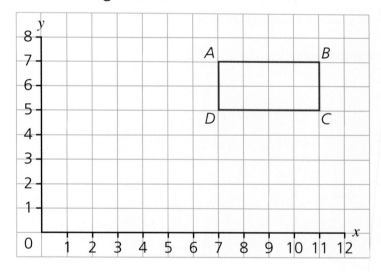

Translate the top left-hand corner.

Copy the rest of the rectangle.

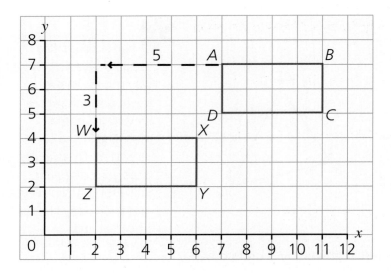

Exercise 11.2

Make a copy of this grid for this exercise.

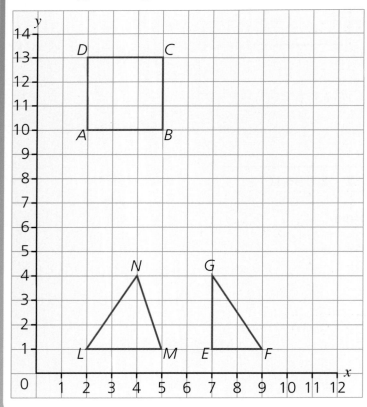

1 Translate *ABCD* 5 units right followed by 4 units down.

   Label the image *PQRS*.

2 Translate *GEF* 6 units left followed by 4 units up.

   Label the image *XYZ*.

3 Translate *LMN* 6 units right followed by 10 units up.

   Label the image *UVW*.

Identifying translations of shapes

To identify the translation that has taken place:

- choose a vertex on the shape and identify the corresponding vertex on the image
- work out the horizontal movement
- work out the vertical movement.

Example:

What translation maps *ABCD* onto *WXYZ*?

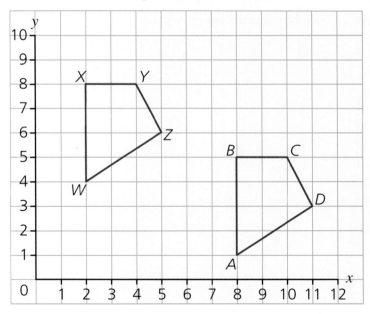

- *A* maps onto *W*.

- Horizontal movement is 6 units to the left.

- Vertical movement is 3 units up.

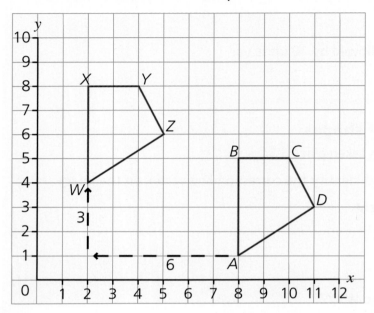

The translation is 6 units to the left followed by 3 units up or −6, +3

Exercise 11.3

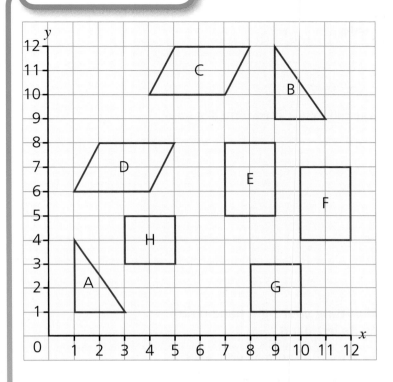

1 Write down the translation that maps triangle A onto triangle B.

2 Write down the translation that maps parallelogram C onto parallelogram D.

3 Write down the translation that maps rectangle E onto rectangle F.

4 Write down the translation that maps square G onto square H.

Reflection

When you look in a mirror, what do you see?

You see a picture or reflection of yourself, but is it exactly like you?

Try standing in front of a mirror and putting your right hand up to touch the glass. Your image is raising its left hand.

The image you see in the mirror is exactly the same as you, except that it has 'flipped over'.

Exercise 12.1

Carefully copy the pictures below. Put a mirror along the dotted line and see how each completed picture should look.
Then remove the mirror and draw the completed picture.

1

2

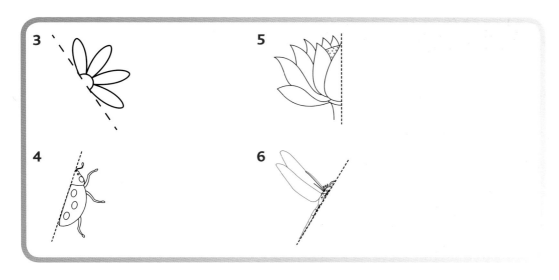

⇨ Lines of symmetry

A picture that has two equal halves is **symmetrical**. The line where the equal halves meet is called a **line of symmetry**.

Some shapes have more than one line of symmetry. This snowflake has six. Can you see where the other three are?

1 Some of these patterns have one line of symmetry and some do not. Copy them into your book and draw the line of symmetry on each pattern if there is one.

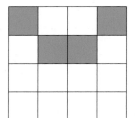 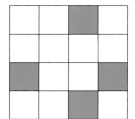 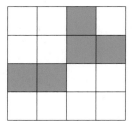 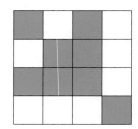

2 These patterns are only partly complete. Copy each pattern and colour in the squares to make each pattern symmetrical about the dotted line.

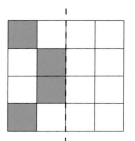 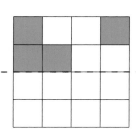 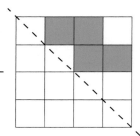 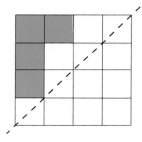

3 Each of these patterns has two or more lines of symmetry. Copy them into your book. Use your mirror to find the lines of symmetry on each pattern and draw them in.

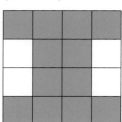 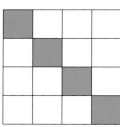 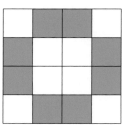 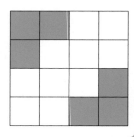

4 These patterns are only partly complete. Copy them into your book and complete each pattern so it has at least two lines of symmetry, as shown by the dotted lines.

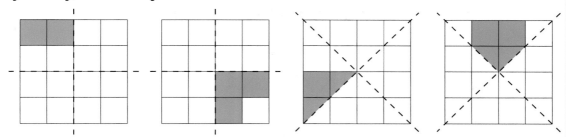

5 Carefully copy this table. Name the polygons and draw all their lines of symmetry.

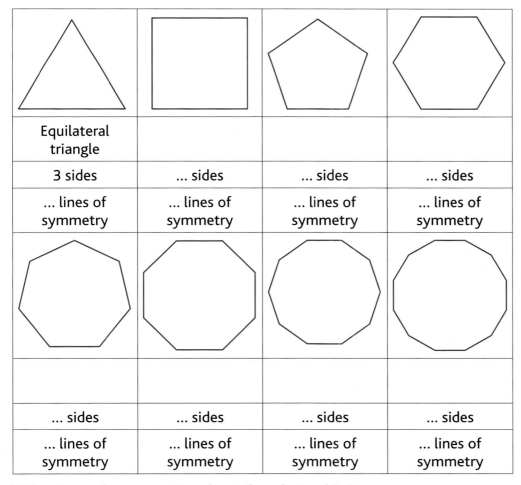

Equilateral triangle			
3 sides	... sides	... sides	... sides
... lines of symmetry	... lines of symmetry	... lines of symmetry	... lines of symmetry
... sides	... sides	... sides	... sides
... lines of symmetry	... lines of symmetry	... lines of symmetry	... lines of symmetry

Write down what you notice about the relationship between the number of sides and the number of lines of symmetry.

6 Copy these shapes and, if they have any lines of symmetry, draw the lines.

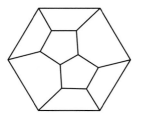 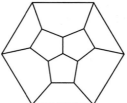 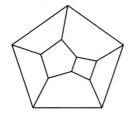

7 Now copy this pattern and colour it in four different ways so that each pattern has a different number of lines of symmetry.

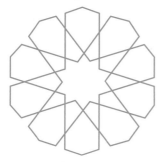

8 Use a computer graphics package to draw the pattern in question 7 and join patterns together to make a whole wall of design. Now design some of your own.

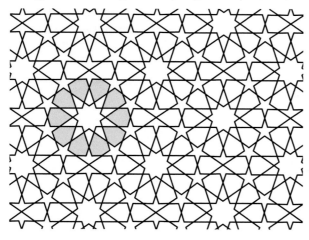

9 Find some symmetrical patterns of your own. Stick them in your exercise book. Draw all their lines of symmetry.

Reflection on a co-ordinate grid

Look at this co-ordinate grid. The point $P(2, 4)$ is to be reflected in the dotted line that is parallel to the x-axis. Put your mirror on the dotted line and work out where the reflection of P will be.

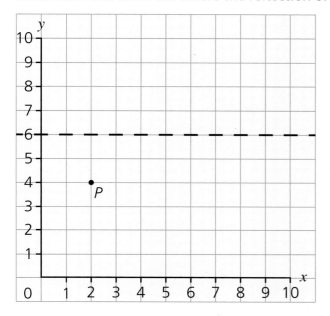

You should have found that the reflection of P will be at (2, 8).

Look at the dotted line. It runs through all the points where y is equal to 6. This line is known as $y = 6$

1 (a) Copy this co-ordinate grid into your book.

Mark the points $A(2, 3)$, $B(4, 2)$ and $C(6, 4)$ carefully.

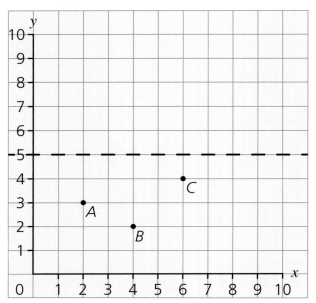

(b) Mark the reflections of points A, B and C in the dotted line
$y = 5$

(c) Label these points A', B' and C'.

(d) Join A to A', B to B' and C to C'. What do you notice?

2 (a) Copy this co-ordinate grid into your book.

Mark the points *P*(2, 3), *Q*(3, 5) and *R*(4, 7) carefully.

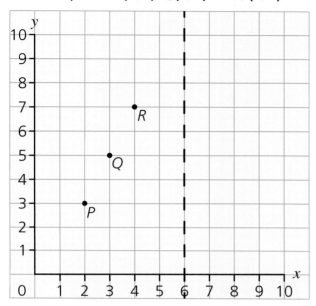

(b) Mark the reflections of points *P*, *Q* and *R* in the dotted line
$x = 6$

(c) Label these points *P'*, *Q'* and *R'*.

(d) Join *P* to *P'*, *Q* to *Q'* and *R* to *R'*. What do you notice?

3 Copy each co-ordinate grid, with the shape on it.

Draw the reflection of each shape in the dotted line.

(a)

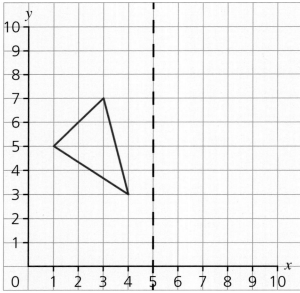

(b)

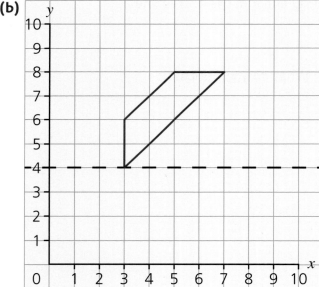

(c)

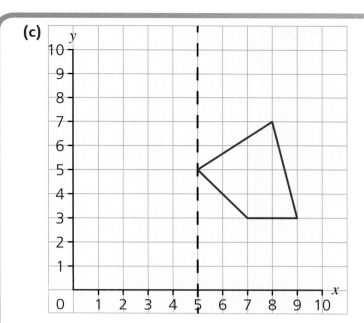

(d)

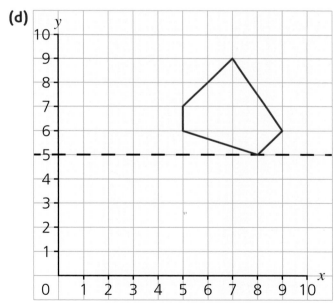

(e)

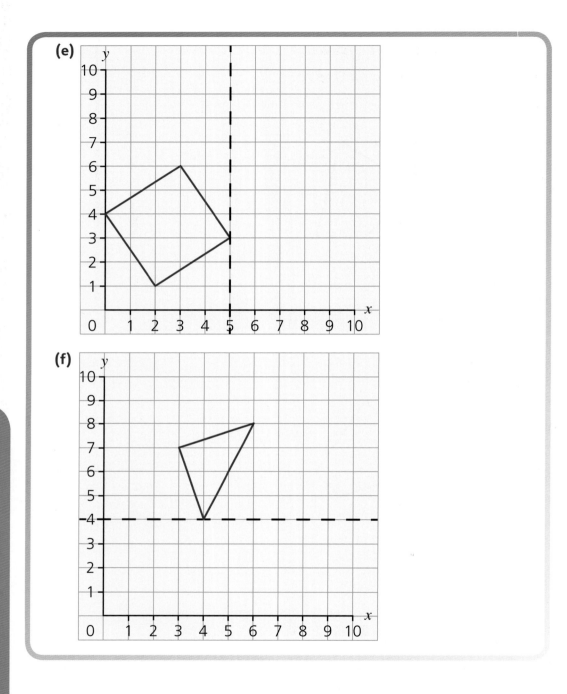

(f)

4 Copy each co-ordinate grid, with the shape on it.

Draw the reflection of each shape in the dotted line.

(a)

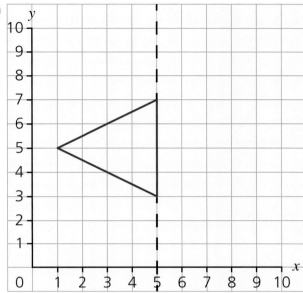

(b)

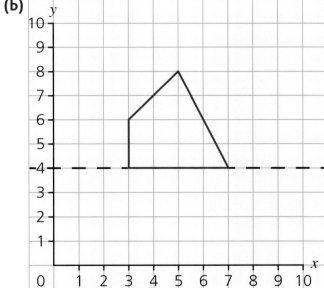

(c)

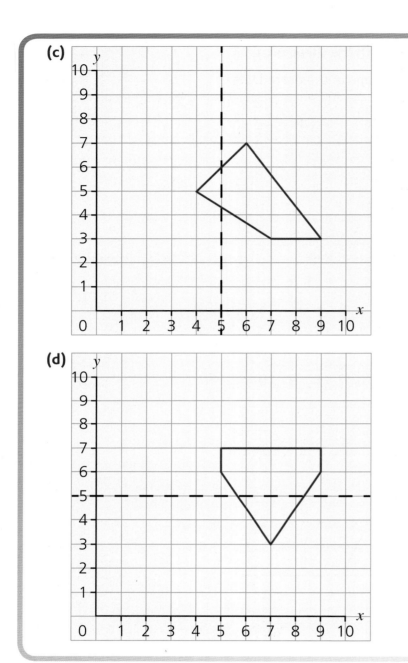

(d)

(e)

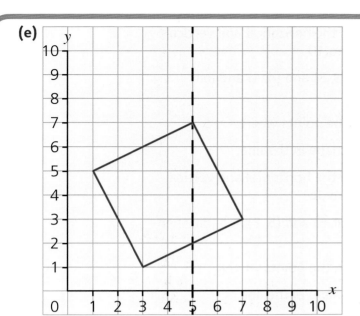

(f)

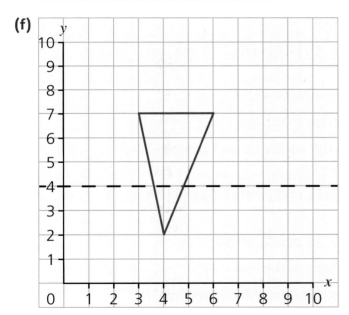

5 (a) Draw a co-ordinate grid with the horizontal and vertical axes both numbered from 0 to 10

(b) Plot the points (3, 4), (4, 7) and (5, 3) and join them up.

(c) Draw a vertical line though the points where $x = 5$

(d) Draw the reflection of your shape in the line.

6 (a) Draw a co-ordinate grid with the horizontal and vertical axes both numbered from 0 to 10

(b) Plot the points $(1, 4)$, $(2, 8)$, $(3, 8)$ and $(4, 4)$ and join them up.

(c) Draw a vertical line though the points where $x = 5$

(d) Draw the reflection of your shape in the line.

7 (a) Draw a co-ordinate grid with the horizontal and vertical axes both numbered from 0 to 10

(b) Plot the points $(1, 1)$, $(2, 3)$, $(4, 5)$ and $(5, 2)$ and join them up.

(c) Draw a horizontal line though the points where $y = 5$

(d) Draw the reflection of your shape in the line.

8 (a) Draw a co-ordinate grid with the horizontal and vertical axes both numbered from 0 to 10

(b) Plot the points $(5, 3)$, $(2, 3)$, $(2, 6)$, $(4, 8)$ and $(5, 8)$ and join them up.

(c) Draw a vertical line though the points where $x = 5$

(d) Draw the reflection of your shape in the line.

9 (a) Draw a co-ordinate grid with the horizontal and vertical axes both numbered from 0 to 10

(b) Plot the points $(1, 5)$, $(2, 3)$, $(3, 5)$, $(4, 3)$ and $(5, 5)$ and join them up.

(c) Draw a horizontal line though the points where $y = 5$

(d) Draw the reflection of your shape in the line.

10 (a) Draw a co-ordinate grid with the horizontal and vertical axes both numbered from 0 to 10

(b) Plot the points $(2, 6)$, $(4, 8)$, $(6, 6)$ and $(4, 5)$ and join them up.

(c) Draw a horizontal line though the points where $y = 6$

(d) Draw the reflection of your shape in the line.

Activity – Snowflakes

Many people make cut-out snowflake shapes with eight points, but real snowflakes have just six points.

Follow these instructions to fold a square of paper and make your own six-pointed snowflake.

1
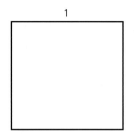

2
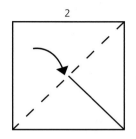

3
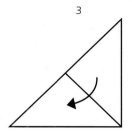

4
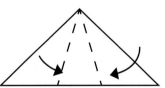

Fold, making sure the three
angles at the top are equal.

5

6

Design and cut out.

7

Here are some more examples.

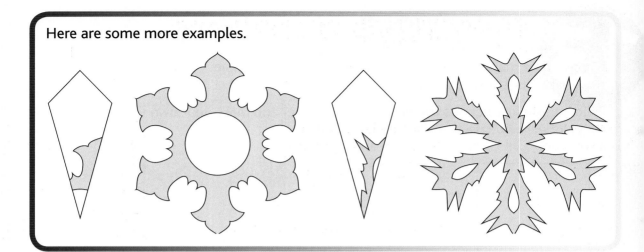

13 Negative numbers

Have you ever watched a film of a rocket being launched? There is a countdown: 'Five, four, three, two, one, blast off!'

What would happen if you wanted to keep counting down?

Look at this thermometer.

You can see that the numbers below zero have a negative sign attached to them. These numbers are called negative numbers.

You can see them on this number line.

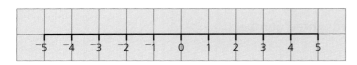

Counting backwards, you would say: 'Five, four, three, two, one, zero, negative one, negative two, negative three, negative four, negative five.'

1 Draw a number line from $^-5$ to 5 and mark it in ones.

2 Put a finger on 5 and count back seven numbers.
Where do you land?

3 Put a finger on $^-5$ and count forwards five numbers.
Where do you land?

4 Put a finger on $^-2$ and count forwards six numbers.
Where do you land?

5 Put a finger on 3 and count backwards eight numbers.
Where do you land?

6 Put a finger on $^-5$ and count forwards eight numbers.
Where do you land?

7 Put a finger on $^-1$ and count backwards three numbers.
Where do you land?

8 Put a finger on $^-2$ and count forwards three numbers.
Where do you land?

⇨ Ordering numbers

Looking at your number line, you can see that 4 is to the right of $^-4$.
This means that 4 is greater than $^-4$

You write this as:

$$4 > {}^-4$$

Example:

Write < or > between $^-1$ and 2, to make a true statement.

$^-1$ is less than 2

This is written:

$$^-1 < 2$$

Exercise 13.2

Write < or > between the numbers in each pair.

1 1 and 5

2 3 and 6

3 ⁻2 and 5

4 4 and ⁻1

5 ⁻3 and 3

6 2 and ⁻1

7 3 and ⁻4

8 ⁻4 and ⁻1

9 ⁻2 and ⁻5

10 ⁻5 and 1

11 ⁻10 and 9

12 ⁻3 and ⁻7

13 ⁻9 and ⁻1

14 ⁻2 and 7

15 12 and ⁻15

16 20 and ⁻15

17 ⁻5 and ⁻15

18 12 and ⁻2

19 ⁻3 and 10

20 14 and ⁻12

You can now put numbers in the correct order.

Exercise 13.3

Put the numbers in each list in order, starting with the smallest.

1 ⁻1, 5, 1

2 ⁻1, 1, ⁻3

3 0, 4, ⁻5

4 ⁻2, ⁻5, 0

5 3, ⁻5, ⁻3

6 2, ⁻1, ⁻3, 1

7 3, 6, 0, ⁻3

8 ⁻1, ⁻4, ⁻10, 0

9 ⁻12, ⁻15, ⁻3, ⁻7

10 6, ⁻16, 0, ⁻6

Put the numbers in each list in order, starting with the largest.

11 ⁻1, 6, ⁻3

12 ⁻4, 5, ⁻2

13 0, ⁻4, 5

14 ⁻5, ⁻1, 5

15 4, ⁻5, 3

16 6, ⁻10, ⁻3, 0

17 ⁻4, 5, 0, ⁻1

18 ⁻10, ⁻15, ⁻8, 0

19 ⁻11, 15, ⁻13, ⁻8

20 12, ⁻15, 0, ⁻5

⇨ Negative numbers in context

Temperature

Look again at a thermometer. Thermometers are used to measure temperature.

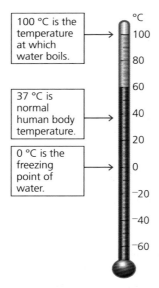

100 °C is the temperature at which water boils.

37 °C is normal human body temperature.

0 °C is the freezing point of water.

As 0 °C is the freezing point of water, you may hear someone say, for example: 'It is two degrees below freezing,' instead of: 'It is negative two degrees,' when talking about temperature.

Exercise 13.4

For questions 1–10, copy this thermometer and mark it to show the temperature.

1 The lowest temperature on Mount Everest: ⁻45 °C

2 The lowest temperature at the South Pole: ⁻82 °C

3 The lowest temperature in Mexico: ⁻32 °C

4 The lowest temperature in Thailand: ⁻1 °C

5 The lowest temperature in England: ⁻26 °C

6 The lowest temperature in Wales: ⁻23 °C

7 The lowest temperature in Iceland: ⁻33 °C

8 The lowest temperature in Portugal: ⁻21 °C

9 The lowest temperature in Malta: 1 °C

10 The lowest temperature in South Africa: ⁻18 °C

11 The temperature at noon is 15 °C and at night it is ⁻2 °C
   What is the change in temperature?

12 The temperature at noon is 8 °C and at night it is ⁻5 °C
   What is the change in temperature?

13 The temperature at noon is 20 °C and at night it is ⁻6 °C
   What is the change in temperature?

14 The temperature at noon is 5 °C and at night it is ⁻12 °C
   What is the change in temperature?

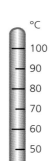

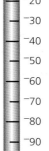

Height

Look at this diagram of a lake between two hills.

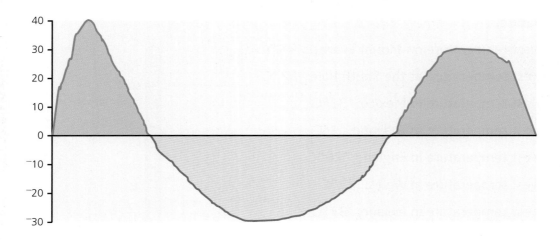

On a map, the hills and the lake are drawn with contour lines.

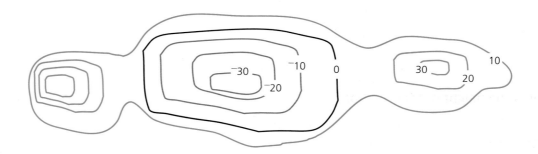

Exercise 13.5

This is a map of part of an area of Scotland. The heights and depths are marked in metres.

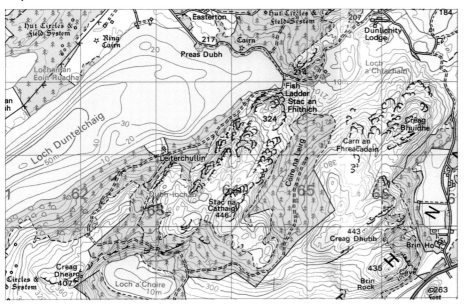

1 What is the greatest depth of Loch Duntelchaig?

2 What is the height of Stac Na Cathaig?

3 What is the difference in height between the deepest part of the Loch and the top of the mountain?

4 What is the greatest depth of Loch a'Choire?

5 What is the difference between the greatest depth of Loch a'Choire and the greatest depth of Loch Duntelchaig?

6 What is the depth of Loch a Chaiachan?

7 How much deeper is Loch Duntelchaig?

8 How deep is Loch Duntelchaig at the point where the number 30 is written?

⇨ Negative co-ordinates

Just as you can extend the number line past zero, you can also extend the axes on the co-ordinate grid.

On this co-ordinate grid, the horizontal and vertical axes both have values from ⁻6 to 6

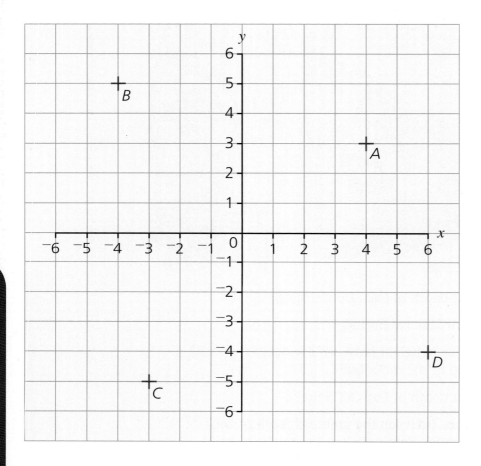

Point A is at (4, 3), B is at (⁻4, 5), C is at (⁻3, ⁻5) and D is at (6, ⁻4).

Exercise 13.6

1 Write down the co-ordinates of points A–K on this co-ordinate grid.

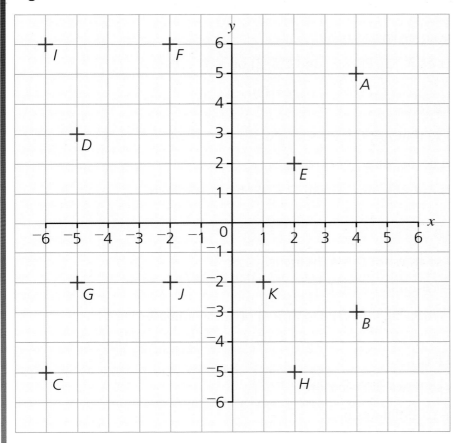

2 Copy the co-ordinate grid above but without the points.
Mark these new points on your grid.

A (2, 6)   F (⁻6, 5)

B (⁻4, 3)   G (⁻5, 1)

C (⁻1, ⁻5)   H (6, ⁻4)

D (4, ⁻3)   I (0, ⁻4)

E (⁻3, ⁻6)   J (⁻6, 0)

3 (a) Mark the points $A(^-2, 3)$, $B(2, 3)$ and $C(2, ^-1)$ on a co-ordinate grid.

(b) Join A to B and B to C.

(c) Mark a point D so that $ABCD$ is a square.

(d) Write down the co-ordinates of D.

4 (a) Mark the points $A(^-4, ^-3)$, $B(^-4, 2)$ and $C(3, 2)$ on a co-ordinate grid.

(b) Join A to B and B to C.

(c) Mark a point D so that $ABCD$ is a rectangle.

(d) Write down the co-ordinates of D.

5 (a) Mark the points $A(4, ^-5)$, $B(6, ^-1)$ and $C(4, 3)$ on a co-ordinate grid.

(b) Join A to B and B to C.

(c) Mark a point D so that $ABCD$ is a rhombus.

(d) Write down the co-ordinates of D.

6 (a) Mark the points $A(3, ^-5)$, $B(5, ^-3)$ and $C(3, 4)$ on a co-ordinate grid.

(b) Join A to B and B to C.

(c) Mark a point D so that $ABCD$ is a kite.

(d) Write down the co-ordinates of D.

Activity – Negative number dice game

You need two dice.

One is a normal die numbered from 1 to 6, the other is numbered from ⁻1 to ⁻6

Play with a partner. Roll both dice together. You win a point if you are the first to call out the difference in value between the numbers correctly.

For example, if you roll a ⁻3 and a 5 then the answer is 8
A number line may help you.

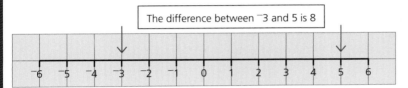

The difference between ⁻3 and 5 is 8

14 Decimals

You know that the value of a digit depends on its place value. For whole numbers, the place value might be counted in millions, thousands, hundreds, tens or units. For numbers less than one, the place value could be tenths, hundredths, thousandths or millionths.

Just as a decimal point separates the pennies and the pounds in amounts of money, the decimal point separates the whole numbers from the decimal fractions in numbers. It does not have a column of its own, but sits on the imaginary line that separates units and tenths.

⇨ Place value

The table shows how to extend the number columns after the decimal point.

Hundreds	Tens	Units	.	tenths	hundredths	thousandths
100	10	1	.	$\frac{1}{10}$	$\frac{1}{100}$	$\frac{1}{1000}$

The value for each column is 10 times smaller than the value of its left-hand neighbour.

$$100 \div 10 = 10 \qquad 10 \div 10 = 1 \qquad 1 \div 10 = \frac{1}{10} \qquad \frac{1}{10} \div 10 = \frac{1}{100} \qquad \frac{1}{100} \div 10 = \frac{1}{1000}$$

The position of the digit tells you its value.

Examples:

Write down the real value of each underlined digit.

(i)

T	U ·	t	h	th
	5 ·	1	_7_	3

7 is in the hundredths column so it is $\frac{7}{100}$

(ii)

T	U ·	t	h	th
	5 ·	1	7	_3_

3 is in the thousandths column so it is $\frac{3}{1000}$

(iii)

T	U ·	t	h	th
	5 ·	_1_	7	3

1 is in the tenths column so it is $\frac{1}{10}$

You can also use place value to write down a number with the digits in the correct place when you are given the number in words.

Examples:

Write down these numbers with the digits in the correct places.

Then write down how you would say the number.

(i) 3 units, 4 tenths, 8 hundredths and 6 thousandths

T	U ·	t	h	th
	3 ·	4	8	6

Three point four eight six

(ii) 1 ten, 2 units, 1 hundredth and 5 thousandths

T	U ·	t	h	th
1	2 ·	0	1	5

Twelve point zero one five

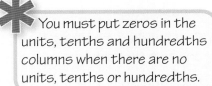

You must put a zero in the tenths column when there are no tenths.

(iii) 2 tens and 8 thousandths

T	U ·	t	h	th
2	0 ·	0	0	8

Twenty point zero zero eight

You must put zeros in the units, tenths and hundredths columns when there are no units, tenths or hundredths.

Exercise 14.1

For questions 1–20, write down the real value of the underlined digit. It may help to rewrite them with column headings, as for the first four.

1

T	U	·	t	h	th
2	1	·	5	3	<u>4</u>

2

T	U	·	t	h	th
1	7	·	<u>2</u>	1	6

3

T	U	·	t	h	th
3	<u>0</u>	·	3	1	7

4

Th	H	T	U	·	t	h	th
5	0	4	3	·	1	<u>2</u>	5

5 1<u>4</u>.435

6 3.0<u>4</u>5

7 5.1<u>0</u>7

8 <u>1</u>25.759

9 3.00<u>6</u>

10 5.<u>0</u>79

11 <u>4</u>02.042

12 402.0<u>4</u>2

13 4<u>0</u>2.042

14 <u>7</u>002.057

15 7002.05<u>7</u>

16 7002.<u>0</u>57

17 <u>3</u>205.305

18 320<u>5</u>.305

19 3205.30<u>5</u>

20 3205.<u>3</u>05

For questions 21–28, write down:

(a) the numbers with the digits in the correct places

(b) how you would say the number.

21 Five units, three tenths, four hundredths and six thousandths

22 Two tens, four units, one tenth, five hundredths and seven thousandths

23 One hundred, two tens, six units, four tenths, nine hundredths and two thousandths

24 Five thousands, one unit, three tenths and four thousandths

25 Five tenths, three hundredths and seven thousandths

26 Four tens, five tenths and eight thousandths

27 Six hundreds, four units, four hundredths and six thousandths

28 Five hundreds and nine thousandths

⇨ Decimals on the number line

The decimals 0.1, 0.5 and 0.75 are marked on this 0–1 number line.

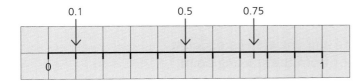

Now zoom in on the number line and look at a smaller range of numbers.

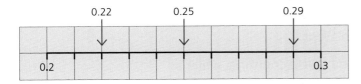

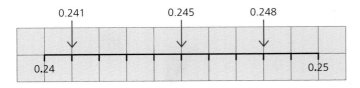

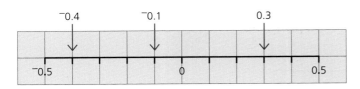

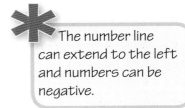

The number line can extend to the left and numbers can be negative.

Exercise 14.2

1 Draw a large number line, from ⁻5 to 5 in steps of 0.25

Copy this grid and cut it into a set of cards.

Starting point: 3	Starting point: 0	Starting point: ⁻2	Step: 0.5	Step: ⁻0.5	Step: 0.1
Starting point: 2	Starting point: ⁻1	Starting point: ⁻4	Step: 0.2	Step: ⁻0.2	Step: 1.5

Put the starting cards in one pile and the step cards in a second pile.

Take turns to pick up one starting card and one step card. Count either backwards or forwards ten steps from the starting point, in the given steps. Your partner will point to the correct place on the number line to help you.

For example, if you drew starting point 1 and step ⁻0.25, you would count:

1   0.75   0.5   0.25   0   minus 0.25   minus 0.5   minus 0.75

and so on until you have counted ten steps.

Your partner then draws two cards and starts counting, while you check the place on the number line.

For questions 2–7, write down the numbers shown by the arrows.

2

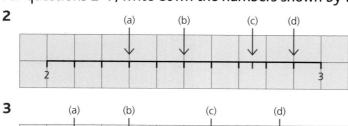

3

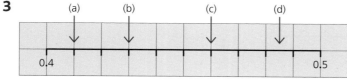

4

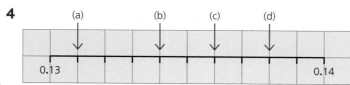

5

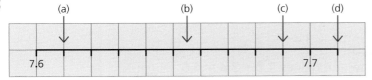

7.6 ... 7.7

6

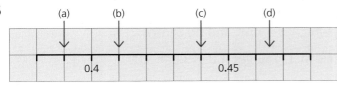

0.4 ... 0.45

7

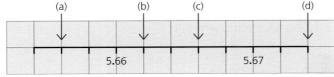

5.66 ... 5.67

8 Draw a number line from 6 to 7 and mark these numbers on it.

  (a) 6.1   **(b)** 6.25   **(c)** 6.6   **(d)** 6.75

9 Draw a number line from 0.7 to 0.8 and mark these numbers on it.

  (a) 0.72   **(b)** 0.74   **(c)** 0.77   **(d)** 0.79

10 Draw a number line from 2.12 to 2.13 and mark these numbers on it.

  (a) 2.121   **(b)** 2.125   **(c)** 2.127   **(d)** 2.126

11 Draw a number line from 4.5 to 4.6 and mark these numbers on it.

  (a) 4.51   **(b)** 4.525   **(c)** 5.56   **(d)** 5.575

12 Draw a number line from 0.34 to 0.35 and mark these numbers on it.

  (a) 0.342   **(b)** 0.344   **(c)** 0.347   **(d)** 0.3485

13 Draw a number line from 7.22 to 7.23 and mark these numbers on it.

  (a) 7.222   **(b)** 7.224   **(c)** 7.226   **(d)** 7.2295

⇨ Mental calculation with decimals

Addition and subtraction

Think how you would work out 1.2 + 3.4

Adding the tenths and then the units gives 1.2 + 3.4 = 4.6

Now think about 1.2 + 3.8

Adding the tenths gives 10 tenths, which is 1 unit and no tenths.

If you then add the units, plus the extra 1, you get 1.2 + 3.8 = 5.0 or 5

Consider 3.45 + 1.55

As you add the hundredths you get 10 hundredths, which is 1 tenth and no hundredths.

If you continue adding, you get 3.45 + 1.55 = 5.00 or 5

What about subtraction?

Think how you would work out 6.45 − 1.3

Subtract in the normal way, taking care to subtract the 3 tenths from the 4 tenths.

6.45 − 1.3 = 5.15

Now consider 4.6 − 2.45

There are no hundredths in 4.6 to take 5 from, so think of this as: 4.60 − 2.45

Just as with normal subtraction, it can help to think of 60 − 45 = ? as 45 + ? = 60

4.60 − 2.45 = 2.15

Exercise 14.3

1 Play this game with a partner. Copy the numbers on this grid and cut it into a set of cards.

1.9	2.35	2.9	1.35
5.1	6.3	1.25	0.75
6.72	7.45	1.55	6.25
3.45	2.7	5.05	7.04
4.16	5.26	5.96	3.7
4.3	5.75	2.35	6.25
12.1	4.12	15.3	0.07
0.05	3.61	6.09	5.01
5.29	3.54	3.12	7.38
1.7	4.3	2.8	1.2
5.4	4.6	6.5	0.5

Shuffle the cards and deal them, face down, into two packs.

You and your partner each take the top card from your own pile. Look at the numbers on the cards and quickly add them together. Call out the answer. You win the two cards if you do this before your partner. When you have used up all the cards, play the game again but, this time, subtract the smaller number from the larger number.

For questions 2–20, write down the answers to the calculations.

2 $7.4 + 2.1$

3 $4.25 + 1.34$

4 $2.15 + 4.85$

5 $1.05 + 3.45$

6 $2.06 + 4.51$

7 $3.5 - 1.4$

8 $2.35 - 1.12$

9 $3.76 - 1.6$

10 $4.28 - 2.8$

11 $4.55 - 3.56$

12	12 + 1.75	17	3.1 − 1.9
13	35.7 + 7.35	18	3.17 − 1.83
14	4 + 3.4 + 0.6	19	25.35 − 3.65
15	45.3 + 0.75	20	12.34 − 2.66
16	3.45 + 12.55		

Complements of one

In some of the additions above, the decimal parts of the numbers added up to 1. For example, in question 20:

$$0.34 + 0.66 = 1$$

0.66 is the **complement** of 0.34 (because it completes the addition to 1).

Example:

What is the complement of 0.73?

The complement of 0.73 is 0.27 because $0.73 + 0.27 = 1$

Exercise 14.4

For questions 1–20, find the complement to one for each number.

Write your answer as an addition, as in the example.

1	0.1	6	0.45
2	0.4	7	0.85
3	0.3	8	0.05
4	0.5	9	0.19
5	0.25	10	0.34
11	0.71	16	0.475
12	0.67	17	0.635
13	0.88	18	0.111
14	0.22	19	0.528
15	0.125	20	0.514

21 From your calculations above, write down what you notice about the pairs of numbers. Check with your partner.

Have you both written down the same things?

Write a rule to explain to someone how they can quickly find the complement.

For questions 22–35, use your rule to write down the answer to these subtractions.

22 1 − 0.65   **29** 1 − 0.28

23 1 − 0.24   **30** 1 − 0.247

24 1 − 0.17   **31** 1 − 0.159

25 1 − 0.39   **32** 1 − 0.363

26 1 − 0.87   **33** 1 − 0.477

27 1 − 0.92   **34** 1 − 0.223

28 1 − 0.56   **35** 1 − 0.178

⇨ Multiplication with decimals

In Chapter 5, you used multiplication tables when multiplying whole numbers. You can multiply decimals in the same way.

$$0.8 \times 4 = 3.2$$

$$0.07 \times 6 = 0.42$$

$$1.2 \times 7 = 8.4$$

There is one very simple rule about where to put the decimal point.

The number of digits after the decimal point in the question is the same as the number of digits after the decimal point in the answer.

If you look at the examples above you will see that this is true, but be careful when either number in the multiplication ends in 5

$$0.4 \times 5 = 2.0 = 2$$

$$0.005 \times 6 = 0.030 = 0.03$$

- Write the 0 in the correct place when you first do the multiplication.

- Check the decimal point is correct and then rewrite the answer without the final 0

Work out the answer to each multiplication.

1 0.3 × 5

2 2 × 0.09

3 0.004 × 6

4 0.005 × 7

5 3 × 1.2

6 8 × 0.012

7 8 × 0.005

8 0.11 × 9

9 0.008 × 7

10 0.005 × 12

Double check that the decimal point is in the correct place.

11 0.7 × 8

12 0.008 × 5

13 4 × 0.05

14 0.008 × 12

15 1.1 × 11

16 8 × 0.07

17 9 × 0.007

18 1.2 × 6

19 0.012 × 5

20 9 × 0.12

⇨ Division with decimals

Division is the reverse of multiplication.

If 0.8 × 4 = 3.2, then 3.2 ÷ 4 = 0.8

If 0.07 × 6 = 0.42, then 0.42 ÷ 6 = 0.07

If 1.2 × 7 = 8.4, then 8.4 ÷ 7 = 1.2

It is a good idea to check each division by making sure that the associated multiplication is true.

Examples:

Check these calculations.

(i) 0.144 ÷ 12 = 0.12 ✗   Check 12 × 0.12 = 1.44   My answer is incorrect.

0.144 ÷ 12 = 0.012 ✓   Check 12 × 0.012 = 0.144   My answer is correct.

(ii) 0.04 ÷ 5 = 0.08 ✗   Check 5 × 0.08 = 0.4   My answer is incorrect.

0.04 ÷ 5 = 0.008 ✓   Check 5 × 0.008 = 0.040   My answer is correct.

Exercise 14.6

Work out the answer to each division.

1 3.6 ÷ 4

2 2.4 ÷ 8

3 3.5 ÷ 7

4 1.2 ÷ 4

5 0.12 ÷ 3

6 0.45 ÷ 5

7 0.56 ÷ 7

8 0.009 ÷ 3

9 0.012 ÷ 6

10 0.072 ÷ 9

Check that the decimal point is in the correct place, by multiplying.

11 2 ÷ 5

12 0.2 ÷ 5

13 0.02 ÷ 5

14 0.048 ÷ 6

15 5.4 ÷ 9

16 0.63 ÷ 7

17 0.024 ÷ 3

18 2.8 ÷ 7

19 0.064 ÷ 8

20 0.96 ÷ 12

21 1.21 ÷ 11

22 4.0 ÷ 5

23 0.4 ÷ 5

24 0.04 ÷ 5

25 0.3 ÷ 5

26 0.6 ÷ 12

27 0.06 ÷ 5

28 1.08 ÷ 9

29 0.072 ÷ 12

30 1.32 ÷ 11

Multiplying by 10, 100 and 1000

In Chapter 5, you saw that when you multiply a number by 10, 100 or 1000 the digits move to the left and you wrote zeros in any column that no longer had a digit in it. The number of places the digits move depends on the numbers of 0s in the number you are multiplying by.

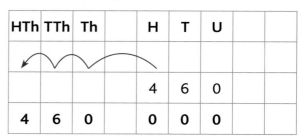

HTh	TTh	Th		H	T	U	
				4	6	0	
4	6	0		0	0	0	

460×1000

$\qquad = 460\,000$

The same is true when you multiply a decimal by 10, 100 or 1000

H	T	U	·	t	h	th	
		0	·	6	5		
		6	·	5			
				2	·	7	
	2	7	0				
		0	·	4	6	5	
	4	6	5				

$0 \cdot 65 \times 10$

$\qquad = 6 \cdot 50$

Digits move 1 place to the left.

$2 \cdot 7 \times 100$

$\qquad = 270$

Digits move 2 places to the left.

$0 \cdot 465 \times 1000$

$\qquad = 465$

Digits move 3 places to the left.

Exercise 14.7

Calculate the answer to each multiplication. Show all your working, including any carried numbers.

1 1.6×10

2 0.6×100

3 0.05×1000

4 5.2×10

5 0.125×100

6 7.12×10

14 Decimals

7 0.007 × 1000

8 0.25 × 100

9 0.065 × 10

10 5.3 × 1000

11 4.05 × 10

12 2.1 × 100

13 4.8 × 1000

14 0.456 × 10

15 0.352 × 100

16 5.06 × 10

17 6.07 × 1000

18 4.09 × 100

19 0.065 × 10

20 8.405 × 1000

Dividing by 10, 100 and 1000

When you divide by 10, 100 or 1000 the digits move to the right. The number of places they move depends on the numbers of 0s in the number you are dividing by. When divided by 10 they move one place, divided by 100 they move two places and divided by 1000 they move three places.

H	T	U ·	t	h	th	
		3 ·	7			
		0 ·	3	7		
	1	2 ·	8			
		0 ·	1	2	8	
2	5	4				
		0 ·	2	5	4	

3·7 ÷ 10

= 0·37

Digits move 1 place to the right.

12·8 ÷ 100

= 0·128

Digits move 2 places to the right.

254 ÷ 1000

= 0·254

Digits move 3 places to the right.

Calculate the answer to each division.

1 9 ÷ 10

2 5 ÷ 100

3 17 ÷ 1000

4 3.5 ÷ 100

5 0.4 ÷ 10

6 4.2 ÷ 1000

7 63 ÷ 100

8 52.3 ÷ 1000

9 5.07 ÷ 1000

10 31.4 ÷ 100

11 950 ÷ 1000

12 50 ÷ 100

13 9.4 ÷ 1000

14 0.4 ÷ 100

15 42.5 ÷ 10

16 3.12 ÷ 1000

17 40.5 ÷ 100

18 408 ÷ 1000

19 25.4 ÷ 10

20 707 ÷ 100

⇨ Ordering decimals

When you are comparing numbers and considering which is larger, it helps to think of their place-value column headings.

Example:

Order these numbers, smallest first.

30   3.03   3.003   30.3

Use a place-value grid.

H	T	U	•	t	h	th
	3	0				
		3	•	0	3	
		3	•	0	0	3
	3	0	•	3		

You can see that:

- 30.3 is bigger than 30 because it has an extra 3 tenths.

- 3.03 is bigger than 3.003 because 3 hundredths are bigger than 3 thousandths.

In order:

3.003   3.03   30   30.3

Exercise 14.9

1 Copy each pair of numbers and write < or > between them.

   (a) 5.9 and 5.2

   (b) 10.001 and 10.01

   (c) 5.55 and 5.055

   (d) 2.022 and 2.2

   (e) 0.15 and 0.105

   (f) 3.3 and 3.03

   (g) 7.012 and 7.102

   (h) 8.503 and 8.035

   (i) 99.095 and 99.059

   (j) 3.033 and 3.303

2 Write each set of numbers in order, starting with the smallest.

   (a) 20.1, 2.1, 21

   (b) 0.77, 0.707, 0.077

   (c) 5.055, 55, 5.5

   (d) 4.044, 4.04, 40

   (e) 600, 60.06, 60.6

3 Write each set of numbers in order, starting with the largest.

   (a) 90.9, 9.099, 90.09

   (b) 33.03, 30.03, 33.303

   (c) 7.007, 77, 77.07

   (d) 14.5, 14.05, 15.04

   (e) 2.031, 3.201, 2.301

⇨ Rounding decimals

When you think about 3 thousandths, you can see that it is a very small number. Sometimes you do not need to include all the decimal places in an answer. You can round to fewer decimal places or to a whole number.

Think about the calculation 4 ÷ 7

	U	·	t	h	th	tth
	0	·	5	7	1	4
7	4	·	⁴0	⁵0	¹0	³0

Step 1: 7 into 4 will not go, carry the 4

Step 2: 7 into 40 is 5 remainder 5, carry the 5

Step 3: 7 into 50 is 7 remainder 1, carry the 1

Step 4: 7 into 10 is 1 remainder 3, carry the 3

Step 5: 7 into 30 is 4 remainder 2, carry the 2

You can see this calculation could go on for a long time, but you can round the decimal numbers, just as you rounded whole numbers in Chapter 3

● If a number falls below the halfway mark (0, 1, 2, 3 or 4), round down.

● If a number falls at or above the halfway mark (5, 6, 7, 8 or 9), round up.

Look at 0.5714 on the number line.

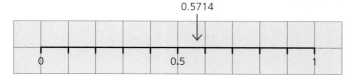

0.5714 is between 0 and 1

It is more than 0.5 so round up.

You say that 0.5714 is 1, correct to the nearest whole number.

Now consider the first decimal place.

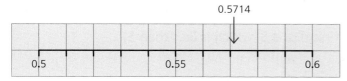

0.5714 is between 0.5 and 0.6

It is more than 0.55 so round up.

Then 0.5714 is 0.6 correct to 1 decimal place (1 d.p.).

Now consider the second decimal place.

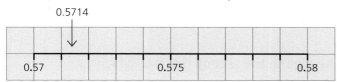

0.5714 is between 0.57 and 0.58

It is less than 0.575 so round down.

Then 0.5714 is 0.57 correct to 2 decimal places (2 d.p.).

Now consider the third decimal place.

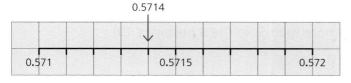

0.5714 is between 0.571 and 0.572

It is less than 0.5715 so round down.

Then 0.5714 is 0.571 correct to 3 decimal places (3 d.p.).

Now you can probably see a simple rule.

1 Count the number of decimal places that you need.

2 Look at the digit to the right.

3 If it is 5 or more, round up your digit.

4 If it is 4 or less, leave your digit as it is.

Examples:

(i) Round 4.375 to:

    (a) the nearest whole number

        4.375 = 4   (The digit in the first d.p. is 3, which is less than 5)

    (b) 1 decimal place

        4.375 = 4.4 (to 1 d.p.)   (The digit in the second d.p. is 7, which is more than 5)

    (c) 2 decimal places.

        4.375 = 4.38 (to 2 d.p.)   (The digit in the third d.p. is 5)

(ii) Round 0.4098 to:

    (a) 1 decimal place

        0.4098 = 0.4 (to 1 d.p.)   (The digit in the second d.p. is 0, which is less than 5)

    (b) 2 decimal places

        0.4098 = 4.41 (to 2 d.p.)   (The digit in the third d.p. is 9, which is more than 5)

    (c) 3 decimal places

        0.4098 = 4.410 (to 3 d.p.)   (The digit in the fourth d.p. is 8, which is more than 5, so the 9 becomes 10)

Exercise 14.10

1 Round each of these numbers to the nearest whole number.

(a) 13.9 (c) 35.074 (e) 0.5

(b) 1025.815 (d) 405.5 (f) 9.909

2 Round each of these numbers to one decimal place.

(a) 34.19 (c) 45.06 (e) 2.069

(b) 2.63 (d) 308.04 (f) 9.957

3 Round each of these numbers to two decimal places.

(a) 1.453 (c) 100.569 (e) 7.1809

(b) 15.056 (d) 34.999 (f) 25.9161

4 Round each of these numbers to three decimal places.

(a) 17.5609 (c) 1.0607 (e) 3.9999

(b) 3.14257 (d) 12.01309 (f) 45.0995

5 Round each of these numbers to:

(i) the nearest whole number

(ii) one decimal place

(iii) two decimal places.

(a) 32.905 (c) 25.095 (e) 11.089

(b) 102.904 (d) 0.5672 (f) 9.595

6 Round each of these numbers to:

(i) one decimal place

(ii) two decimal places

(iii) three decimal places.

(a) 11.7284 (e) 12.87593 (i) 4.87952

(b) 9.63298 (f) 0.9805 (j) 0.4999

(c) 0.4055 (g) 3.2132 (k) 11.5089

(d) 105.4593 (h) 15.8967 (l) 6.3995

⇨ Decimal patterns

Look at this number line. It starts below 0 and runs from ⁻2 to 1.8 in steps of 1.2

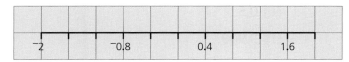

0, 0.3, 0.6, 0.9   What would come next? $0.9 + 0.3 = 1.2$

⁻2, ⁻1.6, ⁻1.2, ⁻0.8   What would come next? $⁻0.8 + 0.4 = ⁻0.4$

To complete number patterns you need to follow these steps.

1 Work out the difference between two adjacent terms in the pattern.

2 Add or subtract to find the missing term.

Examples:

Find the missing terms in these patterns.

(i)   2.7,   3,   3.3,   3.6,   ...,   ...

The difference is $3.6 - 3.3 = 0.3$

The missing terms are: $3.6 + 0.3 = 3.9$

and $3.9 + 0.3 = 4.2$

The pattern is: 2.7, 3, 3.3,   3.6,   **3.9, 4.2**

(ii)   ⁻1.5,   ...,   ⁻0.7,   ⁻0.3,   ...,   0.5

The step is the difference between ⁻0.7 and ⁻0.3 which is 0.4

The missing terms are: $0.5 - 0.4 = 0.1$

and $⁻0.7 - 0.4 = ⁻1.1$

The pattern is: ⁻1.5, **⁻1.1**, ⁻0.7, ⁻0.3, **0.1**, 0.5

14 Decimals

Exercise 14.11

Find the missing terms in each pattern.

1 0, 0.5, 1, 1.5, ..., ...

2 0, 0.4, 0.8, 1.2, ..., ...

3 0, 0.7, 1.4, 2.1, ..., ...

4 0.3, 0.8, 1.3, 1.8, ..., ...

5 2.4, 3, 3.6, 4.2, ..., ...

6 ⁻3.5, ⁻3, ⁻2.5, ⁻2, ..., ...

7 ⁻1.6, ⁻1.2, ⁻0.8, ⁻0.4, ..., ...

8 ⁻2.7, ⁻1.9, ⁻1.1, ⁻0.3, ..., ...

9 ..., ..., 0, 0.5, 1, 1.5

10 ..., ..., 0, 0.7, 1.4, 2.1

11 ..., ..., 0.3, 0.8, 1.3, 1.8

12 ..., ..., ⁻0.4, 0.5, 1.4, 2.3

13 ..., ⁻0.6, 0, ..., 1.2, 1.8

14 ⁻1.2, ..., 0.2, 0.9, 1.6, ...

15 ⁻1.6, ..., 0.8, ..., 3.2, 4.4

16 ..., 1, 2.5, 4, 5.5, ...

17 ..., 0, ..., 1.4, 2.1, 2.8

18 ..., 1, 2.2, ..., 4.6, 5.8

19 ⁻2.3, ..., ⁻0.7, ..., 0.9, 1.7

20 ⁻3.5, ..., ⁻1.1, 0.1, ..., 2.5

⇨ Problem solving

Exercise 14.12

1 I count back from 0.8 in steps of ⁻0.2

   (a) How many steps do I need, to reach zero?

   (b) How many steps do I make to reach ⁻0.6?

2 I count forward from ⁻1.2 in steps of 0.3

   (a) How many steps do I need, to reach zero?

   (b) How many steps do I make to pass 2?

For questions 3–6, one number will always be a whole number.

3 Find two numbers with a sum of 4.2 and a product of 0.8

4 Find two numbers with a sum of 4.4 and a product of 1.6

5 Find two numbers with a difference of 4.4 and a product of 3

6 Find two numbers with a difference of 2.7 and a product of 5.2

7 Think of a number between 0 and 1 that can be rounded to 0.8

   (a) What is the largest number you can think of?

   (b) What is the smallest number you can think of?

8 Think of a number between 0 and 1 that can be rounded to 0.5

   (a) What is the largest number you can think of?

   (b) What is the smallest number you can think of?

9 Think of number between 0 and 10 that can be rounded to 4

   (a) What is the largest number you can think of?

   (b) What is the smallest number you can think of?

10 Answer the following questions using:

   ● no more than one of each of the digits 1–9

   ● any of the four operations $+$, $-$, $\times$, $\div$

   ● no more than three zeros

   ● no more than three decimal points.

   For example:

   $0.4 + 0.6 = 1$

   (a) How many addition calculations can you make that add up to 1?

   (b) Can you make all the whole numbers from 1 to 10, using at least one decimal in your sentence?

Activity – Tricky triangles

Here are some patterns made of dots.

Pattern 1   Pattern 2   Pattern 3   Pattern 4

1 Draw the next four patterns.

2 Copy and complete the table for patterns 5 to 8.

Pattern number	Number of dots	Pattern number × next pattern number
1	1	1 × 2 = 2
2	3	2 × 3 = 6
3	6	3 × 4 = 12
4	10	4 × 5 = 20
5		
6		
7		
8		
9		
10		

3 Can you see a relationship between the numbers in the last two columns?

Use it to complete the final two rows of the table.

The numbers in the second column are called **triangle numbers**. This is because they can be drawn as triangles.

We can also make the triangle numbers by adding **consecutive** whole numbers.

You can see that this works by looking at the number of dots in each row of the patterns you have drawn.

Consecutive means 'following on, one after another'.

4 Continue the pattern below up to the 10th triangle number.

$1 = 1$

$3 = 1 + 2$

$6 = 1 + 2 + 3$

$10 = 1 + 2 + 3 + 4$

5 Use what you have learned to answer these questions.

(a) What is the 15th triangle number?

(b) What is the sum of all the numbers from 1 to 50?

(c) What is the sum of all the numbers from 1 to 100?

(d) What is the sum of all the numbers from 21 to 40?

 **More decimals**

⇨ Formal written addition and subtraction

If a calculation is too difficult to do mentally, write the numbers in a frame. When the numbers have decimals, it is important to write the decimal points in the correct place.

Examples:

(i)   1104 + 7.4 + 0.455

Th	H	T	U ·	t	h	th
1	1	0	4 ·			
			7 ·	4		
			0 ·	4	5	5
1	1	1	1 ·	8	5	5
		1				

Write each number in the frame so that the decimal points are aligned vertically, like a neat column of buttons. Then add as normal.

(ii)   24.4 − 2.735

T	U ·	t	h	th
2	³4 ·	¹³4	⁹0	¹0
	2 ·	7	3	5
2	1 ·	6	6	5

Write each number in the frame, with the decimal points aligned.

Write zeros in the decimal hundredths and thousandths columns for the first number.

Subtract as normal.

Work out the answers to these additions and subtractions.

Show all your working, including any carried numbers.

1 7.4 + 2.56

2 101.3 + 12.655

3 12 + 0.12

4 15 + 0.155

5 24.4 + 3.405

6 12.6 − 2.45

7 105.7 − 3.65

8 2.45 − 1.9

9 3.1 − 0.125

10 34 − 3.107

11 12 + 4.5 + 0.355

12 14.5 + 105 + 2.007

13 3.4 + 6.505 + 24

14 30 − 2.625

15 200 − 11.745

16 6.4 + 0.045 + 236

17 244 − 4.607

18 125 + 4.5 + 6.258

19 34.46 + 7.2 + 5.109

20 207 − 12.107

⇨ Written multiplication

When you are multiplying with decimals, align the decimal points vertically – just as with addition and subtraction.

Examples:

(i) 3.164 × 4

T	U ·	t	h	th
	3 ·	1	6	4
		×		4
1	2 ·	6	5	6
1		2	1	

3.164 × 4 = 12.656

Start with an estimate: 3 × 4 = 12

So you will need to include the tens column in the frame.

Multiply as normal.

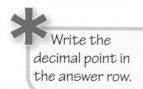
Write the decimal point in the answer row.

(ii) 5.105 × 4

T	U	·	t	h	th
	5	·	1	0	5
			×		4
2	0	·	4	2	0
2				2	

5.105 × 4 = 20.42

Start with an estimate: 5 × 4 = 20

Multiply as normal.

● Write the decimal point in the answer row.

● When you write down your final answer, you do not need to write down the final 0.

Exercise 15.2

Calculate the answers to these multiplications.

* Show all your working, including any carried numbers.

1 3.23 × 4

2 1.45 × 3

3 3.65 × 4

4 3.213 × 6

5 4.745 × 8

6 3.908 × 9

7 5.432 × 7

8 4.086 × 5

9 2.542 × 8

10 0.458 × 6

11 35.604 × 7

12 1.904 × 9

13 4.563 × 5

14 10.745 × 8

15 5.072 × 5

16 12.003 × 9

17 25.781 × 8

18 3.962 × 6

19 35.198 × 7

20 6.348 × 9

⇨ Written division

Dividing by a single-digit integer

Just as before, keep the decimal points aligned vertically.

> Write the decimal point in the answer line above the decimal point in the question.

Examples:

(i)   6.15 ÷ 5

	U	·	t	h
	1	·	2	3
5	6	·¹1		¹5

Step 1: 6 ÷ 5 = 1 r1   Write 1 on the answer line and carry 1

Step 2: 11 ÷ 5 = 2 r1   Write 2 on the answer line and carry 1

Step 3: 15 ÷ 5 = 3   Write 3 on the answer line.

6.15 ÷ 5 = 1.23

(ii)   10.32 ÷ 4

	T	U	·	t	h
		2	·	5	8
4	1	¹0	·²3	³2	

Step 1: You cannot divide 4 into 1   Carry the 1 to the units column.

Step 2: 10 ÷ 4 = 2 r2   Write 2 on the answer line and carry 2

Step 3: 23 ÷ 4 = 5 r3   Write 5 on the answer line and carry 3

Step 4: 32 ÷ 4 = 8   Write 8 on the answer line.

10.32 ÷ 4 = 2.58

(iii)   3.164 ÷ 4

	U	·	t	h	th
	0	·	7	9	1
4	3	·³1	³6	4	

Step 1: You cannot divide 4 into 3
        Carry the 3 to the tenths column.

Step 2: 31 ÷ 4 = 7 r3   Write 7 on the answer line and carry 3

Step 3: 36 ÷ 4 = 9   Write 9 on the answer line.

Step 4: 4 ÷ 4 = 1   Write 1 on the answer line.

3.164 ÷ 4 = 0.791

Exercise 15.3

Calculate the answers to these divisions.

1 $5.8 \div 2$

2 $8.7 \div 3$

3 $9.2 \div 4$

4 $8.5 \div 5$

5 $7.8 \div 6$

6 $5.6 \div 7$

7 $7.2 \div 8$

8 $6.3 \div 9$

9 $33.2 \div 4$

10 $48.5 \div 5$

11 $7.56 \div 9$

12 $9.03 \div 7$

13 $8.16 \div 6$

14 $8.88 \div 3$

15 $3.76 \div 8$

16 $9.48 \div 4$

17 $9.72 \div 2$

18 $8.35 \div 5$

19 $6.72 \div 4$

20 $1.96 \div 7$

21 $9.472 \div 8$

22 $0.805 \div 5$

23 $0.266 \div 7$

24 $8.865 \div 3$

25 $9.402 \div 6$

26 $5.316 \div 2$

27 $8.862 \div 7$

28 $7.945 \div 5$

29 $9.176 \div 4$

30 $8.232 \div 8$

Decimal division with a remainder

You will recall from earlier work that some division calculations do not produce an exact answer. You are left with a remainder.

Examples:

(i) Divide 5.3 by 2

	U	.	t	h
		2	. 6	
2	5		¹3	

	U	.	t	h
		2	. 6	5
2	5	.	¹3	¹0

$5.3 \div 2 = 2.65$

Step 1: $5 \div 2 = 2$ r1   Write 2 on the answer line, carry 1

Step 2: $13 \div 2 = 6$ r1   Write 6 on the answer line, carry 1

Step 3: $10 \div 2 = 5$ Write 5 on the answer line.

5.3 is the same as 5.30 so you can continue to divide because you can write a 0 at the end of 5.3

(ii) Divide 6.5 by 4

	U	.	t	h	th
		1	. 6	2	5
4	6	.	²5	¹0	²0

Step 1: $6 \div 4 = 1$ r2   Write 1 on the answer line and carry 2

Step 2: $25 \div 4 = 6$ r1   Write 6 on the answer line and carry 1

Step 3: Write a zero at the end.

Step 4: $10 \div 4 = 2$ r2   Write 2 on the answer line and carry 2

Step 5: Write another zero at the end.

Step 6: $20 \div 4 = 5$

$6.5 \div 4 = 1.625$

You can write a decimal point and extra 0s at the end of a whole number, without changing its value. For example, 7.0 is the same as 7 and 4.00 is the same as 4. This is useful when you are dividing whole numbers.

You can write down as many 0s as you need, to complete the division.

Examples:

(i) Calculate $9 \div 2$

	U	·	t
	4	·	5
2	9	·	^{1}0

Write down one extra 0

$9 \div 2 = 4.5$

(ii) Calculate $13 \div 4$

	T	U	·	t	h
		3	·	2	5
4	1	3	·	^{1}0	^{2}0

Write down two extra 0s.

$13 \div 4 = 3.25$

(iii) Calculate $67 \div 8$

	T	U	·	t	h	
		8	·	3	7	5
8	6	7	·	^{3}0	^{6}0	^{4}0

Write down three extra 0s.

$67 \div 8 = 8.375$

Calculate the answers to these divisions.

1 $5.3 \div 2$	**6** $3.8 \div 8$
2 $1.8 \div 4$	**7** $14.7 \div 2$
3 $7.6 \div 5$	**8** $33.1 \div 4$
4 $8.7 \div 6$	**9** $23.9 \div 5$
5 $17.2 \div 8$	**10** $19.5 \div 6$
11 $1.98 \div 4$	**16** $5 \div 2$
12 $7.12 \div 5$	**17** $14 \div 4$
13 $6.3 \div 6$	**18** $17 \div 5$
14 $1.85 \div 2$	**19** $3 \div 8$
15 $0.12 \div 8$	**20** $47 \div 4$
21 $27 \div 6$	**26** $5.12 \div 5$
22 $72 \div 5$	**27** $7.29 \div 6$
23 $20 \div 8$	**28** $10.64 \div 8$
24 $65 \div 4$	**29** $4.2 \div 8$
25 $31 \div 8$	**30** $8.5 \div 4$

⇨ Problem solving

When you are solving problems involving decimals, write down the numbers carefully and make sure you show your calculations clearly. Estimating will help you double check that the decimal point is in the correct place.

Exercise 15.5

1 Three numbers add up to 10

Two of the numbers are 3.75 and 2.68

What is the third number?

2 Four numbers add up to 100

Three of the numbers are 4.65, 28.6 and 45.008

What is the fourth number?

3 Write down four pairs of numbers, each with two places of decimals, that add up to ten.

4 Write down four pairs of numbers, each with three places of decimals, that add up to ten.

5 Ali ran 100 m in 12.32 seconds. Yusain was 1.05 seconds faster. What was Yusain's time?

6 Irina ran 200 m in 27.38 seconds. Julieta was 2.56 seconds slower. What was Julieta's time?

7 I want to divide 30 minutes into eight equal time slots.

How long will each slot be?

8 Imran writes down eight equal numbers that add up to 100. What are the numbers?

9 I think of three numbers. The second is twice as big as the first and the third is twice as big as the second. If the first number is 3.75, what is the sum of my three numbers?

10 I have four numbers. The second is equal to the first, the third is twice as big as the second and the fourth is four times as big as the third. If the fourth number is 7, what is the sum of my four numbers?

11 I have three numbers. The second is twice as big as the first and the third is twice as big as the second.

If the numbers add up to 29.75, what are my three numbers?

12 I have four numbers. The second is equal to the first, the third is twice as big as the second and the fourth is four times as big as the third.

If the numbers add up to 14.1, what are my four numbers?

⇨ Putting it together

Examples:

(i) Add 2045 + 19.64 + 0.375

Th	H	T	U ·	t	h	th
2	0	4	5 ·			
		1	9 ·	6	4	
			0 ·	3	7	5
2	0	6	5 ·	0	1	5
			1	1	1	

Write each number so that the decimal points are aligned vertically.

Add as normal.

2045 + 19.64 + 0.375 = 2065.015

(ii) Subtract 43.2 − 1.752

T	U ·	t	h	th
4	^{2}3 ·^{11}2	^{9}0	^{1}0	
	1 ·	7	5	2
4	1 ·	4	4	8

Write each number so that the decimal points are aligned vertically.

Write zeros in the decimal hundredths and thousandths columns where necessary.

Subtract as normal.

43.2 − 1.752 = 41.448

(iii) Multiply 4.256 × 3

T	U ·	t	h	th
	4 ·	2	5	6
		×		3
1	2 ·	7	6	8
1		1	1	

Start with an estimate of 3 × 4 (12) so include a tens column for your answer.

Multiply as normal.

4.256 × 3 = 12.768

(iv) Multiply 6.485 × 6

T	U · t	H	th
	6 · 4	8	5
	×		6
3	8 · 9	1	0
3	2 5	3	

Estimate: 6 × 6 = 36

Multiply as normal.

When you write down your final answer, you do not need to write the final 0

6.485 × 6 = 38.91

(v) Divide 3.74 ÷ 4

	U · t	h	th
	0 · 9	3	5
4	3 · ³7	¹4	²0

You cannot divide 4 into 3 — Write 0 on the answer line and carry 3

37 ÷ 4 = 9 r1 — Write 9 on the answer line and carry 1

14 ÷ 4 = 3 r2 — Write 3 on the answer line, write down a 0 and carry 2

20 ÷ 4 = 5 — Write 5 on the answer line.

3.74 ÷ 4 = 0.935

Exercise 15.6: Summary exercise

1 Calculate the answers to these. Show all your working, including any carried numbers.

(a) 4.5 + 17 + 0.73

(b) 100 + 4.2 + 0.006

(c) 45 + 7.35 + 2.625

(d) 120 − 0.56

(e) 4 − 3.506

(f) 19 − 4.543

(g) 356 + 5.72 + 0.357

(h) 324 − 105.009

2 Calculate the answers to these. Show all your working, including any carried numbers.

(a) 4.35×5

(b) 5.125×4

(c) 63.072×8

(d) 0.145×9

(e) 3×5.642

(f) 8×1.505

(g) 12×0.514

(h) 9×5.609

3 Calculate the answers to these. Show all your working, including any carried numbers.

(a) $9.35 \div 5$

(b) $5.12 \div 4$

(c) $9.216 \div 8$

(d) $0.354 \div 6$

(e) $1.404 \div 9$

(f) $8.456 \div 7$

(g) $5.022 \div 3$

(h) $8.505 \div 5$

4 Calculate the answers to these. Write any remainders as decimals.

(a) $1.2 \div 5$

(b) $7.1 \div 4$

(c) $9.2 \div 8$

(d) $2.1 \div 6$

(e) $3.4 \div 8$

(f) $8.2 \div 5$

(g) $5.1 \div 6$

(h) $7.6 \div 8$

5 I have three numbers. The second is three times as big as the first and the third is three times as big as the second. If the first number is 3.45, what is the sum of the three numbers?

6 One number is twice as big as another and together they add up to 10.11

What are the two numbers?

Activity – Chequered tiles

Square black and white patterned tiles are placed in a row.

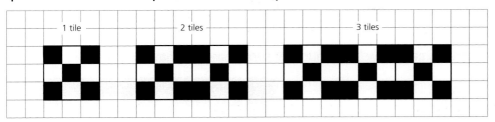

1 Draw a row of four tiles.

2 Copy and complete the table. Extend it up to 10 tiles.

Number of tiles	Number of black squares	Number of white squares	Total number of squares
1			
2			
3			
4			
5			

3 (a) How many black squares are there in a row of 20 tiles?

(b) How many white squares are there in a row of 24 tiles?

(c) What is the total number of squares in a row of 30 tiles?

(d) How many tiles have a total of 225 black squares?

(e) How many tiles have a total of 160 white squares?

(f) How many tiles have a total of 234 squares altogether?

(g) If there are 900 squares altogether, how many of them are white?

 Decimals, fractions and percentages

Decimals and **fractions** can show 'how much' of something you have.

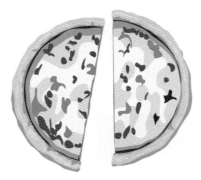

Will and Ali share a pizza.

They have $\frac{1}{2}$ a margherita each.

Oliver weighs 3.45 kg.

A **percentage** is just a special kind of fraction. You can use percentages to compare quantities, when you need to show how much bigger or smaller one quantity is, compared to the other.

This packet is 33% bigger than the usual size.

The prices of items in this shop are 25% lower than they usually are.

In this chapter you will learn about the relationships between decimals, fractions and percentages. First, though, remind yourself of the place value headings of decimal numbers.

Hundreds	Tens	Units	•	tenths	hundredths	thousandths
100	10	1	•	$\frac{1}{10}$	$\frac{1}{100}$	$\frac{1}{1000}$

⇨ Fractions, decimals and percentages on the number line

Look at this number line. It is numbered from 0 to 1 and from 0% to 100%.

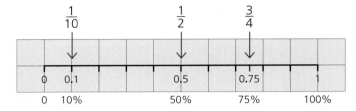

You can see that: $0.1 = \dfrac{1}{10} = 10\%$

$0.5 = \dfrac{1}{2} = 50\%$

$0.75 = \dfrac{3}{4} = 75\%$

Always write fractions in their lowest terms.

From these you can work out other equivalent fractions, decimals and percentages.

Example:

$0.2 = \dfrac{2}{10} = \dfrac{1}{5} = 20\%$

Exercise 16.1

1 Draw a number line from 0 to 1 and mark on it $\dfrac{1}{4}$, $\dfrac{1}{2}$ and $\dfrac{3}{4}$
   Then mark on it the equivalent decimals and percentages.

2 Draw a number line from 0 to 1 and mark on it $\dfrac{1}{10}$, $\dfrac{3}{10}$, $\dfrac{7}{10}$ and $\dfrac{9}{10}$
   Then mark on it the equivalent decimals and percentages.

3 Draw a number line from 0 to 1 and mark on it $\dfrac{1}{5}$, $\dfrac{2}{5}$, $\dfrac{3}{5}$ and $\dfrac{4}{5}$
   Then mark on it the equivalent decimals and percentages.

⇨ Writing decimals as fractions

To write a decimal as a fraction, you write the number over a
power of 10 (10, 100, 1000, ...).

Tenths

If there is just **one** place of decimals to the right of the decimal
point, you have **tenths**.

Examples:

Write each decimal as a fraction in its lowest terms.

(i) $0.3 = \frac{3}{10}$ This fraction is in its lowest terms so there is nothing more
to do.

(ii) $0.2 = \frac{2}{10}$ This fraction is not in its lowest terms. The top and bottom
can both be divided by 2

$0.2 = \frac{2}{10} = \frac{1}{5}$

(iii) $0.5 = \frac{5}{10}$ This fraction is not in its lowest terms. The top and bottom
can both be divided by 5

$0.5 = \frac{5}{10} = \frac{1}{2}$

Hundredths

If there are **two** places of decimals, you have **hundredths**. Again,
always express fractions in their lowest terms.

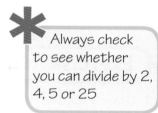

Always check
to see whether
you can divide by 2,
4, 5 or 25

Examples:

Write each decimal as a fraction in its lowest terms.

(i) $0.09 = \frac{9}{100}$ This fraction is already in its lowest terms.

(ii) $0.61 = \frac{61}{100}$ This fraction is already in its lowest terms.

(iii) **0.06** = $\frac{6}{100}$ = $\frac{3}{50}$ Divide top and bottom by 2

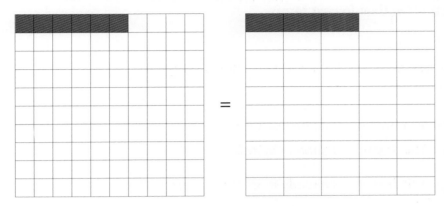

(iv) **0.28** = $\frac{28}{100}$ = $\frac{7}{25}$ Divide top and bottom of the fraction by 4

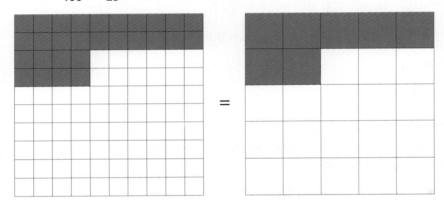

When a decimal includes a **whole number**, the whole number remains as it is and you just need to work with the numbers to the right of the decimal point.

(v) **1.05** = $1\frac{5}{100}$ = $1\frac{1}{20}$ Divide top and bottom of the fraction by 5

(vi) **4.75** = $4\frac{75}{100}$ = $4\frac{3}{4}$ Divide top and bottom of the fraction by 25

Thousandths

If there are **three** places of decimals, you have **thousandths**. Again, always express fractions in their lowest terms.

Always check to see whether you can divide by 2, 4, 5 or 25

Examples:

Write each decimal as a fraction in its lowest terms.

(i) $0.007 = \frac{7}{1000}$ This fraction is already in its lowest terms.

(ii) $0.023 = \frac{23}{1000}$ This fraction is already in its lowest terms.

(iii) $0.014 = \frac{14}{1000} = \frac{7}{500}$ Divide top and bottom by 2

(iv) $0.105 = \frac{105}{1000} = \frac{21}{200}$ Divide top and bottom by 5

(v) $5.025 = 5\frac{25}{1000} = 5\frac{1}{40}$ Divide top and bottom by 25

Exercise 16.2

Write each decimal as a fraction or a mixed number. Make sure that each fraction is in its lowest terms.

1 0.1	**6** 0.16
2 0.9	**7** 0.15
3 0.4	**8** 0.46
4 0.05	**9** 0.145
5 0.009	**10** 0.015
11 0.45	**16** 1.88
12 0.022	**17** 2.085
13 0.605	**18** 3.072
14 0.04	**19** 6.8
15 0.082	**20** 7.18

⇨ Writing fractions as decimals

In Chapter 5 you recognised that a fraction is another way of showing a division. For example, $\frac{1}{4}$ is one part out of a whole divided into four equal parts. You can use this to turn fractions into decimals.

Example:

Write $\frac{1}{4}$ as a decimal.

U	•	t	h
	0	• 2	5
4	1	• ¹0	²0

$\frac{1}{4} = 1 \div 4$

$= 0.25$

Exercise 16.3

Use division to write these fractions as decimals. Show your working.

1 $\frac{1}{2}$ 4 $\frac{1}{4}$ 7 $\frac{5}{8}$ 10 $\frac{1}{5}$

2 $\frac{1}{8}$ 5 $\frac{3}{8}$ 8 $\frac{3}{4}$

3 $\frac{2}{5}$ 6 $\frac{7}{8}$ 9 $\frac{4}{5}$

You do not always need to use the division method. For some fractions, you can use what you know about decimal places to convert them to decimals.

Examples:

Write each fraction as a decimal.

(i) $\frac{3}{10} = 0.3$ You know that the heading for the **first** place of decimals is **tenths**, so you can write 3 tenths as 0.3

(ii) $\frac{9}{100} = 0.09$ You know that the heading for the **second** place of decimals is **hundredths**, so you can write 9 hundredths as 0.09

(iii) $\frac{16}{100} = 0.16$ You know that the heading for the **second** place of decimals is **hundredths**, so you can write 16 hundredths as 0.16

(iv) $\frac{61}{1000} = 0.061$ You know that the heading for the **third** places of decimals is **thousandths**, so you can write 61 thousandths as 0.061

Halves, fifths, quarters, twentieths, twenty-fifths and fiftieths don't match any column headings for decimal places. However:

- 2 and 5 are factors of 10

- 4, 20, 25 and 50 are factors of 100

This means that you can write fractions such as $\frac{1}{2}$ and $\frac{4}{5}$ as equivalent fractions in tenths.

Also, you can write $\frac{3}{4}$, $\frac{9}{20}$, $\frac{8}{25}$ and $\frac{7}{50}$ as equivalent fractions in hundredths. Then it is easy to write them as decimals.

Examples:

Write these fractions as decimals.

(i) $\frac{1}{2} = \frac{5}{10} = 0.5$ Multiply top and bottom of the fraction by 5

(ii) $\frac{3}{4} = \frac{75}{100} = 0.75$ Multiply top and bottom of the fraction by 25

(iii) $\frac{4}{5} = 0.8$ Multiply top and bottom of the fraction by 2

(iv) $\frac{9}{20} = \frac{45}{100} = 0.45$ Multiply top and bottom of the fraction by 5

(v) $\frac{8}{25} = \frac{32}{100} = 0.32$ Multiply top and bottom of the fraction by 4

Similarly, 200, 250, 500 and 125 are factors of 1000 and therefore you can write fractions such as $\frac{7}{200}$, $\frac{49}{250}$ and $\frac{1}{125}$ as equivalent fractions in thousandths and then change them directly to decimals.

Examples:

Write these fractions as decimals.

(i) $\frac{7}{500} = \frac{14}{1000} = 0.014$ Multiply top and bottom of the fraction by 2

(ii) $\frac{1}{8} = \frac{125}{1000} = 0.125$ Multiply top and bottom of the fraction by 125

It is useful to remember that $\frac{1}{8} = 0.125$ and, from that, work out the other decimal equivalents of eighths.

As before, whole numbers remain as they are.

Examples:

Write these mixed numbers as decimals.

(i) $2\frac{3}{8} = 2\frac{375}{1000} = 2.375$ Multiply top and bottom of the fraction by 125

(ii) $5\frac{9}{20} = 5\frac{45}{100} = 5.45$ Multiply top and bottom of the fraction by 5

Exercise 16.4

Use equivalent fractions, or your knowledge of fractions and decimals, to write these fractions as decimals.

1 $\frac{9}{10}$

2 $\frac{2}{5}$

3 $\frac{17}{100}$

4 $\frac{9}{50}$

5 $\frac{3}{20}$

6 $\frac{4}{25}$

7 $\frac{27}{50}$

8 $\frac{3}{5}$

9 $\frac{7}{10}$

10 $\frac{19}{20}$

11 $\frac{7}{1000}$

12 $\frac{1}{8}$

13 $\frac{7}{200}$

14 $\frac{23}{500}$

15 $\frac{17}{20}$

16 $\frac{2}{25}$

17 $1\frac{1}{10}$

18 $2\frac{1}{8}$

19 $5\frac{18}{25}$

20 $7\frac{3}{4}$

21 $\frac{101}{250}$ 26 $2\frac{3}{8}$

22 $\frac{7}{8}$ 27 $1\frac{17}{25}$

23 $\frac{21}{25}$ 28 $2\frac{1}{100}$

24 $\frac{1}{5}$ 29 $2\frac{4}{25}$

25 $\frac{27}{200}$ 30 $1\frac{203}{500}$

⇨ Writing percentages as fractions

Percentage, shown by the sign %, comes from the Latin *per centum*, which means 'out of a hundred'.

Whenever you see the percentage sign (%) you can write the percentage as hundredths. So, for example, 10% is 10 hundredths ($\frac{10}{100}$). You may then need to rewrite the fraction in its lowest terms.

Examples:

Write each percentage as a fraction in its lowest terms.

(i)   **50%** $= \frac{50}{100} = \frac{1}{2}$ Divide the top and bottom of the fraction by 50

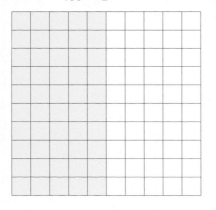 =

(ii) **15%** $= \frac{15}{100} = \frac{3}{20}$ Divide the top and bottom of the fraction by 5

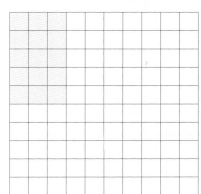 =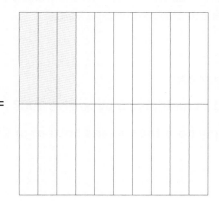

Exercise 16.5

Write these percentages as fractions in their lowest terms.

1 50%		**6** 10%	
2 25%		**7** 35%	
3 75%		**8** 17%	
4 16%		**9** 8%	
5 20%		**10** 80%	

11 65%	**16** 40%
12 14%	**17** 42%
13 24%	**18** 44%
14 72%	**19** 45%
15 4%	**20** 5%

⇨ Writing fractions as percentages

You will need to change all fractions into their equivalent hundredths before you can work out the percentage value.

Example:

Write $\frac{9}{20}$ as a percentage.

What do you need to multiply 20 by to give 100?

You need to multiply both the top and bottom of the fraction by 5

$\frac{9}{20} = \frac{45}{100} = 45\%$

Exercise 16.6

Write these fractions as percentages.

1 $\frac{13}{100}$　　　　　　6 $\frac{4}{5}$

2 $\frac{11}{50}$　　　　　　7 $\frac{1}{4}$

3 $\frac{9}{25}$　　　　　　8 $\frac{1}{2}$

4 $\frac{7}{20}$　　　　　　9 $\frac{23}{50}$

5 $\frac{1}{10}$　　　　　10 $\frac{1}{5}$

11 $\frac{1}{20}$　　　　　16 $\frac{18}{25}$

12 $\frac{7}{10}$　　　　　17 $\frac{17}{20}$

13 $\frac{12}{25}$　　　　　18 $\frac{3}{5}$

14 $\frac{3}{4}$　　　　　19 $\frac{3}{50}$

15 $\frac{39}{50}$　　　　　20 $\frac{3}{25}$

⇨ Writing decimals as percentages

To write a decimal as a percentage, think of the decimal in hundredths, that is, with two decimal places.

Examples:

Write each decimal as a percentage.

(i) $0.23 = \frac{23}{100} = 23\%$

(ii) This time you have to remember to write a 0 after the 7 to show two decimal places.

$0.7 = 0.70 = \frac{70}{100} = 70\%$

Exercise 16.7

Write these decimals as percentages.

1 0.47	6 0.81
2 0.36	7 0.18
3 0.89	8 0.5
4 0.6	9 0.55
5 0.06	10 0.05

⇨ Writing percentages as decimals

Since a percentage is equivalent to decimal hundredths, you will need to use two decimal places when writing a percentage as a decimal.

Examples:

Write each percentage as a decimal.

(i) $15\% = \frac{15}{100} = 0.15$

(ii) $70\% = \frac{70}{100} = 0.70 = 0.7$

(iii) $7\% = \frac{7}{100} = 0.07$ Be careful not to write 0.7

(iv) $37.5\% = \frac{37.5}{100}$ or $\frac{375}{1000} = 0.375$

Write these percentages as decimals.

1 48%	**6** 8%
2 65%	**7** 80%
3 50%	**8** 12.5%
4 5%	**9** 125%
5 19%	**10** 40.5%

⇨ Conversions – to sum up

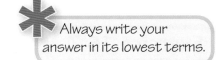

Always write your answer in its lowest terms.

To convert decimals to fractions

One decimal place is tenths	$0.8 = \dfrac{8}{10} = \dfrac{4}{5}$	Divide top and bottom by 2
Two decimal places are hundredths	$0.45 = \dfrac{45}{100} = \dfrac{9}{20}$	Divide top and bottom by 5
Three decimal places are thousandths	$0.204 = \dfrac{204}{1000} = \dfrac{51}{250}$	Divide top and bottom by 4

To convert fractions to decimals

Divide the top number by the bottom number.

$\dfrac{1}{4} = 1.00 \div 4 = 0.25$

or turn the fraction into **tenths** or **hundredths**.

$\dfrac{3}{5} = \dfrac{6}{10} = 0.6$ Multiply top and bottom by 2

$\dfrac{11}{25} = \dfrac{44}{100} = 0.44$ Multiply top and bottom by 4

$\dfrac{31}{200} = \dfrac{155}{1000} = 0.155$ Multiply top and bottom by 5

To convert percentages to fractions

Write the percentage as **hundredths** and then rewrite the fraction in its lowest terms.

$36\% = \dfrac{36}{100} = \dfrac{9}{25}$ Divide top and bottom by 4

To convert fractions to percentages

Write the fraction in **hundredths**.

$\frac{19}{50} = \frac{38}{100} = 38\%$ Multiply top and bottom by 2

To convert decimals to percentages

Use **two decimal places**.

$0.37 = 37\%$

$0.2 = 0.20 = 20\%$

To convert percentages to decimals

Write in **hundredths**.

$39\% = \frac{39}{100} = 0.39$

$6\% = \frac{6}{100} = 0.06$

Useful facts

These are some very commonly used fractions, decimals and percentages that are worth learning.

$\frac{1}{4} = 0.25 = 25\%$

$\frac{1}{2} = 0.5 = 50\%$

$\frac{3}{4} = 0.75 = 75\%$

It is also helpful to know these:

$\frac{1}{10} = 0.1 = 10\%$

$\frac{1}{5} = 0.2 = 20\%$

and these if you really want to be on top of things!

$\frac{1}{100} = 0.01 = 1\%$ $\frac{1}{50} = 0.02 = 2\%$

$\frac{1}{25} = 0.04 = 4\%$ $\frac{1}{20} = 0.05 = 5\%$

$\frac{1}{8} = 0.125 = 12.5\%$ $\frac{3}{8} = 0.375 = 37.5\%$

$\frac{5}{8} = 0.625 = 62.5\%$ $\frac{7}{8} = 0.875 = 87.5\%$

This table shows equivalent fractions (in their lowest terms), decimals and percentages.

Copy it and fill in the gaps.

Fraction	Decimal	Percentage
$\frac{37}{100}$		
	0.71	
		43%
	0.25	
		75%
$\frac{1}{2}$		
		70%
$\frac{3}{10}$		
	0.9	
$\frac{1}{8}$		
	0.4	
		80%
	0.375	
		42%
$\frac{9}{50}$		
		16%
$\frac{11}{250}$		
	0.306	
$\frac{9}{20}$		
	0.35	
		65%

⇨ Problem solving

Solving problems with decimals, fractions and percentages often involves comparing them. The best way to compare them is to turn them all into decimals.

Example:

Put these in order, starting with the smallest.

$\frac{9}{20}$ 44%   0.444

Convert to decimals:

$\frac{9}{20} = \frac{45}{100} = 0.45$ 44% = 0.44   0.444

In order, they are: 0.44, 0.444, 0.45

Answer: 44%,   0.444, $\frac{9}{20}$

Exercise 16.10

1 Which is the larger in each pair?

(a) 0.6   or $\frac{4}{5}$ (c) 65%   or $\frac{7}{10}$

(b) 30%   or $\frac{7}{20}$ (d) 0.69   or $\frac{17}{25}$

2 Which is the smaller in each pair?

(a) $\frac{1}{5}$ or   0.3   (c) 23%   or $\frac{3}{20}$

(b) 90%   or $\frac{47}{50}$ (d) $\frac{3}{4}$ or   0.7

3 Write each group in order of size, starting with the smallest.

(a) $\frac{1}{4}$ 0.23   24%

(b) 0.6 $\frac{31}{50}$ 61%

(c) $\frac{8}{25}$ 30%   0.31

4 Write each group in order of size, starting with the largest.

(a) 0.3   4% $\frac{1}{20}$

(b) 72%   0.68 $\frac{7}{10}$

(c) 0.14   16% $\frac{3}{20}$

5 Feisal scores 57% in a test. Samira gets $\frac{3}{5}$ of the paper correct.
Who got the higher mark?

6 Two shops sell a pair of ballet shoes at the same original price, then both shops have a sale. Tutus offer 25% off the price and Pirouette give a $\frac{1}{5}$ discount. Which shop has the lower sale price?

7 Zak scores $\frac{13}{20}$ on an exercise. What percentage is this?

8 Richard is given 68% on an essay marked out of 25

How many actual marks did he get?

9 Milly is given the choice of having her pocket money increased by either $\frac{1}{5}$ or 5%. Which choice gives her the larger increase?

10 In a 100-metre race Anne has completed 0.46 of the distance, Jane has covered 38% of the course and Catherine $\frac{11}{25}$ of it.
Which girl is nearest to the finish?

17 Money and measures

⇨ Units of currency

A country's system of money is called its **currency**. The currency in the UK is **sterling**. This is because our earliest form of money was small silver coins that looked like stars. The word for star in Old English was *steorra* and so a little star was called *steorraling*.

The UK now uses two units of currency, which are pounds and pennies or pence.

There are 100 pence in one pound.

100p = £1

For amounts that are not an exact amount of pounds, you use a decimal point to separate the pounds from the pence.

158p = £1.58

£12 565.95 = 1 256 595p

Other countries have different currencies.

The currency in the USA is the dollar.
1 dollar ($1) = 100 cents (100c)

In much of Europe, the currency is the euro.
1 euro (€1) = 100 cents (100c)

In China, the currency is the yuan.
1 yuan (¥1) = 10 jiao (10 角) or 100 fen (100 分)

Exercise 17.1

1 Convert each larger unit to the smaller unit.

(a) £5 to pence

(b) €15 to cents

(c) $180 to cents

(d) £15.45 to pence

(e) £1235.07 to pence

(f) €120.65 to cents

(g) £150 000 to pence

(h) $20 000 to cents

(i) €3500 to cents

(j) £125.45 to pence

(k) ¥15 to jiao

(l) ¥1405 to fen

2 Convert each smaller unit to the larger unit.

(a) 1200p to pounds

(b) 570c to dollars

(c) 15 950c to euros

(d) 12 435p to pounds

(e) 350 568c to dollars

(f) 1 250 000c to euros

(g) 1 305 009p to pounds

(h) 345 905c to euros

(i) 1350 角 to yuan

(j) 435 角 to yuan

(k) 13 567 分 to yuan

(l) 1239 分 to jiao

⇨ Money problems

You use money all the time when you go shopping. It is very important that you can calculate how much you are spending and how much change you will receive.

Another useful word, when you are shopping, is **dozen**.
1 dozen is twelve, so a dozen eggs means 12 eggs.

Exercise 17.2

Answer these questions by carefully writing out your calculations and showing all your working. Some questions will need two stages of working.

1 I find a 10p coin, two 50p coins, three £2 coins, six £1 coins and a 20p coin on the floor in my bedroom.

How much money is that?

2 I have a £5 note and I buy a packet of biscuits for £1.74

(a) How much change do I get?

(b) What is the minimum number of coins I will receive for change?

3 I have saved £19.72 and I want to buy a new computer game that costs £29.95

How much more money do I need?

4 In our supermarket I can buy six eggs for £1.32 or a dozen eggs for £2.52

(a) What is the cost of one egg, if I buy the packet of six?

(b) What is the cost of one egg, if I buy a dozen eggs?

5 A box of eight doughnuts costs $2.72

What is the cost of one doughnut, in cents?

6 It costs £8.64 for an adult to go to the cinema and £6.12 for a child. What is the total cost for:

(a) 1 adult and 3 children

(b) 2 adults and 4 children

(c) my class of 20 children and 2 teachers?

7 On holiday, I buy six croissants for €4.92 and a packet of butter for 96c.

(a) How much do I spend in total?

(b) How much change do I get from a €10 note?

(c) What is the cost of one croissant?

8 (a) My friends and I compare what we bought at the weekend. Calculate how much each of us spent.

(i) My shopping

1 ruler at £2.25

2 pens at £1.75 each

1 pack of pencils at £1.60

Chocolate at 39p

A packet of mints at 77p

(ii) Amy's shopping

Raisins at 45p

Dried mangos at £2.69

A fruit bar at £1.99

A notebook at £1.65

(iii) Michael's shopping

Scissors at £2.70

Rubber bands at £1.25

A box of doughnuts at £2.75

A pencil case at 95p

2 pencils at 35p each

(b) If we all started with £10, how much change did we each receive?

9 A café buys milk in 6-pint bottles for £1.99 each.

It sells quarter-pint glasses of milk for 45p.

How much profit does the café make if they sell:

(a) 10 glasses of milk

(b) 24 glasses of milk

(c) 4 glasses of milk?

10 Copy and complete this shopping list.

4 cans of beans at 72p each	£____
____ packets of bacon at £1.45 each	£4.35
2 dozen eggs at £____ a dozen	£5.70
Total:	____

11 Copy and complete this shopping list.

2 kg of carrots at £1.56 per kg	£____
__ cabbages at 90p each	£5.40
3 kg potatoes at £____ per kg	£4.05
Total:	____

12 Calculate the total cost of the ingredients in this sponge cake recipe:

125 g of butter at £6 per kg

100 g of sugar at £1.60 per kg

250 g of flour at 72p per kg

2 eggs at £1.32 for 6

13 We are going to make some cakes to sell at the school fair.

(a) Using the recipe and prices above, what will it cost us to buy all the ingredients to make 12 cakes?

(b) We shall also need three pots of jam at 95p per pot, four litres of cream at £2.25 per litre and icing sugar at £1.71 per pack.

(i) What is the total cost now?

(ii) What is the cost of making each cake?

(c) We sell each cake for £6.50. How much profit do we make?

14 (a) I put £1.20 a week from my pocket money into my piggy bank. How much money do I have after 50 weeks?

(b) My sister put £5 a month into her piggy bank.

How much does she have after 12 months?

(c) My brother put 1p in his piggy bank the first month, 2p the second month, 4p the third month and 8p the fourth month, and so on. How much did he save in 12 months?

⇨ Metric units of length

You already know most of the metric units for length. You are going to revise these again and practise decimal values.

10 millimetres (mm)   = 1 centimetre (cm)

100 centimetres (cm)   = 1 metre (m)

1000 millimetres (mm) = 1 metre (m)

1000 metres (m)   = 1 kilometre (km)

To complete this exercise, you will need a ruler and a long measuring tape.

For these questions, draw a table like this:

Object	Estimate	Measurement
Length of room		
Width of room		
Height of room		

1 Look around the classroom. You will see various pieces of furniture, objects and people. Write down an estimate for each measurement, using millimetres, centimetres or metres as appropriate.

(a) The length, width and height of the classroom

(b) The height and width of the door into the classroom

(c) The height and width of the largest window

(d) The height of the seat of your chair

(e) The width of your desk

(f) The length of your pencil

(g) The width of your pencil

2 Now you have made your estimates, work with your partner to measure each distance. How accurate were your estimates?

Converting units of length

When you are changing from a larger unit to a smaller one, multiply.

When you are writing down your calculations, remember to change the units and use the equals sign correctly.

Examples:

(i)   Convert 6 m to centimetres (cm). $6 m = 6 \times 100 \, cm$
$$= 600 \, cm$$

(ii) Convert 0.04 m to millimetres (mm).
$$0.04 \, m = 0.04 \times 1000 \, mm$$
$$= 40 \, mm$$

(iii) Convert 0.25 km to millimetres (mm).
$$0.25 \, km = 0.25 \times 1000 \, m = 250 \, m$$
$$= 250 \times 1000 \, mm$$
$$= 250 \, 000 \, mm$$

When you are changing from a smaller unit to a larger one, divide.
Again, remember to use the equals sign correctly.

Examples:

(i)   Convert 5 m to kilometres (km). $5 m = 5 \div 1000 \, km$
$$= 0.005 \, km$$

(ii) Convert 25 mm to centimetres (cm).
$$25 \, mm = 25 \div 10 \, cm$$
$$= 2.5 \, cm$$

(iii) Convert 42 cm to metres (m). $42 \, cm = 42 \div 100 \, m$
$$= 0.42 \, m$$

Exercise 17.4

1 Convert these lengths to millimetres.
   (a) 4 cm   **(b)** 3 m   **(c)** 500 m   **(d)** 50 cm

2 Convert these lengths to kilometres.
   (a) 5000 m   **(b)** 60 m   **(c)** 450 m   **(d)** 5 m

3 Convert these lengths to metres.
   (a) 425 cm   **(b)** 30 cm   **(c)** 50 mm   **(d)** 7 mm

4 Convert these lengths to centimetres.

(a) 72 mm   (b) 4 m   (c) 3 mm   (d) 6 km

5 Convert these lengths to metres.

(a) 3 cm   (b) 56 mm   (c) 45 km   (d) 0.7 km

6 Write these lengths in the units shown in brackets.

(a) 0.4 km (m)   (f) 0.075 km (m)

(b) 750 m (km)   (g) 0.063 km (cm)

(c) 0.3 m (mm)   (h) 0.045 m (cm)

(d) 7 mm (cm)   (i) 35 m (km)

(e) 1250 m (km)   (j) 452 mm (m)

⇨ Metric units of mass

The weight of an object is what keeps it on the ground. It is the force with which the Earth pulls the object towards itself.

The mass of the object is a measure of how much of it there is.

You already know most of the metric units for mass. You are going to revise these again and practise decimal values.

1000 milligrams (mg) = 1 gram (g)

1000 grams (g)   = 1 kilogram (kg)

1000 kilograms (kg)   = 1 metric tonne (t)

Exercise 17.5

To complete this exercise, you will need some weighing scales.

Draw up a table like this.

Object	Estimate	Measurement
(a) Mass of text book		
(b) Mass of maths book		
(c) Mass of pencil case		
(d) Mass of chair		
(e) Mass of partner		
(f) Mass of ...		

1 Write down an estimate for the above measures, using milligrams, grams or kilograms as appropriate. Fill in the estimate column.

You can add any extra objects that your teacher gives you.

2 Now you have made your estimates, work with your partner to weigh the objects.

How accurate were your estimates?

Converting units of mass

When you are changing from a larger unit to a smaller one, multiply. When you are writing down your calculations, remember to change the units and use the equals sign correctly.

Examples:

(i) Convert 80 g to milligrams (mg).

$$80\,g = 80 \times 1000\,mg$$
$$= 80\,000\,mg$$

(ii) Convert 0.75 kg to grams (g).

$$0.75\,kg = 0.75 \times 1000\,g$$
$$= 750\,g$$

(iii) Convert 0.04 t to kilograms (kg).

$$0.04\,t = 0.04 \times 1000\,kg$$
$$= 40\,kg$$

When you are changing from a smaller unit to a larger one, divide. Again, remember to use the equals sign correctly.

Examples:

(i) Convert 70 g to kilograms (kg).

$$70\,g = 70 \div 1000\,kg$$
$$= 0.07\,kg$$

(ii) Convert 350 mg to grams (g).

$$350\,mg = 350 \div 1000\,g$$
$$= 0.350\,g$$

(iii) Convert 4250 kg to tonnes (t).

$$4250\,kg = 4250 \div 1000\,t$$
$$= 4.25\,t$$

Exercise 17.6

1 Convert these weights to milligrams.
   (a) 4 g   **(b)** 35 g   **(c)** 1250 g   **(d)** 0.3 g

2 Write these weights in kilograms.
   (a) 7000 g   **(b)** 3125 g   **(c)** 16 g   **(d)** 7 g

3 Convert these weights to grams.
   (a) 1250 mg   **(b)** 47 mg   **(c)** 715 mg   **(d)** 6.5 mg

4 Write these weights in tonnes.
   (a) 4675 kg   **(b)** 312 kg   **(c)** 25 kg   **(d)** 1 235 643

5 Convert these weights to grams.
   (a) 35 406 mg   **(b)** 5.4 kg   **(c)** 0.052 kg   **(d)** 72 mg

6 Write these weights in the units shown in brackets.

(a) 0.6 kg (g)

(b) 625 mg (g)

(c) 0.073 t (kg)

(d) 7.5 kg (g)

(e) 425 mg (g)

(f) 0.015 t (kg)

(g) 35 g (kg)

(h) 725 kg (t)

(i) 4.2 g (mg)

(j) 12 345 kg (t)

⇨ Metric units of capacity

There are two units of capacity.

1000 millilitres (ml) = 1 litre (l)

Capacity is a fluid measure. It is the amount of space inside a container.

Volume is generally a solid measure. It is the amount of space taken up by a solid object.

Exercise 17.7

To complete this exercise, you will need a measuring jug.

1 Ask your teacher for a collection of cups, jugs, cartons and buckets.

Estimate the capacity of each container, in millilitres or litres. Draw up a table like this, to record your results.

Object	Estimate	Measurement

2 Now you have made your estimates, you need to check your answers by measuring with water. It is probably best to do this outside.

Converting units of capacity

As before, when you are changing from a larger unit to a smaller one, multiply. When you are writing down your calculations, remember to change the units and use the equals sign correctly.

Examples:

(i) Convert 8l to millilitres (ml).

$$8l = 8 \times 1000\,ml$$
$$= 8000\,l$$

(ii) Convert 0.05l to millilitres (ml).

$$0.05l = 0.05 \times 1000\,ml$$
$$= 50\,ml$$

When you are changing from a smaller unit to a larger one, divide. Again, remember to use the equals sign correctly.

Examples:

(i) Convert 7500ml to litres (l).

$$7500\,ml = 7500 \div 1000\,l$$
$$= 7.5\,l$$

(ii) Convert 450ml to litres (l).

$$450\,ml = 450 \div 1000\,l$$
$$= 0.45\,l$$

Exercise 17.8

1 Convert these capacities to millilitres.

(a) 6l   (c) 0.75l   (e) 18l   (g) 0.007l

(b) 1.5l   (d) 0.03l   (f) 120l   (h) 0.065l

2 Write these capacities in litres.

(a) 7000ml   (c) 12400ml   (e) 25ml   (g) 155670ml

(b) 150ml   (d) 5ml   (f) 6125ml   (h) 470ml

3 Write these capacities in the units shown in brackets.

(a) 0.6l (ml)   (c) 650ml (l)   (e) 0.045l (ml)   (g) 14500ml (l)

(b) 720l (ml)   (d) 420ml (l)   (f) 35ml (l)   (h) 0.007l (ml)

⇒ Problem solving

Before you answer this type of question, look at the units in which you need to give the answer. It will help if you make any changes to units first.

Example:

In a French supermarket, salami costs €35 per kilogram.
What is the cost of 200 g of the salami?

Cost per kilogram = €35
Cost per gram = €35 ÷ 1000
= €0.035

Cost of 200 g = €200 × 0.035
= €100 × 2 × 0.035
= €7

Exercise 17.9

Use your knowledge of metric units and money to solve these problems. Show all your working carefully, even if you are calculating mentally.

1 Graham buys six oranges that weigh 240 g each.

How much do they weigh altogether?

2 A fencing panel is 1.90 m long.

What is the total length of seven panels placed end to end?

3 In a box there are six fruit cakes, each with mass 1.75 kg.

What is the total mass of the cakes?

4 A two-litre bottle of lemonade is poured equally into eight glasses. How much is there in each glass? Give your answer in millilitres.

5 It is 1920 km from John O'Groats (the UK's most northern point) to Land's End (the UK's most south-western point). I am planning to cycle this in 12 days.

How far must I cycle each day?

6 A £2 coin has a diameter of 2.84 cm. How long is a straight line of 200 two-pound coins when they are laid side by side? Give your answer in metres.

7 French Camembert costs €13.40 per kilogram.

How much does René pay for 300 g of Camembert?

8 I have to fill the classroom fish tank with clean water. The fish tank holds 10 litres and the small jug I have to use holds 400 ml. How many full jugs do I need, to fill the tank?

9 A baby elephant weighs 264 km at birth, increasing to 4 tonnes when fully grown. How many tonnes does the elephant gain?

10 On a picnic we take one cake weighing 1.35 kg, a bottle of fruit juice weighing 2.25 kg, six sandwiches weighing 225 g each, 1.5 kg of apples and three bars of chocolate weighing 125 g each.

What is the total weight of our picnic, in kilograms?

11 My garden has a left and right length of 15 m and a width of 12 m. If fencing panels are 90 cm wide, how many will I need to build a fence around the three sides of my garden?

12 What is better value, a 1 kg rich fruit cake costing £12 or a 913 g iced Christmas cake costing £11?

(If your answer is not exact, you may wish to round to the nearest penny. Will this make a difference to your answer?)

⇨ Imperial units

The units you have been looking at so far are metric units. Now you will think about some common imperial units.

Inches, feet, yards and miles

Centimetres were brought into use in Europe at the end of the nineteenth century, although they were not adopted in the United Kingdom until the 1970s. Before this we used imperial units and we still use some of them today.

Your school ruler is 30 cm long, but it might also be marked as
12 inches or **1 foot**.

In the imperial system for measurement of length:

12 inches (in)   = 1 foot (ft)

3 feet (ft)   = 1 yard (yd)

1760 yards (yd) = 1 mile (mi)

Exercise 17.10

1 Work out the answers to these, in inches.

(a) $\frac{1}{2}$ of 1 foot   **(c)** $\frac{1}{3}$ of 1 foot   **(e)** $\frac{3}{4}$ of 1 foot

(b) $\frac{1}{4}$ of 1 foot   **(d)** $\frac{1}{6}$ of 1 foot   **(f)** $\frac{5}{6}$ of 1 foot

2 Work out the answers to these, in feet and inches.

(a) $\frac{1}{2}$ of 1 yard   **(c)** $\frac{1}{3}$ of 1 yard   **(e)** $\frac{3}{4}$ of 1 yard

(b) $\frac{1}{4}$ of 1 yard   **(d)** $\frac{1}{6}$ of 1 yard   **(f)** $\frac{5}{6}$ of 1 yard

3 Work out the answers to these, in yards.

(a) $\frac{1}{2}$ of 1 mile   **(c)** $\frac{1}{8}$ of 1 mile   **(e)** $\frac{3}{4}$ of 1 mile

(b) $\frac{1}{4}$ of 1 mile   **(d)** $\frac{1}{5}$ of 1 mile   **(f)** $\frac{5}{8}$ of 1 mile

4 Simon is six inches taller than Sue. If Sue is 4 ft 10 in, how tall is Simon?

5 Ali is nine inches smaller than Yasmeen. If Yasmeen is 5 ft 3 in, how tall is Ali?

6 I have some blocks that are 1 ft 6 in high, some boxes that are 9 in high and some books that are 3 in thick.

    (a) What is the total height of:

        (i) 3 blocks   **(iv)** 1 block, 2 boxes and 3 books

        (ii) 4 boxes   **(v)** 3 blocks, 4 boxes and 2 books

        (iii) 10 books   **(vi)** 2 blocks, 5 boxes and 6 books?

    (b) What combination of blocks, boxes and books would be exactly:

        (i) 3 feet high   **(iii)** 5 feet high?

        (ii) 4 feet high

Converting units of length

You need to use these approximations when converting between imperial and metric units of length.

≈ means is 'approximately equal to'.

1 foot ≈ 30 cm

1 metre ≈ 3 ft 3 in or 3.25 feet

Exercise 17.11

1 Carefully measure out 3 feet or 1 yard. Measure this distance in centimetres.
Now copy and complete these sentences.

1 yard = ___ cm

1 yard = ___ m

1 foot = ___ cm

2 Carefully measure out 1 metre. Measure this distance in inches.
Then copy and complete these sentences.

1 metre = ___ ft ___ in

10 centimetres = ___ in

3 Estimate these lengths in feet and inches:
- The height of your desk
- The height of the door
- The height of this textbook

Now measure the above objects in feet and inches and see how accurate you were. Estimate and measure some other distances in feet and inches.

4 1 foot ≈ 30 cm

What is 1 foot in **(a)** millimetres **(b)** metres?

5 (a) Use the approximation in question 4 to find what length, in metres, is approximately equal to:
   - **(i)** 2 feet
   - **(iii)** 2 yards
   - **(v)** 15 feet
   - **(ii)** 10 feet
   - **(iv)** 10 yards
   - **(vi)** 12 yards

(b) What length, in centimetres, is approximately equal to:
   - **(i)** 6 inches
   - **(iii)** 4 inches
   - **(v)** 15 inches
   - **(ii)** 9 inches
   - **(iv)** 3 inches
   - **(vi)** 1 foot 6 inches?

6 1 metre ≈ 3 ft 3 ins or 3.25 feet.
What length, in feet and inches, is approximately equal to:
   - **(a)** 2 metres
   - **(c)** 10 metres
   - **(e)** 1.5 metres
   - **(b)** 5 metres
   - **(d)** 6 metres
   - **(f)** 2.5 metres?

7 When Helena measured her bathroom, she wrote down its width as 6 feet 6 inches and its length as 10 feet.
What are the approximate measurements of the room, in metres?

8 I measured my sister's height as 4 feet 6 inches.
What is this in **(a)** centimetres **(b)** metres?

9 I measured the height of my bedroom as 2.4 metres.
What is this in feet and inches?

10 1 kilometre is approximately equal to $\frac{5}{8}$ mile (0.625 miles or 1100 yards).

   (a) What distance, in miles, is approximately equal to:

      (i) 80 km   **(iii)** 400 km   **(v)** 160 km

      (ii) 4 km   **(iv)** 16 km   **(vi)** 1000 km?

   (b) What distance, in kilometres, is approximately equal to:

      (i) 100 miles   **(iii)** 50 miles   **(v)** 500 miles

      (ii) 1000 miles   **(iv)** 10 miles   **(vi)** 60 miles?

11 A marathon race is just over 26 miles.
Approximately how far is this, in kilometres?

12 In a triathlon, an athlete swims for 4 km, runs for 40 km and cycles for 180 km.
What is the approximate total distance, in miles?

Ounces, pounds, stones and tons

In the imperial system for measurement of weight:

16 ounces (oz)   = 1 pound (lb)

14 pounds (lb)   = 1 stone (st)

2240 pounds (lb) = 1 ton (t)

Exercise 17.12

1 Write each of these amounts in pounds and ounces.

   (a) 20 ounces   **(c)** 50 ounces   **(e)** 80 ounces

   (b) 40 ounces   **(d)** 32 ounces   **(f)** 100 ounces

2 Work out the answers to these, in ounces.

   (a) $\frac{1}{2}$ lb   **(c)** $\frac{1}{8}$ pound   **(e)** $\frac{3}{4}$ pound

   (b) $\frac{1}{4}$ pound   **(d)** $1\frac{1}{4}$ lb   **(f)** $2\frac{3}{8}$ lb

3 Work out the answers to these, in pounds and ounces.

(a) $\frac{1}{2}$ of 1 stone   (c) $\frac{1}{8}$ of 1 stone   (e) $3\frac{1}{2}$ stone

(b) $\frac{1}{4}$ of 1 stone   (d) $1\frac{1}{4}$ stone   (f) $\frac{3}{4}$ of 1 stone

4 A box weighs 4 lb 8 oz. If a second box is 10 oz heavier, how heavy is the second box?

5 An envelope weighs 12 oz. It is 8 oz lighter than a second envelope. What does the second envelope weigh?

6 I have six weights for my weighing scales.

A: $1\frac{1}{2}$ lb, B: 1 lb, C: 8 oz, D: 5 oz, E: 3 oz and F: 1 oz

(a) What is the total weight of:

    (i) 2 × weight A, weight B and 3 × weight C

    (ii) 4 × weight A, 4 × weight D and 7 × weight F

    (iii) 3 × weight A, 2 × weight D and 3 × weight E?

(b) What combination of weights do I need to weigh:

    (i) $\frac{3}{4}$ lb   (ii) 5 lb 15 oz?

Converting units of weight

Have a look at a pack of butter and a bag of flour.

When the UK used imperial units, packs of butter were sold in packs weighing $\frac{1}{2}$ lb.

When the UK adopted the metric system, butter was sold in packs of 250 g.

You will need both imperial and metric measuring scales for this exercise.

1 (a) Fill a plastic pot with pencils until you have a pound weight. Weigh the pot and pencils, in kilograms.
Then copy and complete the sentence below.

1 pound = ___ kg

(b) Add more pencils until you have a kilogram weight.
Then weigh the pot, in pounds and ounces.

Copy and complete this sentence.

1 kg = ___ lb ___ oz

2 Draw up a table like this.

Dimension	Estimate	Measurement

(a) Estimate the weight of these items, in pounds and ounces.
You can add some others to the list.

(i) Your pencil   (iv) Yourself

(ii) Your textbook   (v) A hole punch

(iii) A table lamp

(b) Now measure the weight of the items, in pounds and ounces. See how accurate you were.

3 1 pound ≈ 450 g

What is this in   (a) mg   (b) kg?

4 (a) What weight, in grams, is approximately equal to:

(i) 2 lb   (iii) 4 oz   (v) $\frac{1}{3}$ lb

(ii) $\frac{1}{2}$ lb   (iv) 12 oz   (vi) 1.5 lb?

(b) What weight, in kilograms, is approximately equal to:

    (i) 2 lb   **(iii)** 5 lb   **(v)** 15 lb

    (ii) 10 lb   **(iv)** 100 lb   **(vi)** 60 lb?

5 1 kg ≈ 2.2 lb or 2 lb 3 oz

What weight, in pounds and ounces, is approximately equal to:

    (a) 2 kg   **(c)** 10 kg   **(e)** 1.5 kg

    (b) 5 kg   **(d)** 15 kg   **(f)** 100 kg?

6 My mum weighs 60 kg.

How much does she weigh, approximately, in pounds?

7 This is an old recipe for Victoria sponge cake.

For the cake	For the butter icing
3 eggs	4 oz icing sugar
6 oz self-raising flour	2 oz butter
6 oz caster sugar	$\frac{1}{2}$ teaspoon of vanilla extract
6 oz butter	
$\frac{1}{2}$ teaspoon of vanilla extract	
jam to sandwich the cake	

How many grams do I need of each of these ingredients?

(a) Self-raising flour

(b) Butter (for the cake and the icing)

(c) Icing sugar

Pints, quarts and gallons

In the imperial system for measurement of capacity:

2 pints (pt) = 1 quart (qt)

8 pints (pt) = 1 gallon (gal)

Exercise 17.14

1 Write these quantities in pints.

(a) $\frac{1}{2}$ of 1 gallon 　　(c) $\frac{1}{4}$ of 1 gallon 　　(e) $\frac{3}{4}$ of 1 gallon

(b) $\frac{1}{2}$ of 1 quart 　　(d) $\frac{1}{4}$ of 1 quart 　　(f) $\frac{5}{8}$ of 1 gallon

2 Write these quantities in gallons.

(a) 16 pints 　　(c) 40 pints 　　(e) 25 pints

(b) 20 pints 　　(d) 10 pints 　　(f) 200 pints

3 A barrel of beer contains 36 gallons. How many pints is that?

4 I buy a 2-gallon container of lemonade.

How many $\frac{1}{2}$-pint glasses will it fill?

5 How many $1\frac{1}{4}$-pint bottles will it take to fill a 3-gallon bucket?

6 I mix 5 pints of orange juice concentrate with 2 gallons of water.

(a) How many pints of orange squash do I have?

(b) How many $\frac{1}{4}$-pint glasses can I fill?

(c) If I sell each glass of orange squash for 25p, how much money do I collect?

(d) If I paid £2.50 for the orange juice concentrate, how much profit do I make?

Converting units of capacity

As an estimate:

1 pint   ≈ 600 ml

1 gallon ≈ 4.5 litres

1 litre   ≈ 1.7 pints

10 litres ≈ 2.2 gallons

Exercise 17.15

You will need both imperial and metric measuring jugs for this exercise.

1 Carefully measure out 1 pint of water and pour it into a measuring jug marked in millilitres.
Copy and complete this sentence.

1 pint = ___ ml

2 Carefully measure out 1 litre of water and pour it into a measuring jug marked in pints.
Copy and complete this sentence:

1 litre = ___ pints

3 Draw up a table like this.

Dimension	Estimate	Measurement

(a) Use the collection of cups, jugs, cartons and buckets you used in Exercise 17.9. Estimate their volumes, in pints and gallons.

(b) Now measure their volumes in pints and gallons and see how accurate you were.

4 1 pint ≈ 600 ml

What is that in litres?

5 (a) What volume, in litres, is approximately equal to:

    (i) 10 pints   **(iii)** 3 pints   **(v)** 2 gallons

    (ii) 1 quart   **(iv)** 2 quarts   **(vi)** 5 gallons?

(b) What volume, in millilitres, is approximately equal to:

    (i) $\frac{1}{2}$ pint   **(iii)** $\frac{1}{3}$ pint   **(v)** $\frac{5}{6}$ pint

    (ii) $\frac{1}{4}$ pint   **(iv)** $\frac{3}{4}$ pint   **(vi)** $\frac{5}{8}$ pint?

6 (a) 1 litre ≈ 17 pints

    What volume, in pints, is approximately equal to:

    (i) 2 litres   **(iii)** 6 litres   **(v)** 10 litres

    (ii) 5 litres   **(iv)** $1\frac{1}{2}$ litres   **(vi)** $2\frac{1}{2}$ litres?

(b) 10 litres ≈ 2.2 gallons

    What volume, in gallons, is approximately equal to:

    (i) 5 litres   **(iii)** 2 litres   **(v)** 15 litres

    (ii) 20 litres   **(iv)** 100 litres   **(vi)** 25 litres?

7 A bucket holds 2 gallons. How many litres is that?

8 The school swimming pool holds 700 000 gallons of water. If 1 gallon ≈ 4.5 litres, how many litres is that?

9 For the school fair, class 5C is going to make a fruit punch.

These are the ingredients:

3 quarts pineapple juice

$\frac{1}{4}$ pint lemon juice

$\frac{1}{4}$ pint lime juice

$\frac{3}{4}$ pint orange juice

$\frac{3}{4}$ pint sparkling water

(a) Write the ingredients, in litres and millilitres.

(b) If they pour the punch into glasses holding 200 ml each, how many glasses will they fill?

10 To make cement mortar you mix $\frac{1}{4}$ gallon of water, 1 gallon of dry cement powder and 3 gallons of sand.

Rewrite these quantities in litres.

Activity – Using money

Ask your teacher for some imitation money to help you answer these questions.

1 Write down how to make up each amount, using as few coins as possible.

(a) 13p   (c) 36p   (e) £1.60   (g) £6.23

(b) 25p   (d) 78p   (f) £2.85   (h) £9.99

2 How many different ways can you make 20p?

3 In your purse you have five 1p coins, four 2p coins, six 5p coins, seven 10p coins, five 20p coins, three 50p coins, three £1 coins and one £2 coin. You are going to buy:

- one dozen eggs costing £2.35 from the grocer
- cough medicine costing £2.55 from the chemist
- a card costing £1.99 from the stationers'
- a box of chocolates costing £1.74 from the sweet shop.

How can you divide up your coins so that you have the exact money for each shopkeeper?

18 Fractions of quantities

You know that a **fraction** means part of a **whole**. The bottom number tells you how many parts the whole has been divided into. For example, $\frac{1}{2}$ is one part of a whole that has been divided into two equal parts.

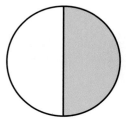

In this chapter you will look at how you can use fractions to talk about parts of a **quantity**.

⇨ Finding a fraction of a quantity

One part of a whole

Suppose you have six apples in a basket and you want to work out how many you would have each, if you shared them equally with a friend. You want to find half of the number of apples.

You can write this as: 'Find $\frac{1}{2}$ of 6.'

To answer this, you need to divide the whole quantity (six apples) into two parts.

You can write this as a division calculation:

$6 \div 2 = 3$

So $\frac{1}{2}$ of 6 apples is 3 apples.

> ✳ You always divide by the number on the bottom of the fraction. You can use a frame to do the division if you need to.

Examples:

(i) Calculate $\frac{1}{2}$ of 20

You need to divide 20 by 2

$\frac{1}{2}$ of 20 = 20 ÷ 2

$\phantom{\frac{1}{2} \text{ of } 20} = 10$

$\frac{1}{2}$ of 20 is 10

(ii) Calculate $\frac{1}{4}$ of 68

You need to divide 68 by 4

Use a division frame if you need to.

		1	7
4	6	8	

$\frac{1}{4}$ of 68 = 68 ÷ 4

$\phantom{\frac{1}{4} \text{ of } 68} = 17$

$\frac{1}{4}$ of 68 is 17

(iii) Archie has 12 bars of chocolate to give away. He wants to divide them equally among his four friends.

How may bars of chocolate will each friend get?

In this sort of word problem you need to think carefully about the numbers involved.

There are 12 bars of chocolate that need to be divided among four people.

You can write this as a division calculation.

12 ÷ 4 = 3

Each friend gets 3 bars of chocolate.

Exercise 18.1

For questions 1–10, find the amounts.

1 $\frac{1}{2}$ of 24

2 $\frac{1}{3}$ of 42

3 $\frac{1}{4}$ of 36

4 $\frac{1}{5}$ of 75

5 $\frac{1}{6}$ of 90

6 $\frac{1}{7}$ of 91

7 $\frac{1}{8}$ of 104

8 $\frac{1}{9}$ of 108

9 $\frac{1}{5}$ of 270

10 $\frac{1}{6}$ of 420

11 Abigail gets half marks on a maths exercise that is marked out of 36. How many marks does she get?

12 There are 18 plums in a bowl. Mark eats $\frac{1}{3}$ of the plums. How many plums does he eat?

13 Balloons are sold in packets of 72

   A quarter of the balloons are red. How many red balloons are there in a packet?

14 'My Plaice' serves 85 people at lunchtime. One fifth of the customers order scampi and chips. How many people is this?

15 A sixth of the packets of crisps in a box of 96 are smokey bacon flavour. How many packets of this flavour are there?

16 A seventh of the 140 yachts in harbour are French. How many is this?

17 Bessie bakes 120 small cakes. She ices one-eighth of them. How many of them are iced?

18 Zac has 144 marbles, of which one-ninth are white. How many white marbles does Zac have?

19 A group of children sit a total of 600 different exams. A quarter of the exams are awarded an A grade. How many exams resulted in an A grade?

20 A cross-channel ferry has 927 passengers on board. One-third of them are children. How many is this?

Remainders

In the last exercise, all of the quantities could be divided exactly by the denominator. In real life, this does not always happen.

Example:

I want to share this chocolate bar between three people.
How many pieces of chocolate will they each get?

There are 28 pieces.

Each person will get one third of the bar.

$\frac{1}{3}$ of $28 = 9$ r1   or $9\frac{1}{3}$

They will each receive 9 whole pieces of chocolate and then $\frac{1}{3}$ of a piece.

Exercise 18.2

Calculate each of these quantities. If the answer is not exact, write the remainder as a fraction in its lowest terms.

1   $\frac{1}{3}$ of 28   6 $\frac{1}{3}$ of 100

2   $\frac{1}{5}$ of 32   7 $\frac{1}{6}$ of 93

3   $\frac{1}{6}$ of 28   8 $\frac{1}{8}$ of 100

4   $\frac{1}{4}$ of 25   9 $\frac{1}{9}$ of 210

5   $\frac{1}{10}$ of 1205   10 $\frac{1}{4}$ of 2014

11   A chocolate bar is divided into 20 pieces. I get one-third of the bar. How many pieces do I get?

12 A pizza is divided into eight slices. We each have one-fifth of the pizza. How many slices is that?

13 A 10-metre length of string is divided into eighths.

What is the length of each piece, in metres?

14 We started out on a journey of 215 km but the car broke down halfway. How many kilometres had we travelled before we broke down?

15 I have to swim 800 m. Each length of the pool is one-sixth of the total. How long is one length of the pool?

16 Mary divided 500 g of sugar equally into six bowls.

How many grams of sugar were there in each bowl?

17 We have 18 bananas to share equally among five of us.

How many whole bananas and what fraction of a banana do we each get?

18 A piece of music normally lasts 25 minutes but it was stopped a quarter of the way through.

How many minutes had the music played for?

19 I draw a line 18 cm long in my exercise book and then divide it into 10 equal parts. How long is each part?

20 A nursery school day of 6 hours is divided into 9 equal periods. How long is each period, in **(a)** hours **(b)** minutes?

More than one part of a whole

You have been looking at simple fractions where you considered just one part of a whole. For example:

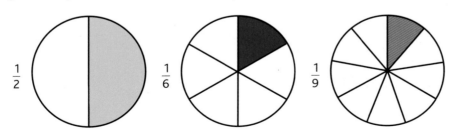

$\frac{1}{2}$ $\frac{1}{6}$ $\frac{1}{9}$

and so on.

Now think about fractions that are made up of more than one part. For example:

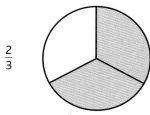

$\frac{2}{3}$ This means 2 parts, each $\frac{1}{3}$ of the whole.

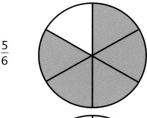

$\frac{5}{6}$ This means 5 parts, each $\frac{1}{6}$ of the whole.

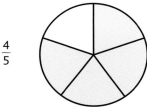

$\frac{4}{5}$ This means 4 parts, each $\frac{1}{5}$ of the whole.

Suppose you need to work out $\frac{4}{5}$ of a quantity.

First you work out what 1 part ($\frac{1}{5}$) is by dividing by 5 (the number on the bottom of the fraction).

Then you work out what 4 parts are by multiplying 1 part by 4 (the number on the top of the fraction).

Examples:

(i)   Calculate $\frac{4}{5}$ of 40

Step 1: Work out what 1 part ($\frac{1}{5}$) is of 40

$\frac{1}{5}$ of 40 = 40 ÷ 5
$\qquad\qquad$ = 8

		8
5	4	0

You now know that $\frac{1}{5}$ of 40 is 8

Step 2: Work out what 4 lots are of $\frac{1}{5}$

$\frac{4}{5}$ of 40 = 4 × 8
$\qquad\qquad$ = 32

$\frac{4}{5}$ of 40 is 32

(ii) Calculate $\frac{5}{6}$ of 60

Step 1: Work out what 1 part $\left(\frac{1}{6}\right)$ is of 60

$$\frac{1}{6} \text{ of } 60 = 60 \div 6$$
$$= 10$$

You now know that $\frac{1}{6}$ of 60 is 10

Step 2: Work out what 5 lots are of $\frac{1}{6}$

$$\frac{5}{6} \text{ of } 60 = 5 \times 10$$
$$= 50$$

$\frac{5}{6}$ of 60 is 50

When you have to solve a word problem involving fractions, take care when identifying the numbers you need to use in your calculation.

Example:

$\frac{2}{3}$ of a class of 15 are going to the cinema today.

How many cinema tickets does the teacher need to buy?

(There is a special offer on so the teacher goes free.)

		5
3	1	5

You need to find $\frac{2}{3}$ of 15

Step 1: $\frac{1}{3}$ of 15 $= 15 \div 3$
$$= 5$$

Step 2: $\frac{2}{3}$ of 15 $= 2 \times 5$
$$= 10$$

The teacher needs to buy 10 tickets.

Exercise 18.3

For questions 1–20, calculate each amount.

1   $\frac{2}{3}$ of 18

2   $\frac{3}{4}$ of 20

3   $\frac{4}{5}$ of 15

4   $\frac{5}{6}$ of 42

5   $\frac{5}{6}$ of 84

6   $\frac{3}{8}$ of 72

7   $\frac{5}{9}$ of 81

8   $\frac{2}{5}$ of 70

9   $\frac{3}{4}$ of 92

10   $\frac{2}{3}$ of 111

11   $\frac{3}{5}$ of 145

12   $\frac{5}{6}$ of 192

13   $\frac{3}{8}$ of 144

14   $\frac{2}{7}$ of 238

15   $\frac{7}{9}$ of 126

16   $\frac{5}{6}$ of 300

17   $\frac{4}{5}$ of 360

18   $\frac{3}{7}$ of 294

19   $\frac{2}{5}$ of 195

20   $\frac{3}{8}$ of 400

21   A gym club has 80 members, of whom $\frac{3}{5}$ are girls.
    How many girls are there?

22   Sixty children have a choice of ice cream. $\frac{3}{4}$ of them choose a
    choc ice. How many is this?

23   130 trains stop at Bunton. $\frac{9}{10}$ of them are on time.
    How many is this?

24   The rounders team won $\frac{5}{8}$ of its 16 matches.
    How many matches did it win?

25   $\frac{2}{5}$ of a packet of mixed nuts are cashews.
    How many cashews are there in a packet of 60 nuts?

26   $\frac{7}{8}$ of the staff at Bargains 4U are aged under 30
    If there are 112 staff, how many are aged under 30?

27   $\frac{5}{6}$ of the 210 children at Grange School have a pet.
    How many is this?

28 A sponsored swim raises £235

How much does the local children's home receive if it is given $\frac{3}{5}$ of the total?

29 Mr Pranav buys 144 tins of Fizzy. Two-thirds of the tins are lemon flavoured and the rest are orange flavoured.
How many of the tins are orange-flavoured Fizzy?

30 There are 40 girls in the Junior School. $\frac{3}{8}$ of them have brothers. How many girls do not have brothers?

⇨ Writing one quantity as a fraction of another quantity

Sometimes you want to write one quantity as a fraction of another. For example, you might want to know what 20p is as a fraction of 60p. In order to work this out there are two simple steps.

Step 1: Make sure the two numbers are in the same units (for example, if you are dealing with money, make sure they are both in pence) and write them as a fraction. The answer will give you the top number as a fraction of the bottom number.

Step 2: Cancel the fraction to its lowest terms.

Examples:

In these examples, the numbers are already in the same units.

(i) Write 9 as a fraction of 30

Step 1: There are no units because 9 and 30 are just numbers so you can just write the fraction.

$$\frac{9}{30}$$

Step 2: Write $\frac{9}{30}$ in its lowest terms.

Look for a factor that is common to 9 and 30

In this case you can divide both top and bottom by 3

$$\frac{9}{30} = \frac{3}{10} \qquad \begin{array}{l} \text{Top: } 9 \div 3 = 3 \\ \text{Bottom: } 30 \div 3 = 10 \end{array}$$

9 as a fraction of 30 is $\frac{3}{10}$

(ii) Write 15 pence as a fraction of 25 pence.

Step 1: Both numbers are in the same units, pence, so you can write the fraction.

$$\frac{15}{25}$$

Step 2: Divide top and bottom by 5 to give the lowest terms.

$$\frac{15}{25} = \frac{3}{5} \qquad \text{Top: } 15 \div 5 = 3$$
$$\text{Bottom: } 25 \div 5 = 5$$

15 pence as a fraction of 25 pence is $\frac{3}{5}$

Exercise 18.4

Write the first quantity as a fraction of the second. Give your answer in its lowest terms.

	First quantity	Second quantity
1	12	18
2	28	40
3	15 pence	30 pence
4	25 pence	60 pence
5	£4	£20
6	£12	£30
7	10 centimetres	35 centimetres
8	48 centimetres	80 centimetres
9	20 metres	30 metres
10	25 metres	100 metres
11	7 kilometres	21 kilometres
12	24 kilometres	50 kilometres
13	35 grams	50 grams

14	130 grams	200 grams
15	4 kilograms	28 kilograms
16	30 kilograms	120 kilograms
17	10 millilitres	17 millilitres
18	400 millilitres	1000 millilitres
19	15 minutes	40 minutes
20	12 minutes	60 minutes

Now look at some examples where the numbers are not always in the same units. For example, you may have amounts in pence and pounds.

If you want to write one quantity as a fraction of another quantity, the units for both quantities must be the same.

Examples:

(i) Write 15 pence as a fraction of £1

Step 1: The units are different. Change £1 to 100 pence (100p = £1).

Then write 15 pence as a fraction of 100 pence.

$$\frac{15}{100}$$

Step 2: Divide top (15) and bottom (100) by 5 to give the lowest terms.

$$\frac{15}{100} = \frac{3}{20} \qquad \text{Top: } 15 \div 5 = 3 \\ \text{Bottom: } 100 \div 5 = 20$$

15 pence as a fraction of £1 is $\frac{3}{20}$

(ii) Write 24 centimetres as a fraction of 1 metre.

Step 1: The units are different. Change 1 metre to 100 centimetres (100 cm = 1 metre). Then write 24 cm as a fraction of 100 cm.

$$\frac{24}{100}$$

Step 2: Divide top (24) and bottom (100) by 4 to give the lowest terms.

$$\frac{24}{100} = \frac{6}{25} \qquad \text{Top: } 24 \div 4 = 6$$
$$\text{Bottom: } 100 \div 4 = 25$$

24 cm as a fraction of 1 m is $\frac{6}{25}$

(iii) Write 400 grams as a fraction of 2 kilograms.

Step 1: The units are different. Change 2 kilograms to 2000 grams (1000 grams = 1 kilogram). Then write 400 g as a fraction of 2000 kg.

$$\frac{400}{2000}$$

Step 2: In this example, the cancelling is done in two stages.

$$\frac{400}{2000} = \frac{4}{20} \qquad \text{First divide 400 and 2000 by 100}$$
$$= \frac{1}{5} \qquad \text{Then divide 4 and 20 by 4}$$

400 g as a fraction of 2 kg is $\frac{1}{5}$

1000 millilitres = 1 litre

100 centimetres = 1 metre

1000 grams = 1 kilogram

90° = 1 right angle

100 cents = $1

Exercise 18.5

Write the first quantity as a fraction of the second. Give your answer in its lowest terms.

	First quantity	Second quantity
1	30 pence	£1
2	5 pence	£1
3	24 pence	£1

4	6 millimetres	1 centimetre
5	50 centimetres	1 metre
6	200 metres	1 kilometre
7	600 grams	1 kilogram
8	400 millilitres	1 litre
9	50 millilitres	1 litre
10	40 minutes	1 hour
11	25 minutes	1 hour
12	45 seconds	1 minute
13	12 seconds	1 minute
14	45°	1 right angle
15	60°	1 right angle
16	40 pence	£2
17	75 cents	$3
18	30 pence	£1.50
19	5 millimetres	5 centimetres
20	50 centimetres	2 metres
21	400 metres	5 kilometres
22	600 grams	3 kilograms
23	120 millilitres	2 litres
24	30 minutes	4 hours
25	20 seconds	10 minutes

 **Percentages**

You learned in Chapter 16 that **percentage (%)** means '**out of 100**'. A percentage is a part of the whole, where 100% represents the whole.

Examples:

(i) If 60% of a class are boys then 40% are girls.
(60 + 40 = 100)

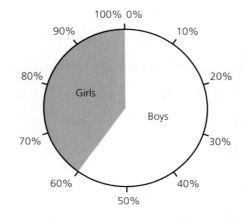

(ii) Edward achieved 80% as his maths exam result. (80 marks out of a possible 100 marks)

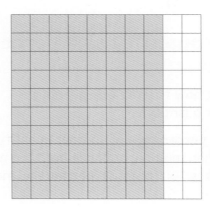

(iii) If 85% of the children have a pencil then 15% do not have a pencil. (100 − 85 = 15)

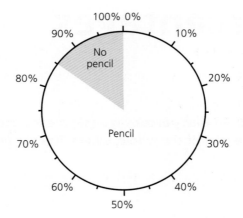

Percentages can be thought of, very simply, as fractions.

$$1\% = \frac{1}{100} \quad \text{1 out of 100}$$

From the examples above:

(i) $60\% = \frac{60}{100}$ and $40\% = \frac{40}{100}$

(ii) $80\% = \frac{80}{100}$

(iii) $85\% = \frac{85}{100}$ and $15\% = \frac{15}{100}$

⇨ Finding one quantity as a percentage of another

In Chapter 18 you learnt how to write one quantity as a **fraction** of another quantity.

To write a quantity as a **percentage** of another quantity, you first write the fraction and then multiply or divide both the numbers so that the bottom number is 100 (because 'percentage' means 'out of 100').

Then you can write the top number as a percentage.

To keep the fraction equivalent (the same), whatever you do to the bottom number you must also do to the top.

Examples:

(i) Write 3 as a percentage of 10

First write 3 as a fraction of 10: $\frac{3}{10}$

Then multiply top and bottom by 10 so that the bottom number is 100

$$\frac{3}{10} = \frac{30}{100}$$

Now you can write the top number as a percentage.

$$\frac{30}{100} = 30\%$$

So 3 as a percentage of 10 is 30%

(ii) Write 11 as a percentage of 20

$$\frac{11}{20} = \frac{55}{100} \qquad \text{Multiply top and bottom by 5}$$

$$= 55\%$$

(iii) Write 6 as a percentage of 25

$$\frac{6}{25} = \frac{24}{100} \qquad \text{Multiply top and bottom by 4}$$

$$= 24\%$$

(iv) What is 30p as a percentage of £2?

$$\frac{30p}{£2} = \frac{30}{200} \qquad \text{Write both numbers in pence.}$$

$$\frac{30}{200} = \frac{15}{100} \qquad \text{Divide top and bottom by 2}$$

$$= 15\%$$

(v) What is 1.5 m as a percentage of 5 m?

$$\frac{1.5m}{5m} = \frac{150}{500} \qquad \text{Write both numbers in centimetres to get rid of the decimals.}$$

$$\frac{150}{500} = \frac{30}{100} \qquad \text{Divide top and bottom by 5}$$

$$= 30\%$$

1 Write the first quantity as a percentage of the second.

	First quantity	Second quantity
(a)	7	10
(b)	17	50
(c)	23	25
(d)	4	5
(e)	12	20
(f)	40p	£8
(g)	£1.80	£3
(h)	27 mm	5 cm
(i)	80 cm	2 m
(j)	480 g	2 kg

2 Four pencils in a box of 10 are red.
What percentage of the pencils are red?

3 Nine children in a class of 20 are girls.
What percentage of the class is girls?

4 Five out of a group of 25 monkeys are chimpanzees.
What percentage of the monkeys are chimpanzees?

5 One in every four cars has satellite navigation.
What percentage of cars is this?

6 Which is the higher mark, 39 out of 50 or 76%?

7 Charlie spends £600 on a holiday. His accommodation costs
£270. What percentage of the total cost does this represent?

8 Gussie buys a hair band for 80 pence. She pays with a £2 coin.
What percentage of the money does she spend?

9 Tom earns £25 a week as a paperboy. In January he was given an increase of £2.50

What was his percentage increase?

10 There are 200 children at Uptown Lower School. 164 of them live within 5 km of the school. What percentage is this?

11 The tape on a roll is 5 m long.

   (a) George uses 50 cm to wrap a packet. What percentage of the roll is this?

   (b) Simone needs 150 cm to wrap her parcel. What percentage of a roll is this?

   (c) Terry needs 3.8 m to wrap her box. What percentage of the roll is this?

12 A can of Fizzy contains 330 millilitres.

What percentage of a litre (1000 ml) is this?

13 Jenny's £3 train fare is increased by 45 pence.

What is the percentage increase?

14 A suit is originally priced at £500

In a sale the price is reduced by £175

What was the percentage decrease?

15 Mr Checker pays £1200 tax when he earns £6000

What is the percentage rate at which tax is paid?

50%, 25% and 75%

You will come across some percentages quite frequently so you should make sure you understand exactly what they mean.

Start by looking more closely at 50%.

$50\% = \dfrac{50}{100}$ You can write this in its lowest terms by dividing the top and bottom numbers by 50

$\qquad = \dfrac{1}{2}$ This is a very familiar fraction!

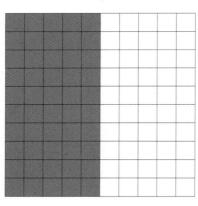

Now look at 25% and 75%.

$25\% = \dfrac{25}{100}$ Write in its lowest terms by dividing the top and bottom numbers by 25

$\qquad = \dfrac{1}{4}$

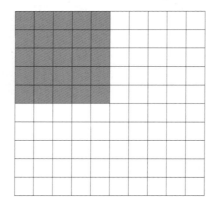

$$75\% = \frac{75}{100}$$
$$= \frac{3}{4}$$

Divide top and bottom by 25

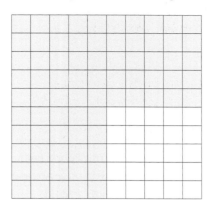

Now you can use what you have learned about these percentages to find 50%, 25% and 75% of a quantity.

Examples:

(i) What is 50% of 28?

50% is the same as a half. To find one half of a quantity you divide by 2

$$50\% \text{ of } 28 = \frac{1}{2} \times 28$$
$$= 28 \div 2$$
$$= 14$$

So 50% of 28 is 14

You should be able to do this in your head. If not, write it out like this.

		1	4
2	2	8	

(ii) What is 25% of £32?

25% is the same as one quarter.

To find one quarter of a quantity you divide by 4, or by 2 and then by 2 again.

$$25\% \text{ of } 32 = \frac{1}{4} \text{ of } 32$$
$$= 32 \div 4 \qquad 32 \div 2 = 16 \text{ then } 16 \div 2 = 8$$
$$= 8$$

So 25% of £32 is £8

(iii) What is 75% of 160 kg?

75% is the same as three quarters. To find three quarters of a quantity, you first find one quarter, and then multiply that by three.

Step 1: $\frac{1}{4}$ of $160 = 160 \div 4$

$= 40$

Step 2: 3 lots of $\frac{1}{4} = 3 \times 40$

$= 120$

So 75% of 160 kg is 120 kg.

Put the correct units in your answer, in this case kg.

Exercise 19.2

1 Calculate 50% of each amount.

(a) 30   (d) $250   (g) £1.36

(b) 124   (e) 850 ml   (h) £5.00

(c) £60   (f) £8.40   (i) $7.50

2 Calculate 25% of each amount.

(a) 120   (d) £36   (g) £16.40

(b) 48   (e) 140 m   (h) £6.00

(c) £80   (f) £4.60   (i) £2.00

3 Calculate 75% of each amount.

(a) 24   (d) £40   (g) £4.60

(b) 60   (e) £600   (h) £9.00

(c) 200   (f) £2.40   (i) 8 m

10%

$$10\% = \frac{10}{100} = \frac{1}{10}$$

The easiest way to find 10% of a quantity is to divide by 10.

Think carefully about **place value** (See Chapter 5).

When you divide by 10 the digits move 1 place to the right.

Examples:

(i) 10% of 70 $= 70 \div 10$

$= 7$

(ii) 10% of £90 $= 90 \div 10$

$= £9$

(iii) 10% of 120 $= 120 \div 10$

$= 12$

(iv) 10% of £360 $= £360 \div 10$

$= £36$

(v) 10% of 400 $= 400 \div 10$

$= 40$

(vi) 10% of £700 $= £700 \div 10$

$= £70$

(vii) 10% of 27 $= 27 \div 10$

$= 2.7$

(viii) 10% of £35 $= £35 \div 10$

$= £3.50$

(ix) 10% of 8 $= 8 \div 10$

$= 0.8$

(x) 10% of £4 $= £4 \div 10$

$= £0.40$ or 40p

(xi) 10% of £2.50 $= 2.50 \div 10$

$= £0.25$ or 25p

Finding one quantity as a percentage of another

Calculate 10% of each amount.

1	60	**6**	200 m
2	250	**7**	900 g
3	46	**8**	£70
4	5	**9**	40 kg
5	£600	**10**	80 l
11	£75	**16**	45 kg
12	£2.80	**17**	15 cm
13	£6.30	**18**	90p
14	£12.50	**19**	50p
15	$27.50	**20**	£3.50

Multiples of 10%

To find multiples of 10% such as 20%, 30%, 40%, and so on, **find 10%** and **multiply**.

Examples:

(i) Calculate 60% of 80

10% of 80 = 8

60% of 80 = 8 × 6   Multiply by 6 because 10 × 6 = 60

= 48

(ii) Calculate 30% of £45

10% of £45 = £4.50

30% of £45 = £4.50 × 3   Multiply by 3 because 10 × 3 = 30

= £13.50

(iii) Calculate 70% of £2.50

10% of £2.50 = 25p

70% of £2.50 = 25p × 7

= £1.75

Exercise 19.4

Calculate each amount.

1 20% of:	(a) 60	(b) £90	(c) £3.50	(d) £4
2 30% of:	(a) 30	(b) £40	(c) £4.50	(d) £6
3 40% of:	(a) 40	(b) £200	(c) £1.20	(d) £8
4 60% of:	(a) 80	(b) £150	(c) £8.50	(d) £9
5 70% of:	(a) 50	(b) £80	(c) £2.40	(d) £10
6 80% of:	(a) 70	(b) £120	(c) £1.80	(d) £3
7 90% of:	(a) 150	(b) £300	(c) £1.20	(d) £5

Fractions of 10%

To find 5%, **find 10%** and **divide by 2**

$10 \div 2 = 5$ so $5\% = \frac{1}{2}$ of 10%

To find $2\frac{1}{2}$% **find 10%, divide by 2 and then by 2 again.**

$5 \div 2 = 2\frac{1}{2}$ so $2\frac{1}{2}\% = \frac{1}{2}$ of 5%

Examples:

(i) What is 5% of £80?

10% of £80 = £8

5% of $80\% = \frac{1}{2}$ of £8

= £4

Finding one quantity as a percentage of another

(ii) What is $2\frac{1}{2}$ % of £120?

      10% of £120   = £12

      5% of £120   = $\frac{1}{2}$ of £12   Halve 10% to give 5%.

                       = £6

      $2\frac{1}{2}$ % of £120   = $\frac{1}{2}$ of £6   Halve 5% to give $2\frac{1}{2}$%.

                       = £3

      $2\frac{1}{2}$ % of £120   = £3

Exercise 19.5

1 Calculate 5% of each amount.

  (a) 40   **(e)** £30   **(i)** £5.00   **(m)** 400 kg

  (b) 180   **(f)** £42   **(j)** £2.40   **(n)** 920 m

  (c) 260   **(g)** £128   **(k)** £3.80   **(o)** 1200 l

  (d) £60   **(h)** £8.00   **(l)** £21.60

2 Calculate $2\frac{1}{2}$% of each amount.

  (a) 80   **(d)** £120   **(g)** £1.60   **(j)** £20

  (b) 320   **(e)** £50   **(h)** £4.80

  (c) 280   **(f)** £30   **(i)** £12.40

⇨ Problem solving

Exercise 19.6

1 40% of a class are girls. What percentage of the class are boys?

2 82% of children eat fresh vegetables for lunch. What percentage of children do not eat fresh vegetables for lunch?

3 Richard achieves 50% on a test marked out of 40.
How many marks does he score?

4 Jane eats 25% of a 200-gram bar of chocolate.
How many grams of chocolate are left?

5 75% of the 160 boys at school have a sister. How many boys is this?

6 There are 60 apples in a box. 10% cannot be eaten because they
are too bruised. How many of the apples can be eaten?

7 Carlo's bill at the Pizza Parlour is £27.50

He leaves a tip of 10% of the bill. How much tip does he leave?

8 There are 60 chocolates in a box. 45% have toffee centres.
How many is this?

9 25% of a packet of balloons are coloured red. If there are 50 red
balloons, how many balloons are there altogether in the packet?

10 A group of 120 visits the Tower of London. 10% are adults
and 65% are boys. How many of the party are girls?

11 Train fares increase by $2\frac{1}{2}$%. What is the new price of a
ticket that cost £18 before the increase?

12 There are 80 tins of soup on the shop shelf. $12\frac{1}{2}$% of them
contain tomato soup. How many tins of tomato soup are there?

In the next exercise you will need to understand some important
words associated with percentages.

● **Profit:** This is the money you gain when you sell something for
more than it costs you to make or buy.

● **Loss:** This is the money you lose when you sell something for less
than it costs to make or buy.

● **Discount:** This is an amount by which the price of something is
reduced, so the customer pays less.

Exercise 19.7

1 Ian makes a table for £80

He sells it, making a profit of 60%. How much is his profit?

2 Disco Dave buys a DVD player for £180

Since he pays with cash he is given a 5% discount. How much does he save?

3 A bicycle is priced at £320

Victoria is given 15% off the price (discount) of the bicycle as a prize for winning a cycle safety competition.
How much does Victoria have to pay for the bicycle?

4 In a sale, the price of everything is reduced (discounted) by 20%.
By how much are these items reduced?

(a) Jacket priced at £200   (c) Shirt priced at £35

(b) Trousers priced at £110   (d) Belt priced at £4

5 Aston pays £7.50 for a model car and sells it to Martin, making a profit of 40%. How much does Martin pay for the car?

6 It costs a farmer £300 to produce a tonne of apples. Unfortunately, he has to sell at a loss of 5%. How much does he sell a tonne of apples for?

Exercise 19.8: Summary exercise

For questions 1–5, write the first quantity as a percentage of the second.

	First quantity	Second quantity
1	7	20
2	11p	25p
3	30p	£5
4	700 g	2 kg
5	75 cm	2.5 m

For questions 6–17, calculate each quantity.

6 50% of 36   12 10% of 250

7 50% of £5   13 10% of £6

8 25% of 68   14 10% of £0.70

9 25% of £12   15 5% of 60

10 75% of 40   16 5% of £40

11 75% of 92   17 $2\frac{1}{2}$% of 120

18 Christine scores 50% in her maths test, which is marked out of 64
How many marks does she get?

19 25% of the 112 patients in hospital arrived by ambulance.
How many patients arrived by ambulance?

20 75% of the loaves in a baker's van are white. If there are 96 loaves altogether, how many white loaves are there?

21 For one day, a clothes shop reduces all prices by 10%. How much does Marcus save, buying a jacket originally priced at £160?

22 A charge of 10% is added to the bill if a Chinese meal is delivered. How much is added, if the meal costs £32.80?

23 40% of the 65 biscuits in a tin are chocolate-covered.
How many chocolate-covered biscuits are there?

24 15% of the mass of a cherry cake is made up of cherries. What is the mass of cherries in a cake that has a total mass of 500 grams?

25 A bowls club has 260 members of whom only 45% are aged under 60

How many members are aged 60 or over?

26 There are 1600 books in the school library, of which $2\frac{1}{2}$% are books of poetry. How many books of poetry are there in the library?

20 Long multiplication

When you multiply a number by another number with more than one digit the multiplication calculation is called **long multiplication**. There are two informal ways of doing long multiplication.

⇨ Informal method using factors

Sometimes it is easier to break a multiplication down into steps, using factors. You did this mentally in Chapter 5

When the numbers are too big for you to calculate mentally, you can write them down in a frame and calculate formally.

Multiplying by 35, for example, is the same as multiplying by 5 and then by 7

This is because 5 and 7 are the factors of 35

$$8 \times 35 = 8 \times 5 \times 7$$

You can do the calculation in two steps.

Step 1: $8 \times 5 = 40$

Step 2: $40 \times 7 = 280$

This method can be very helpful when you are multiplying by numbers larger than 12, as long as these numbers have factors.

Examples:

(i) Multiply 57 by 15
You know that $15 = 5 \times 3$

Step 1: Multiply by 5

	H	T	U
		5	7
×			5
	2	8	5
		3	

$7 \times 5 = 35$

$5 \times 5 = 25$ and add the carried 3

Step 2: Multiply by 3

	H	T	U
	2	8	5
×			3
	8	5	5
	2	1	

$5 \times 3 = 15$

$8 \times 3 = 24$ plus the carried 1

$2 \times 3 = 6$ and add the carried 2

$57 \times 15 = 855$

(ii) Multiply 476 by 28

You know that 28 = 7 × 4

Step 1: Multiply by 7

	Th	H	T	U
		4	7	6
×				7
	3	3	3	2
		5	4	

$6 \times 7 = 42$

$7 \times 7 = 49$ and add the carried 4

$4 \times 7 = 28$ and add the carried 5

Step 2: Multiply by 4

	TTh	Th		H	T	U
		3		3	3	2
×						4
	1	3		3	2	8
		1		1		

$2 \times 4 = 8$

$3 \times 4 = 12$

$3 \times 4 = 12$ and add the carried 1

$3 \times 4 = 12$ and add the carried 1

476 × 28 = 13 328

Exercise 20.1

Use factors to multiply these numbers.

1 31 × 15

2 57 × 28

3 93 × 12

4 47 × 24

5 71 × 18

6 67 × 32

7 29 × 25

8 83 × 14

9 25 × 35

10 51 × 16

11 63 × 48	**16** 46 × 56
12 73 × 54	**17** 28 × 42
13 23 × 72	**18** 53 × 36
14 85 × 63	**19** 17 × 64
15 19 × 49	**20** 37 × 45
21 417 × 12	**26** 231 × 56
22 539 × 35	**27** 782 × 32
23 346 × 42	**28** 853 × 63
24 189 × 27	**29** 604 × 24
25 817 × 18	**30** 138 × 72

⇨ Informal method using partitioning

Examples:

(i)   Multiply 64 by 37

Method 1: Partitioning one of the numbers

64 × 37 = 64 × (30 + 7)

Partition (split) 37 into tens and units.

Step 1: Calculate 64 × 30

64 × 30 = 64 × 10 × 3

$\qquad\quad$ = 640 × 3   64 × 10 = 640

$\qquad\quad$ = 1920

Step 2: Calculate 64 × 7

	H	T	U
		6	4
×			7
	4	4	8
		2	

Step 3: Add the answers to Step 1 and Step 2 together.

	Th	H	T	U
	1	9	2	0
+		4	4	8
	2	3	6	8
	1			

64 × 37 = 2368

Method 2: Partitioning both numbers

Partition (split) both the numbers, using a grid like this.

×	60	4	
30	1800	120	= 1920
7	420	28	= 448
			= 2368

(ii)   Multiply 473 by 29

Method 1: Partitioning one of the numbers

$473 \times 29 = 473 \times (20 + 9)$

Step 1: Calculate 473×20

$$473 \times 20 = 473 \times 10 \times 2$$
$$= 4730 \times 2$$
$$= 9460$$

Step 2: Calculate 473×9

	Th	H	T	U
		4	7	3
×				9
	4	2	5	7
		6	2	

Step 3: Add the answers to Step 1 and Step 2

	TTh	Th		H	T	U
		9		4	6	0
+		4		2	5	7
	1	3		7	1	7
				1		

$473 \times 29 = 13\,717$

Method 2: Partitioning both numbers

×	400	70	3		
20	8000	1400	60	=	9460
9	3600	630	27	=	4257
				=	13\,717

Use an informal method to multiply these numbers.

1	93 × 13	6	48 × 54
2	47 × 19	7	18 × 57
3	37 × 23	8	49 × 17
4	91 × 27	9	36 × 29
5	69 × 39	10	87 × 65
11	415 × 23	16	563 × 47
12	643 × 34	17	271 × 53
13	132 × 17	18	737 × 63
14	218 × 92	19	817 × 71
15	426 × 73	20	903 × 87
21	1319 × 56	26	3412 × 28
22	1472 × 45	27	4806 × 34
23	1035 × 27	28	3154 × 62
24	1050 × 49	29	4072 × 29
25	5006 × 37	30	3070 × 74

⇨ The formal method

These examples show the informal method above written in a formal way. Look carefully at how the frame is set up. This is done step by step in the first example and then all in one in the next two.

Examples:

(i) Multiply 64 by 37

Step 1: Estimate: $60 \times 40 = 2400$

You will need 4 columns and a space between the frame and your margin.

Step 2: Set up the frame.

	Th	H	T	U	
			6	4	
×			3	7	
					× 7
				0	× 30

Write down the number you are multiplying by, next to each answer row.

Write the 0 in place.

Step 3: Multiply by the units (7).

	Th	H	T	U	
			6	4	
×			3	7	
		4	4₂	8	× 7
				0	× 30

$7 \times 4 = 28$

Write 8 in the units column and carry the 2 tens.

$7 \times 6 = 42$ and add the carried 2 to make 44

Step 4: Multiply by the tens (30).

	Th	H	T	U	
			6	4	
×			3	7	
		4	4_2	8	× 7
	1	9_1	2	0	× 30

$3 \times 4 = 12$ Write 2 in the tens column and carry the hundred.

$3 \times 6 = 18$ and add the carried 1 to make 19

Step 5: Add the two results.

	Th	H	T	U	
			6	4	
×			3	7	
		4	4_2	8	× 7
	1	9_1	2	0	× 30
	2	3	6	8	
	1				

(ii) Multiply 473 by 29

Step 1: Estimate: $500 \times 30 = 15\,000$

Step 2: Set up the frame and complete the calculation.

	TTh	Th		H	T	U	
				4	7	3	
×					2	9	
		4		2_6	5_2	7	× 9
		9_1		4	6	0	× 20
	1	3		7	1	7	
				1			

Multiply 473 by 9

Multiply 473 by 20
This will end in 0

Add the two results.

(iii) Multiply 4764 by 68

Step 1: Estimate: $5000 \times 70 = 350\,000$

Step 2: Set up the frame and complete the calculation.

	HTh	TTh	Th		H	T	U	
			4		7	6	4	
×						6	8	
		3	8_6		1_5	1_3	2	× 8
	2	8_4	5_3		8_2	4	0	× 60
	3	2	3		9	5	2	
	1	1						

Multiply 4764 by 8

Multiply 4764 by 60. This will end in 0

Add the two results.

Exercise 20.3

Use the formal method to multiply these numbers.

1	47 × 23	**6**	39 × 75
2	72 × 51	**7**	52 × 92
3	67 × 83	**8**	82 × 63
4	95 × 34	**9**	59 × 37
5	26 × 47	**10**	17 × 89
11	253 × 17	**16**	519 × 84
12	729 × 41	**17**	183 × 97
13	347 × 78	**18**	485 × 57
14	806 × 23	**19**	650 × 63
15	632 × 37	**20**	701 × 29
21	1425 × 24	**26**	1517 × 32
22	2531 × 35	**27**	2045 × 46
23	1072 × 46	**28**	6352 × 78
24	4010 × 55	**29**	9157 × 84
25	3104 × 26	**30**	7597 × 79

⇨ Problem solving

Exercise 20.4

1 A bus can carry 86 passengers when full.
What is the maximum number of people that 15 buses can carry?

2 A carton contains 48 packets of butter.
How many packets are there in 36 cartons?

3 Fifty years ago grandfather's car travelled 37 miles on 1 gallon
of petrol. How many miles could he cover on 16 gallons?

4 February has 28 days. How many hours are there in February?

5 A sheet of sticky labels consists of 32 rows each containing 42 labels. How many labels are there in a sheet?

6 There are 26 rows of seats in the Grand Theatre. Each row has 38 seats in it. How many rows are in the theatre?

7 An ICT expert is paid £435 per day.
How much does she earn in 21 days?

8 Ozzie is paid to shear 260 sheep in a day.
How many sheep does he shear in 25 days?

9 A bicycle shop takes delivery of 18 bicycles that cost £329 each. How much does it cost the shop owner to buy these bicycles?

10 72 people each pay £963 for a cruise. How much do they pay altogether?

11 It costs £1375 to go on an adventure cruise in the Mediterranean. How much would it cost a party of 24 people?

12 Interactive whiteboards cost £2374
How much would it cost a school to buy 37?

13 25 children are going on a school trip. The cost is £34.75 each. How much is the total cost for all the children?

14 Theatre tickets cost £17.64 for children and £23.73 for adults. What is the total cost for a party of 28 children and 14 adults?

15 There are 1760 yards in a mile.
How many yards are there in 38 miles?

16 (a) There are 16 ounces in a pound and 14 pounds in a stone. How any ounces are in a stone?

   (b) There are 2240 pounds in a ton.
   How many ounces are there in a ton?

17 A computer costs £675 but there is 25% off the price in the sale. What is the sale price of the computer?

18 A washing machine costs £242 but there is a 15% delivery charge. What is the total price?

19 A restaurant bill came to £85.50 and a 12% service charge was added on. What was the total price, including service?

20 Five teachers are taking 37 children to a wild-life park. Entry costs £16 for a child and £18.50 for an adult, but they are getting a 24% discount as they are a school party. What is the total cost of the trip?

21 More division

⇨ Division using factors

In Chapter 5 you learned how to use factors to divide mentally. Now you are going to learn how to use the formal written method of division by factors.

Miss Plunkett wants to divide a box of 288 strawberries among the 16 children in her class.

She knows that the calculation 288 ÷ 16 will give the number of strawberries each child will receive. Unfortunately, Miss Plunkett does not know her 16 times table! What can she do? She does know her 2 to 10 times tables. Miss Plunkett decides to divide the children into two groups and give each group half the strawberries. Now there are two groups of 8 children and each group has 144 strawberries.

Each child will receive 144 ÷ 8 = 18 strawberries.

Miss Plunkett could write her calculations like this.

		1	4	4
2		2	8	8

		1	8
8		1	4	⁶4

Miss Plunkett has divided by 2 and by 8, the factors of 16 (2 × 8 = 16)

Example:

Divide 819 by 21

You know that $21 = 3 \times 7$

Step 1: Divide by 3

	2	7	3
3	8	²1	9

Step 2: Divide by 7

		3	9
7	2	7	⁶3

$819 \div 21 = 39$

It does not matter in which order you divide.

Example:

Divide 7904 by 32

You know that $32 = 4 \times 8$

Step 1: Divide by 4

	1	9	7	6
4	7	³9	³0	²4

Step 2: Divide by 8

		2	4	7
8	1	9	³7	⁵6

or:

Step 1: Divide by 8

		9	8	8
8	7	9	⁷0	⁶4

Step 2: Divide by 4

	2	4	7
4	9	¹8	²8

Use factors to divide these numbers. All the answers are exact – there are no remainders.

1	$270 \div 18$	**6**	$602 \div 14$
2	$864 \div 24$	**7**	$928 \div 32$
3	$780 \div 15$	**8**	$987 \div 21$
4	$532 \div 28$	**9**	$828 \div 36$
5	$912 \div 16$	**10**	$798 \div 42$
11	$1140 \div 15$	**16**	$2716 \div 28$
12	$1024 \div 16$	**17**	$1665 \div 45$
13	$1806 \div 21$	**18**	$2296 \div 56$
14	$1536 \div 24$	**19**	$2142 \div 63$
15	$1863 \div 27$	**20**	$4214 \div 49$
21	$7749 \div 63$	**26**	$10\,374 \div 21$
22	$4000 \div 32$	**27**	$25\,788 \div 42$
23	$4464 \div 24$	**28**	$15\,552 \div 48$
24	$7560 \div 35$	**29**	$31\,416 \div 56$
25	$9548 \div 28$	**30**	$39\,024 \div 72$

⇨ Problem solving

Exercise 21.2

1 35 children divide 280 apples equally among themselves. How many apples does each child receive?

2 In a car park there is room for 630 cars in 15 equal rows. How many parking spaces are there in a row?

3 414 chairs are laid out in the church hall in 18 equal rows. How many chairs are there in a row?

4 768 recruits are divided into 24 squads. How many recruits are there in a squad?

5 Geoff uses 48 litres of petrol to travel 1104 kilometres on his motorcycle. How far can he go on 1 litre of petrol?

6 Eggs are placed on trays that hold 64 eggs. How many trays are needed to hold 1088 eggs?

7 27 teachers share a Lotto win of £6966 equally. What is each teacher's share?

8 Harriet has 1728 box files, which are all the same size. She arranges them on 32 shelves, which are all the same length. How many box files does she put on one shelf?

9 Norman buys 16 packets of tulip bulbs. How many bulbs are there in a packet, if the total number of bulbs is 1200?

10 56 tubes of Witties contain 2128 chocolate drops altogether. How many drops are there in a tube?

 # Area and perimeter

When you study a shape, there are two dimensions you can measure:

- the distance round the outside, which is called the perimeter
- the amount of space inside the shape, which is called the area.

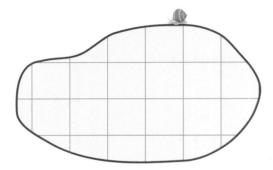

One way to think of the perimeter is to imagine a sea snail, or **peri**winkle, crawling along the outside of your shape. The snail trail it leaves behind goes right around the shape and marks out the perimeter. The **peri**meter is a length and is measured in millimetres, centimetres or metres (or feet and inches).

It is not easy to measure the curved line with a ruler so you can use string.

Lay a piece of string around the shape. Mark the string where it meets up, when you have laid it all the way round. Then pull it tight and measure it, from the end to the mark you made, against your ruler. You will see it measures 17 cm.

The **area** is the space inside the shape, measured in squares. If you draw your shape on centimetre-squared paper you can estimate the area in **square centimetres** (cm²).

		1	2	3	
4	5	6	7	8	9
10	11	12	13	14	15

		1	2	3	
4	5	6	7	8	9
10	11	12	13	14	15
	16	17	18	19	

Looking at the diagram, you can see that 15 whole or very nearly whole squares have been numbered, inside the shape, but there is still quite a lot of area that has not been counted yet. The method is to count all the squares that are more than half inside the shape.

The area of the shape is 19 square centimetres (cm²).

Exercise 22.1

For each shape, use string and tracing paper to estimate:

(a) the perimeter
(b) the area.

1

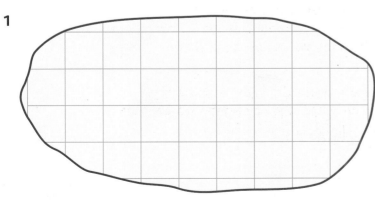

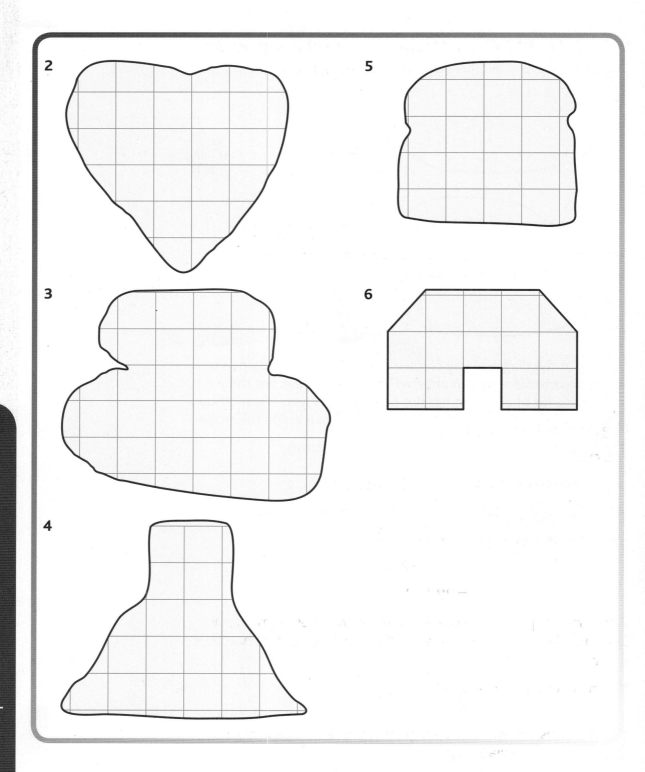

2

5

3

6

4

⇨ Perimeters of rectangles and squares

The perimeter of a shape is the distance around the outside.

Look at these four shapes.

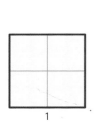 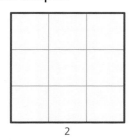 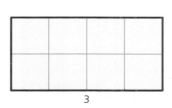 

As the sides are straight you can see the exact lengths of the height and width of the rectangle.

The perimeter of rectangle 1 is: 2 + 2 + 2 + 2 = 8 cm.

The perimeter of rectangle 2 is: 3 + 3 + 3 + 3 = 12 cm.

The perimeter of rectangle 3 is: 4 + 2 + 4 + 2 = 12 cm.

The perimeter of rectangle 4 is: 2 + 3 + 2 + 3 = 10 cm.

So to calculate the perimeters of the rectangles, you add the lengths of all the sides together.

The rule is:

perimeter = side 1 + side 2 + side 3 + side 4

If l stands for the length and w stands for the width, then:

Perimeter of a rectangle $= l + w + l + w$

$$= 2 \times l + 2 \times w$$

$$= 2(l + w)$$

A square is a special rectangle in which all the sides are the same length. If the length of one side is l, then the lengths of all the sides will be l.

Perimeter of a square $= 4 \times l$
$$= 4l$$

When you use letters to write a general rule, it is called a **formula**. The plural of formula is formulae.

You can use the formulae to calculate the perimeters of squares and rectangles.

Squares are also rectangles.

Examples:

(i) Calculate the perimeter of a rectangle of length 8 cm and width 5 cm.

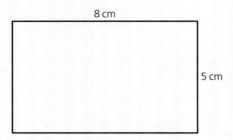

Perimeter $= 2l + 2w$

$\qquad = 2 \times 8 + 2 \times 5$

$\qquad = 16 + 10$

$\qquad = 26$ cm

(ii) Calculate the perimeter of a square of side 7 cm.

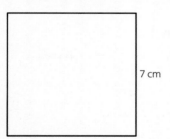

Perimeter $= 4l$

$\qquad = 4 \times 7$

$\qquad = 28$ cm

These are the stages in finding the perimeter.

1 Draw a quick sketch of the shape.

2 Write down the formula, using letters.

3 Write the correct numbers in the formula.

4 Calculate to find the answer.

5 Write down the correct units.

In the examples, you saw the words 'length' and 'width', but the sides of a rectangle can also be called **base** and **height**.

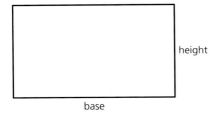

Exercise 22.2

1 Calculate the perimeter of each of these shapes.

(a)

5 cm

3 cm

(c)

20 m

15 m

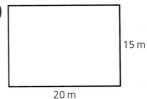

(b)

15 mm

4 mm

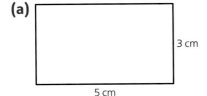

(d)

1.8 km

1.8 km

2 Calculate the perimeters of rectangles with these measurements.

    (a) length = 7 cm, width = 3 cm

    (b) base = 5.5 m, height = 4 m

3 A square has sides of length 25 m. What is its perimeter?

4 Calculate the perimeter of each of these shapes. Give your answer in the units of the longest side.

(a)

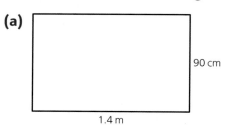

90 cm

1.4 m

(b)

400 m

2.1 km

(c)

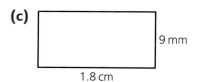

9 mm

1.8 cm

(d)

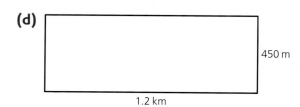

450 m

1.2 km

Finding missing lengths

You can also use the formula to find the missing lengths in a square or rectangle, if you know the perimeter.

Examples:

(i) A rectangle has a perimeter of 36 m and height 5 m.
What is the length, b, of the base of the rectangle?

$$\text{Perimeter} = 2b + 2h$$
$$36 = 2b + 10$$
$$2b = 26$$
$$b = 13\,\text{m}$$

(ii) A square has a perimeter of 144 mm. What is the length, a, of its sides?

$$\text{Perimeter} = 4 \times a$$
$$144 = 4 \times a$$
$$a = 144 \div 4$$
$$a = 36\,\text{mm}$$

Exercise 22.3

1 A rectangle has a perimeter of 30 cm.

What is its height, h, if its base is 10 cm long?

2 A square has a perimeter of 36 cm.

What is the length, s, of its sides?

3 A rectangle has a perimeter of 100 km.

What is its length, l, if it is 10 km wide?

4 A square has a perimeter of 200 mm.

What is the length, a, of its sides?

5 A rectangle has a perimeter of 55 m.

What is its width, w, if it is 13 m long?

6 A rectangle has a perimeter of 2 m.

What is its base, b, if it is 45 cm high?

7 A rectangle has a perimeter of 5 m.

What is its length, l, if it is 95 cm wide?

8 A square has a perimeter of 5 cm.

What is the length of its sides, x?

⇨ Perimeters of composite shapes

Sometimes you will see shapes that are not squares or rectangles but are combinations of these shapes. You can find their perimeter by following these steps.

1 Find the lengths of all the sides.

2 Add all the lengths together.

Example:

Find the perimeter of this shape.

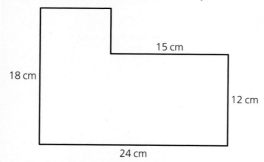

15 cm

18 cm

12 cm

24 cm

You can see that two lengths in this shape are not labelled. You can work them out by comparing the lengths of the parallel sides. Each unknown length is the difference between the given lengths on a pair of parallel sides.

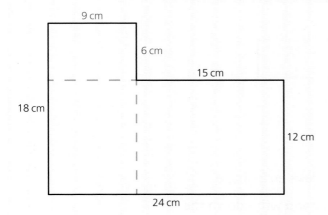

The missing length along the top is $24 - 15 = 9\,\text{cm}$.

The missing vertical length is $18 - 12 = 6\,\text{cm}$.

Check that you have counted all the sides of the shape.

Perimeter $= 24 + 18 + 9 + 6 + 15 + 12$

$\qquad = 84\,\text{cm}$

Exercise 22.4

1 Copy and cut out these rectangles.

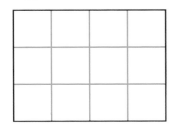 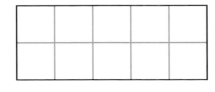

Stick them in your book so that they make an L-shape.

Count the squares round the perimeter and write down the perimeter of your composite shape.

2 Copy and cut out these rectangles.

Stick them in your book so that they make an L-shape.

Count the squares round the perimeter and write down the perimeter of your composite shape.

For questions 3–6, copy and cut out the composite shape and stick it in your exercise book. Write down the length of each side. Then add the lengths of the sides and write down the perimeter of the shape.

3

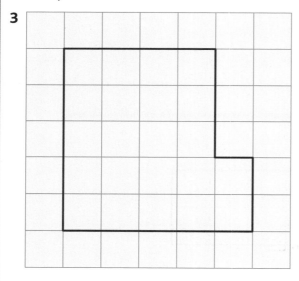

4

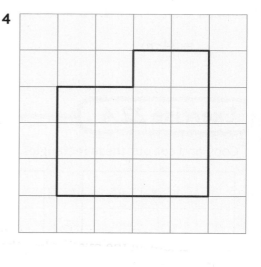

5

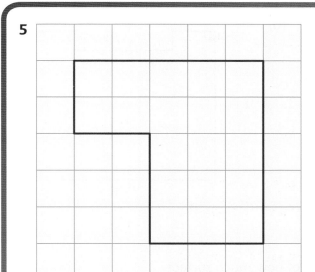

6

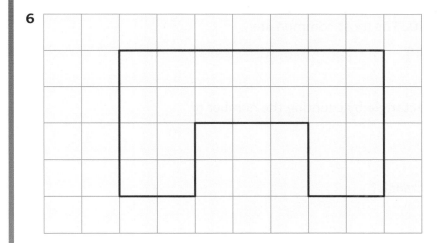

For questions 7–10, copy the composite shape into your exercise book. Calculate all the missing lengths and then calculate the perimeter of each shape.

7

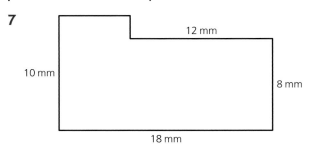

8

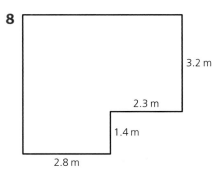

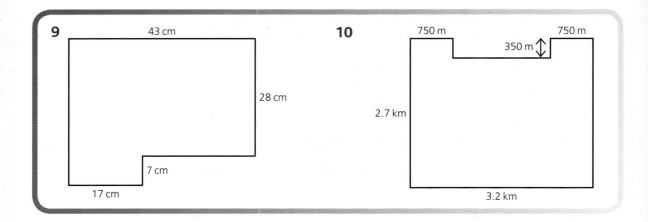

9 43 cm 28 cm 7 cm 17 cm

10 750 m 750 m 350 m 2.7 km 3.2 km

The area of a rectangle

You already know that the **area** is a measure of how much surface is covered by a shape.

It is measured in **square units**. The most common are:

● the square centimetre (cm²)

● the square metre (m²).

You can find the area of a **rectangle** by counting the number of centimetre squares inside it.

Example:

What is the area of this rectangle?

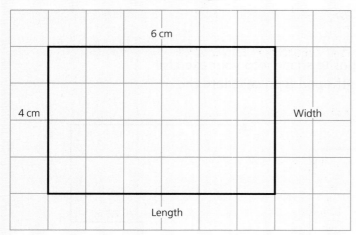

6 cm

4 cm Width

Length

The area of the rectangle is 24 cm². Count the squares – the area of each one is 1 cm².

22 Area and perimeter

However, not all shapes are drawn accurately on centimetre-squared paper. You need a method that will work for **all** rectangles.

Take another look at the rectangle above.

- There are 6 centimetre squares along the length.
- There are 4 centimetres along the width (also called the breadth).
- To find the area quickly, multiply 6 by 4 to give 24

This shows that you can find the area of a rectangle by multiplying the length and the width together.

The formula for this is:

area of a rectangle = length (l) × width (w)

Example:

What is the area of this rectangle?

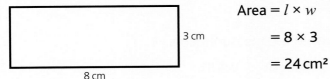

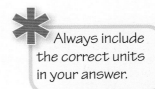

Area = $l \times w$

= 8 × 3

= 24 cm²

Always include the correct units in your answer.

If you are just given the dimensions of the rectangle, it is a good idea to sketch it first.

Example:

Calculate the area of a rectangle that is 7.5 cm long and 5 cm wide.

First sketch the rectangle.

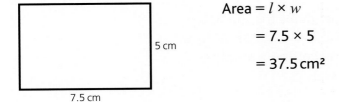

Area = $l \times w$

= 7.5 × 5

= 37.5 cm²

Exercise 22.5

1 Find the area of each of these rectangles.

(a)

6 cm

9 cm

(b)

5 m

24 m

(c)

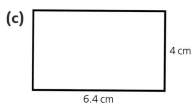

4 cm

6.4 cm

2 Calculate the areas of rectangles with these measurements.

	Length	Width		Length	Width
(a)	7 cm	5 cm	**(f)**	4.3 m	2 m
(b)	12 cm	9 cm	**(g)**	5.8 m	3 m
(c)	15 m	4 m	**(h)**	9.5 cm	6 cm
(d)	50 cm	6 cm	**(i)**	12.3 cm	10 cm
(e)	36 m	8 m	**(j)**	20 cm	0.5 cm

Finding missing lengths of sides

You know that the **factor pairs** of a number make that number when they are multiplied together. You also know that division is the **inverse** of multiplication. So you know that there are three calculations associated with every factor pair.

$$48 = 6 \times 8$$

$$48 \div 6 = 8 \text{ or } \frac{48}{6} = 8$$

and $\quad 48 \div 8 = 6 \text{ or } \frac{48}{8} = 6$

It follows that if **area = length × width** ($A = l \times w$)

then **length = area ÷ width** ($l = A \div w$) or $\dfrac{\text{area}}{\text{width}}$ $\left(l = \dfrac{A}{w}\right)$

and **width = area ÷ length** ($w = A \div l$) or $\dfrac{\text{area}}{\text{length}}$ $\left(w = \dfrac{A}{l}\right)$

Examples:

(i) What is the width of a rectangle that is 10 cm long and has an area of 30 cm²?

Again, you might find a sketch helpful.

Area = 30 cm²

10 cm

$w = A \div l$

$= 30 \div 10$

$= 3\,\text{cm}$

(ii) What is the length of a rectangle that has an area of 56 m² and is 4 m wide?

Area = 56 m²

4 m

$l = A \div w$

$= 56 \div 4$

$= 14\,\text{m}$

1 Calculate the width of each rectangle.

	Area	Length
(a)	18 m²	6 m
(b)	72 cm²	12 cm
(c)	63 m²	9 m
(d)	56 cm²	8 cm
(e)	100 cm²	25 cm

2 Calculate the length of each rectangle.

	Area	Width
(a)	28 m²	4 m
(b)	87 m²	3 m
(c)	125 m²	5 m
(d)	144 cm²	8 cm
(e)	222 cm²	6 cm

⇨ Areas of composite shapes

To find the area of a composite shape:

1 Divide the shape into separate rectangles.

2 Find the area of each rectangle.

3 Add all the areas together.

Sometimes you will need to work out the length or width of some of the individual rectangles before you can calculate the areas. Use the lengths of any parallel lines to help you.

Examples:

(i) Calculate the area of the shape below.
(All measurements are in centimetres.)

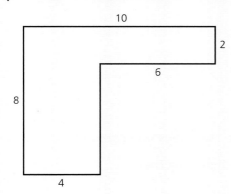

Split the shape into two rectangles. There are two ways you can do this.
Calculate the areas separately and add them together.

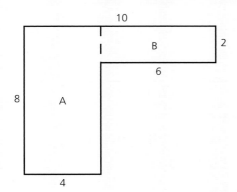

Area A = $l \times w$ or   Area A = $l \times w$
        = 8 × 4   = 10 × 2
        = 32 cm²   = 20 cm²

Area B = $l \times w$ Area B = $l \times w$
        = 6 × 2   = 6 × 4   (length = 8 − 2)
        = 12 cm²   = 24 cm²

A + B = 32 + 12   A + B = 20 + 24
        = 44 cm²   = 44 cm²

(ii) Calculate the area of the shape below. All measurements are in metres.

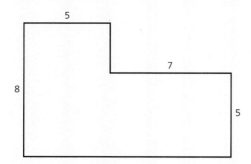

Split the shape into two rectangles. There are two ways you can do this.

Then calculate the areas separately and add them together.

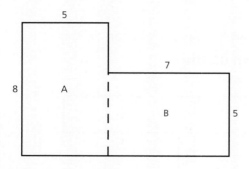 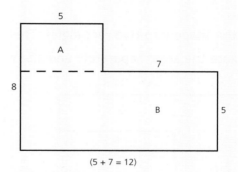

Area A = $l \times w$ or   Area A = $l \times w$

     = 8 × 5   = 5 × 3   (length = 8 − 5)

     = 40 m²   = 15 m²

Area B = $l \times w$ Area B = $l \times w$

     = 7 × 5   = 12 × 5   (length = 5 + 7)

     = 35 m²   = 60 m²

A + B = 40 + 35   A + B = 15 + 60

     = 75 m²   = 75 m²

Exercise 22.7

Calculate the area of each of these shapes.

Questions 1–3: All measurements are in centimetres.

1

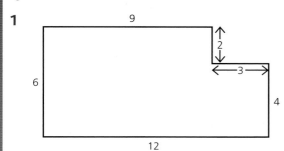

2

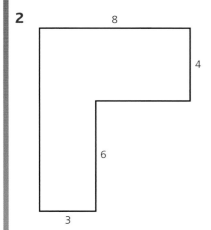

3

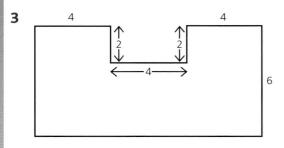

Questions 4–6: All measurements are in metres.

4

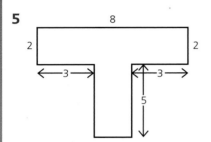

5

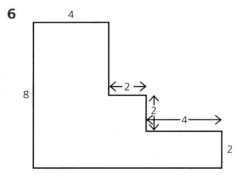

6

⇨ The area of a square

In a **square** the length and width are equal.

You can use the formula for finding the area of a rectangle to find the area of a square.

area = $l \times w$

Because, in a square, $l = w$, you can write this as:

area of a square = $l \times l$ or   area = l^2

Example:

What is the area of a square of side 5 cm?

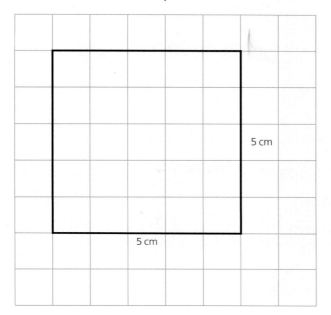

Area = $l \times l$

= 5 × 5

= 25 cm²

Exercise 22.8

Find the areas of squares with sides of these lengths.

1 3m

2 7cm

3 9m

4 11cm

5 20cm

6 6m

Finding the side length of a square

To find the **side length** of a square you need to find that factor which, when multiplied by itself, produces the area.

The side length of a square is the square root of the area:

area = length × length $(A = l^2)$

length = $\sqrt{\text{area}}$ $(l = \sqrt{A})$

Taking a square root is the inverse of squaring a number. The square root is indicated by the symbol $\sqrt{}$.

Example:

What is the side length of a square with area 36 cm²?

$l = \sqrt{A}$

$\quad = \sqrt{36}$

$\quad = 6\,cm$

Exercise 22.9

Find the side lengths of squares with these areas.

1 16 cm²   **3** 4 m²   **5** 100 cm²

2 64 m²   **4** 1 m²   **6** 144 cm²

- Perimeter of a rectangle = $2(l + w)$ or $2 \times l + 2 \times w$
- Perimeter of a square = $4 \times l$
- Area of a rectangle = $l \times w$

  length = $A \div w$

  width = $A \div l$
- Area of a square = l^2

  side length = $\sqrt{A}$

Exercise 22.10: Summary exercise

1 Calculate the perimeter of a rectangle with length 6.7 cm and width 4.3 cm.

2 How wide is a rectangle that is 12 m long, with an area of 48 m²?

3 What is the length of a rectangle with an area of 120 m² and that is 5 m wide?

4 What is the side length of a square of area 9 m²?

5 What is the length of a rectangle that is 8 m wide and has a perimeter of 60 m?

6 The perimeter of a square is 20 cm.

    (a) How long is one side of the square?

    (b) What is the area of the square?

7 Calculate the areas of the rectangles with these measurements.

    (a) length 9 cm, width 4 cm

    (b) length 8.4 m, width 6 m

8 What is the area of a square of side 7 cm?

9 Calculate the perimeter and the area of each of these shapes.

    (a)

2 cm

2 cm

10 cm

12 cm

    (b)

3 m

3 m

4 m

6 m

8 m

10 There is a square of which the area and perimeter have the same numerical value.

    What is the length of a side of this square?

⇨ Problem solving

Exercise 22.11

1 A postcard measures 15 centimetres by 10 centimetres.

   (a) What is its area?

   (b) What is the length of its perimeter?

   Squares of side 2 centimetres are cut from each corner.

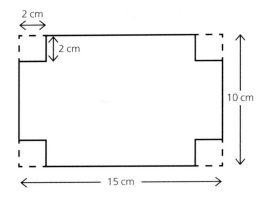

   (c) What is the area of all four squares?

   (d) What is the area of the remaining shape?

   (e) What is the length of the new perimeter?

2 Dr Quack's consulting room is rectangular, measuring 5 metres by 4 metres.

   (a) What is the area of the room?

   He covers the whole floor with carpet that costs £35 per m².

   (b) What is the cost of the carpet?

3 Peter's lawn is a rectangle that measures 20 metres by 16 metres.

(a) What is the area of the lawn?

A packet of weed killer, which costs £1.32, is enough to cover 30 m².

(b) How many packets must he buy to cover the lawn?

(c) What will they cost?

4 Beatrix McGregor has a vegetable patch in the shape of a rectangle. It measures 15 metres by 8 metres.

(a) What is the area of the vegetable patch?

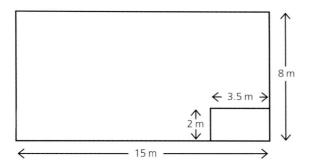

(b) In one corner there is a shed that measures 3.5 metres by 2 metres, as shown in the diagram.
What is the area of the shed floor?

(c) 40 square metres are taken up by paths and the compost heap.
What area remains for Beatrix to grow vegetables?

(d) She wants to surround her total patch with wire.
How many metres of wire will she use?

5 The diagram shows the field where Billy keeps a pair of goats.

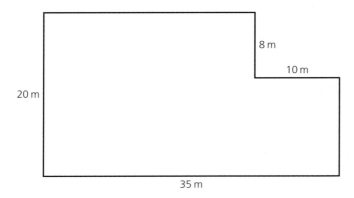

(a) What area do the goats have to graze?

(b) What is the perimeter of the field?

6 The school photograph, which measures 52 centimetres by 20 centimetres, is mounted on white card and then framed, as shown in the diagram.

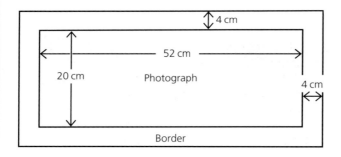

The white border is 4 centimetres wide all the way round.

(a) The picture frame is to be made from one length of wood. How long will this piece of wood need to be?

(b) What is the area of the white border?

7 A groundsman wants to put rope around the edge of the school cricket square. The square is 9 metres wide and has an area of 216 square metres. How much rope does he need?

8 David's patio is a rectangle that measures 8 metres by 5 metres. He paves it with slabs that are 50 centimetre squares.

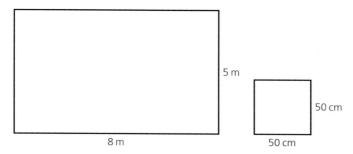

(a) How many slabs can he fit along the length of the patio?

(b) How many slabs can he fit along the width of the patio?

(c) How many slabs must he buy to pave the whole patio?

(d) Slabs cost £1.50 each. How much will David pay for all the slabs?

Activity – A range of rectangles

For these questions, you can assume that the lengths and widths of the rectangles are all a whole number of metres.

1 If the perimeter of a rectangle is 20 metres long, write down all the possible measurements and the corresponding areas.

2 If the area of a rectangle is 20 m², write down all the possible measurements and the corresponding perimeters.

3 John has a rope that is 100 metres long. What is the largest area that John can enclose inside a rectangle made from his rope?

4 Keith is going to rent, from a farmer, a rectangular plot of land that has an area of 100 m². He wants a plot with the largest possible perimeter.

(a) What dimensions should Keith ask the farmer for?

(b) How much rope will he need to enclose the plot?

3D shapes

You are already familiar with many of the most common three-dimensional (3D) shapes.

Face

Cube

Edge

Cuboid

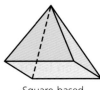

Square-based pyramid

Cone

Triangular prism

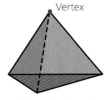

Vertex

Triangular based pyramid

Cylinder

Sphere

 Each 3D shape except the cylinder and the sphere has:

- **faces**, which are 2D (plane) shapes
- **edges**, which are straight lines where the faces meet
- **vertices** (corners), which are points where the edges meet.

The exceptions are the sphere (ball), which has no edges or vertices and the cylinder which has no vertices.

⇨ Nets

To make a model of a 3D shape, you start by drawing its **net** (flattened shape) on paper in two dimensions.

Cube

A **cube** is a 3D shape with six square faces that are all the same size.

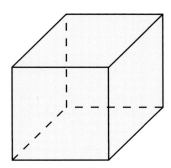

Here is the net of this cube.

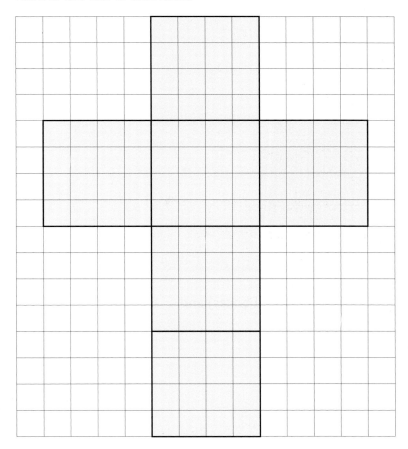

Cuboid

A **cuboid** is a rectangular box with six rectangular faces.

Here is the net of this cuboid.

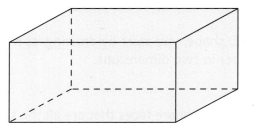

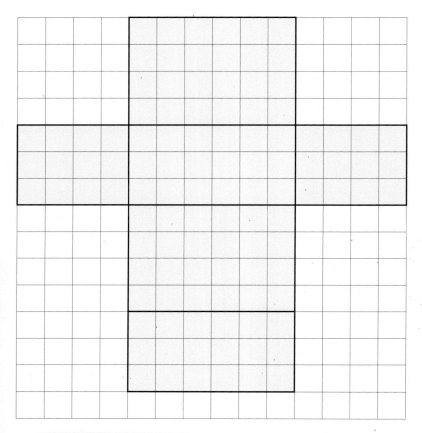

Exercise 23.1

1 Collect some cardboard boxes (for example, cereal boxes) and flatten them out to make their nets.

Answer these questions about each of the nets.

(a) How many faces does the shape have?

(b) How many of its faces are equal in size?

(c) What are the lengths of the sides of the faces?

2 Copy the nets on the previous two pages onto squared paper. Cut them out and fold them along the lines, to make a cube and a cuboid.

3 Other nets have their faces arranged in a different way. Try to draw two different nets for:

(a) a cube

(b) a cuboid.

Other nets

Copy these nets and fold them up, to make models of the solid shapes.

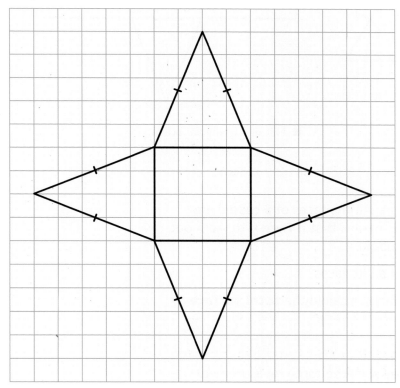

■ Net of a square-based pyramid

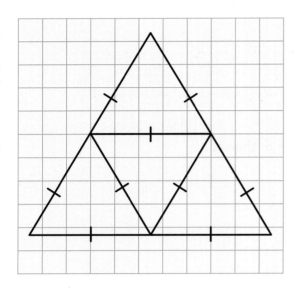

■ Net of a tetrahedron

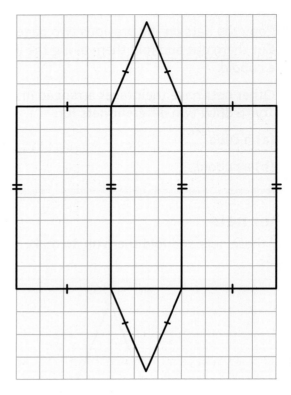

■ Net of a triangular prism

⇨ Surface area

All the faces of a cube are squares. All the faces of a cuboid are either rectangles or squares. This means that it is easy to work out the **surface area** of a cube or cuboid.

A shape's net shows the areas of all its faces.

The sum of the areas of all the faces is called the **total surface area**.

Cube

All six faces of a cube are squares with the same measurements.

You can calculate the area of one square by multiplying the length of one side by the length of another side.

You can then find the total surface area by multiplying the area of one square by 6

Example:

Find the surface area of a cube with edges of 3 cm.

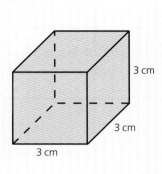

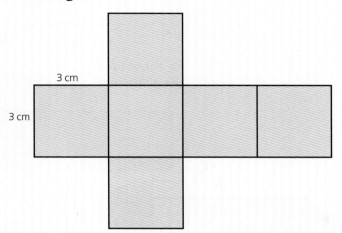

Area of 1 square face = 3 cm × 3 cm

$$= 9 \text{ cm}^2$$

Total surface area = 6 × the area of 1 square

$$= 6 × 9$$

$$= 54 \text{ cm}^2$$

Cuboid

A cuboid has three pairs of equal faces:

● top and bottom

● front and back

● the two ends

To work out the total surface area of a cuboid, you must first work out the area of one face from each pair. Then you can:

● multiply each area by 2 and add the results together *or*

● add the areas together and multiply the result by 2

Example:

Find the surface area of this cuboid.

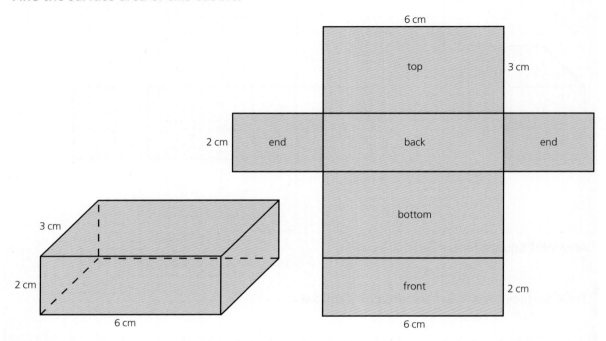

First, identify the pairs of faces and find the area of one face from each pair:

- top and bottom   (Each measures 6 cm × 3 cm.)   Area is 6 × 3 = **18** cm².
- front and back   (Each measures 6 cm × 2 cm.)   Area is 6 × 2 = **12** cm².
- both ends.   (Each measures 3 cm × 2 cm.)   Area is 3 × 2 = **6** cm².

Now work out the total surface area.

Method 1

Surface area = (2 × area of top) + (2 × area of front) + (2 × area of end)

= (2 × 18) + (2 × 12) + (2 × 6)

= 36 + 24 + 12

= 72 cm²

Method 2

Surface area = 2 × [(area of top) + (area of front) + (area of end)]

= 2 × [18 + 12 + 6]

= 2 × 36

= 72 cm²

Exercise 23.2

1 **(a)** On centimetre-squared paper, draw accurately the net of a cube of edge 4 cm.

   (b) Calculate the total surface area of the cube.

2 **(a)** How many faces does a cube have?

   (b) What is the area of one face of cube of edge 8 cm?

   (c) What is the total surface area of the cube?

3 The total surface area of a cube is 600 cm².

   (a) What is the area of one face of the cube?

   (b) What is the length of a side of the cube?

4 A cuboid is 6 centimetres long, 4 centimetres wide and 2 centimetres high.

   (a) On centimetre-squared paper, draw accurately the net of the cuboid.

   (b) Calculate the total surface area of the cuboid.

5 Below is the net of an open cube with the base shaded.

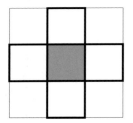

An open cube
has five faces – it
does not have a 'lid'.

Which of these are also nets of open cubes? It may help to copy
them and cut them out.

(a)

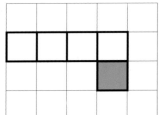

(e)

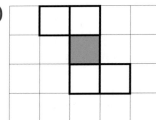

(b)

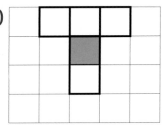

(f)

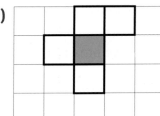

(c)

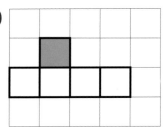

(g)

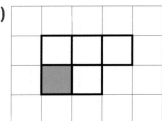

(d)

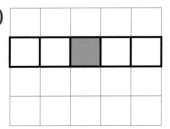

(h)

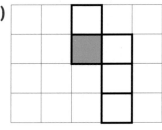

(i)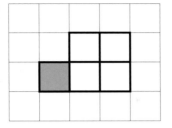

(j)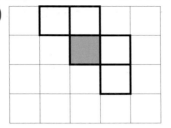

6 Which of these are nets of cuboids?

(a)

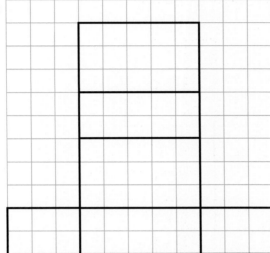

(b)

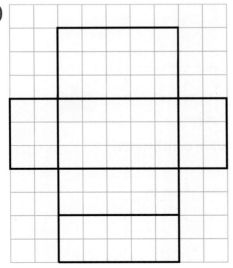

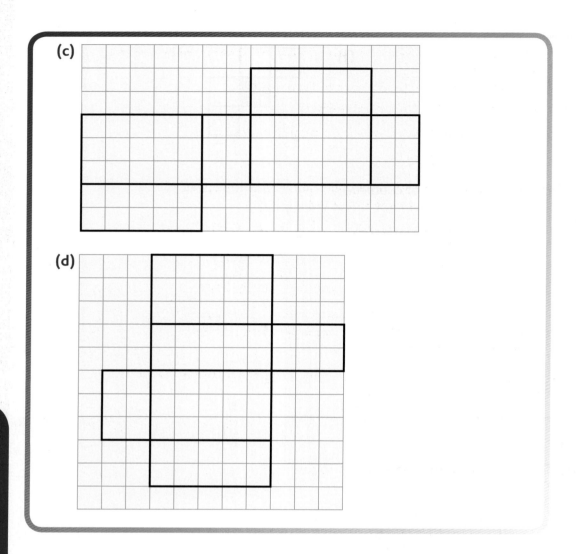

(c)

(d)

⇨ Volume

Volume is the amount of **space** a 3D shape occupies.

It is measured in **cubic units**, for example the **cubic centimetre (cm³)**.

1 cm³ is the space occupied by a cube that measures 1 cm by 1 cm by 1 cm.

Exercise 23.3

1 (a) Fold up the three nets that you made in Exercise 23.1 question 2 and Exercise 23.2 question 4.

   (i) 4 cm by 4 cm by 4 cm   **(iii)** 6 cm by 3 cm by 2 cm

   (ii) 3 cm by 4 cm by 6 cm

(b) Fill each of them with centimetre cubes and count the cubes to find the volume of the cube or cuboid.

2 (a) Work with a partner and make these cuboids from their nets:

   (i) 2 cm by 2 cm by 3 cm   **(iii)** 4 cm by 3 cm by 2 cm

   (ii) 3 cm by 3 cm by 3 cm   **(iv)** 5 cm by 3 cm by 3 cm

(b) Fill each of them with centimetre cubes. Count the cubes and work out the volume of each cuboid. Do you get the same answer when a different side is the base?

3 Work with your partner to find a way of calculating the volume of a cuboid without counting cubes.

Cuboid

This cuboid is 5 cm long, 3 cm wide and 1 cm high.

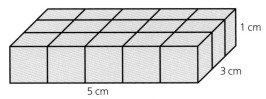

It is made of one layer of 5 × 3 = 15 centimetre cubes.

1 × 15 = 15 so the volume is 15 cm³.

This cuboid is 5 cm long, 3 cm wide and 2 cm high.

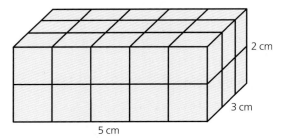

2 cm

3 cm

5 cm

It is made up of two layers of 15 centimetre cubes.

You know there are 15 cm³ in one layer so the volume is
15 × 2 = 30 cm³.

This cuboid is 5 cm long, 3 cm wide and 3 cm high.

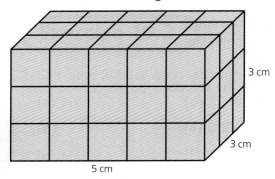

3 cm

3 cm

5 cm

It is made up of three layers of 15 centimetre cubes.

The volume is 15 × 3 = 45 cm³.

If you look at the cuboids above, you can see that, to find the volume of a cuboid, you:

● multiply **length (*l*)** by **width (*w*)** to find the number of cubes in one layer

● multiply the number of cubes in one layer by the number of layers, which is the same as the **height (*h*)**.

This gives the formula:

Volume of a cuboid = length × width × height   or $l × w × h$

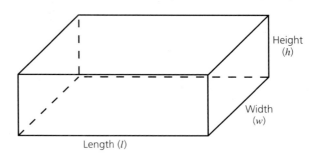

Height (*h*)

Width (*w*)

Length (*l*)

Cube

You can use the same formula to calculate the volume of a cube.

Example:

Find the volume of this cube.

Volume = $l × w × h$

   = 2 × 2 × 2

   = 8 cm³

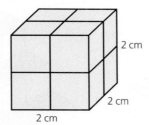

2 cm

2 cm

2 cm

Exercise 23.4

1 Calculate the volumes of the cuboids with these measurements.

	Length	Width	Height
(a)	5 cm	4 cm	3 cm
(b)	6 cm	5 cm	2 cm
(c)	8 cm	7 cm	5 cm
(d)	10 cm	8 cm	8 cm
(e)	20 cm	10 cm	4 cm

2 Calculate the volumes of cubes with these side lengths.

   (a) 4 cm   **(b)** 5 cm   **(c)** 10 cm

3 Work out the volume of each of these solid shapes.

(a)

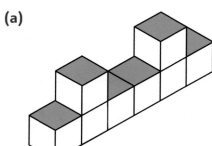

(b)

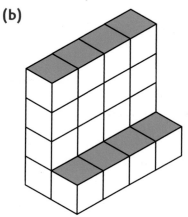

4 Look at the diagram.

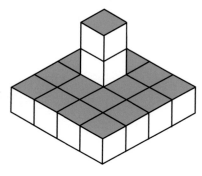

How many extra cubes would you need, to complete a 6 × 3 × 3 cuboid?

5 Look at the diagram.

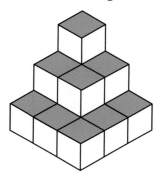

How many extra cubes would you need to complete a 5 × 3 × 4 cuboid?

6 Look at the diagram. A total of 8 cubes has been removed from the middle of the cuboid.

How many extra cubes would you need to make a 5 by 3 by 3 cuboid?

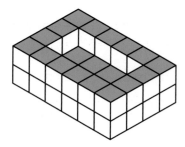

⇒ Problem solving

✳ 1 litre has a volume equal to 1000 cm³.

Exercise 23.5

1 How many ways can you build a quarter-litre (250 cm³) cuboid, using centimetre cubes?

2 A half-litre jug is used to fill a container measuring 30 cm by 50 cm by 20 cm. How many jugfuls will fill the container?

3 Grandfather's biscuit tin measures 20 centimetres by 15 centimetres by 10 centimetres. What is the volume of the biscuits that the tin can hold when it is full?

4 The base of a cereal packet is 22 cm by 7 cm. The packet is 30 cm high.

   (a) What is the volume of the packet?

   (b) The packet is only three-quarters full of cereal. What is the volume of cereal in the packet?

5 A small water trough measures 80 cm by 40 cm by 30 cm.

   (a) What is the volume of the trough?

   (b) How many litres of water are needed to fill the trough from empty?

6 Grandmother keeps her sugar in a tin that is 24 cm long, 12 cm wide and 12 cm deep.

   (a) What is the volume of the tin?

   The tin is empty so she buys three packets of sugar, which each measure 10 cm by 7 cm by 14 cm.

   (b) Will the sugar fit into the tin?

7 A cardboard box has a square base of side 40 cm and is 35 cm high. What is its capacity? Give your answer in litres.

8 A wooden die is a cube of side 3 cm.

    (a) What is the volume of the die?

    (b) The wood used has a mass of 0.7 grams per cm³.
        What is the mass of a die?

9 Toby has a set of 162 building bricks that are 4-centimetre cubes.

    He keeps them in a box that has a base measuring 36 centimetres by 24 centimetres.

    (a) How many bricks are there in the bottom layer?

    (b) How many layers are there when all the bricks are in the box?

10 The aquarium in the dentist's waiting room is 60 cm long and 30 cm wide, and is filled to a depth of 25 cm.

How many litres of water are there in the aquarium?

Activity – One litre

Many things are sold in one-litre containers.

Make a collection of one-litre containers. They might be plastic bottles, cartons or boxes or even just bags. Compare their heights, widths and lengths. Cut them along their joins and open them out, to see their nets. Calculate the total areas of their sides and surfaces.

Write a report on your findings.

Tables and graphs

Quite often you will need to collect data, to gather information. For example, you might record the results of a science experiment, or measure the temperature every day for a month. You can look at this information just as numbers, but it is often easier to see patterns if you display the data pictorially.

⇨ Bar charts, frequency graphs and pictograms

One of the simplest ways to collect information is in a **tally chart** or **frequency table**, like the one below.

Transport	Tally	Frequency
Car	⊮⊮ ⊮⊮ ⊮⊮	15
Bus	⊮⊮ |||	8
Bike	||	2
Walk	⊮⊮	5
Total		**30**

■ How Class 5A come to school

Once you have collected your data, you can display it in a **pictogram**, **frequency graph** or **bar chart**.

This bar chart shows the data from the frequency table.

Types of transport used by pupils in Class 5A to come to school

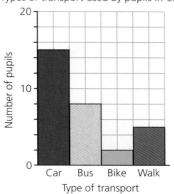

Always give your bar chart a title.

The table below shows some information that Judith collected, about the numbers of hours of sunshine at different airport cities on Boxing Day.

Hours of sunshine on Boxing Day

Airport	Number of hours of sunshine
London, England	1
Nantes, France	7
Dublin, Ireland	4
Beja, Portugal	5
Kirkwall, Scotland	3
Alicante, Spain	9

Judith decides to use a pictogram to display the data, to make it look good and stand out.

Hours of sunshine on Boxing Day 2013

London, England	
Nantes, France	
Dublin, Ireland	
Beja, Portugal	
Kirkwall, Scotland	
Alicante, Spain	

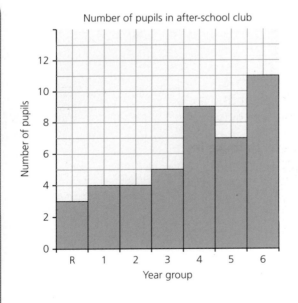

☀ = 2 hours of sunshine

The information in the two tables and diagrams above were about distinct topics. The order of the columns or rows did not matter.

When you collect numerical data, to draw a frequency graph, it must be ordered.

This frequency graph shows the numbers of pupils using an after-school club.

Number of pupils in after-school club

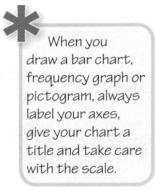

When you draw a bar chart, frequency graph or pictogram, always label your axes, give your chart a title and take care with the scale.

Exercise 24.1

1 Use the frequency graph showing the number of children attending the after-school club to answer these questions.

(a) Which year group had the highest number of children attending after-school club?

(b) Which year group had the lowest number of children attending after-school club?

(c) How many children in Year 3 attended the after-school club?

(d) How many more Year 4 children than Year 1 children attended?

(e) What was the total number of children attending the club?

2 Here is some information Year 5 has collected about how they travel to school. Put this information in a frequency table and then draw a bar graph to show the results.

bus	walk	car	walk	car	car
bike	bus	bus	car	walk	walk
bike	walk	bike	car	car	car
car	car	bus	walk	bus	car
car	bus	car	car	walk	bike

3 Everyone at school can choose a piece of fruit to eat at snack time. The school cook made a note of what everyone chose. The table shows her results.

Type of fruit	Number
Apple	50
Pear	25
Banana	30
Grapes	15
Orange	35
Strawberries	30

Draw a pictogram showing the results of the school cook's survey.

4 Omar rolled a six-sided die 50 times. These are his results.

4	5	6	1	2	2	3	1	3	3
3	1	2	5	6	3	4	4	2	6
5	4	4	2	5	4	6	2	5	4
2	3	3	3	6	3	2	6	1	2
2	5	2	5	3	2	3	5	5	1

(a) Put the results into a frequency table.

(b) Draw a frequency graph to show the results.

(c) What number was rolled most frequently?

(d) What number was rolled least frequently?

5 Jemima measured the amount of rain (in millimetres) that fell every day in April. Here are her results.

0	0	3	5	3	9	15	12	10	3
6	5	7	6	0	0	20	22	13	15
20	16	29	28	8	7	20	14	12	4

(a) Group the amounts of rain in the ranges 0–4 mm, 5–9 mm, 10–14 mm, etc. Put the results into a frequency table.

(b) Draw a frequency graph to show Jemima's results.

(c) What fraction of the days in April had less than 10 mm of rain?

(d) What percentage of the days in April had 20 mm or more of rain?

⇨ Line graphs

If the information you collect is a **measurement** (for example, temperature readings, speed during a journey or the rate of growth of a runner bean plant), you can display it on a line graph.

Example:

Jack recorded his company's sales for one week last October. The figures are in thousands of pounds.

Day of the week	Mon	Tues	Wed	Thurs	Fri	Sat	Sun
Sales / £000s	3	7	15	10	13	8	1

Draw a graph to show this information.

First draw the axes.
- Put the days of the week along the bottom.
- Put the sales figures up the side. Start at 0 and stop at 16
- In the graph below, the scale is 1 square to £1000

Then plot the points, one by one.
- Find the day of the week on the horizontal axis, then move up the graph until you are in line with the correct value on the vertical axis.
- Mark the point with a small cross.

Finally, join the points with straight lines.

It is always a good idea to continue the axis just beyond the largest measurement, in this case 15 (Wednesday).

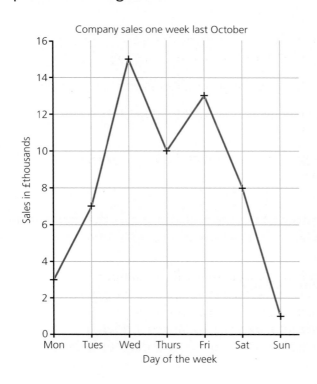

Company sales one week last October

Sometimes you will be asked to use a graph to **estimate** a value. This means that you must read a point off the graph. We use the word estimate because we cannot know whether the answer is exact.

When you read points off a graph, you should always check the scale being used on the axes.

Example:

Sue recorded the temperature in degrees Celsius (°C) every 2 hours last Tuesday.

Here are her results.

Time	8 a.m.	10 a.m.	Noon	2 p.m.	4 p.m	6 p.m
Temperature (°c)	13	17	26	30	28	21

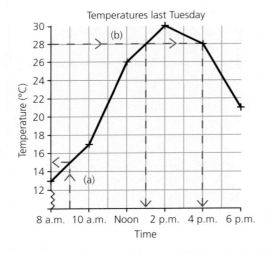

Note: The 'zigzag' at the bottom of the vertical axis shows that part of the temperature scale has been left out. The lowest reading is 13 °C so you don't need to show 0–12 °C.

(a) Estimate the temperature at 9 a.m.

First check the scales.
- The scale on the horizontal axis is 1 square to 1 hour.
- The scale on the vertical axis is 1 square to 2 degrees Celsius.

Now find the value you need to answer the question:
- Find 9 on the time axis.
- Draw a vertical line, from 9 a.m., until you meet the graph line.
- Draw a horizontal line, from that point on the graph line, to the temperature axis.
- Read the value on the temperature axis. For 9 a.m. it is halfway between 14 and 16, which is 15

The temperature at 9 a.m. was 15 °C.

Note: This is an estimate because you do not know that the temperature rose steadily between 8 a.m. and 10 a.m.

(b) When was the temperature more than 28 °C?

This time you know the temperature and need to find a time (or times).
- Find 28 on the temperature axis.
- Draw a horizontal line, from 28 °C, across to the graph line.
- Find the points where your horizontal line crosses the graph line. At each point, draw a horizontal line down to the time axis.
- Read the values on the time axis. They are 1 p.m. and 4 p.m.

The temperature was more than 28 °C between 1 p.m. and 4 p.m.

Note: This is an estimate because you do not know that the temperature was 28 °C at exactly 1 p.m. (You do know that it was 28 °C at 4 p.m.)

1 Ross is feeling unwell on Monday. His mother finds he has a raised temperature and tells him to stay in bed. She takes his temperature twice a day and plots the results on a graph.

A normal body temperature is 37 °C.

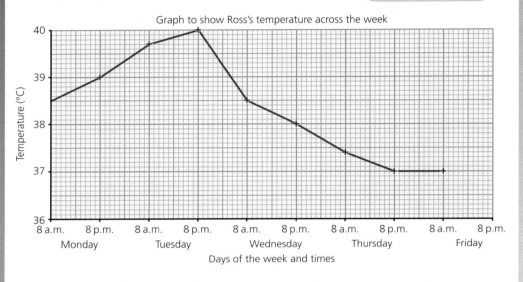

Graph to show Ross's temperature across the week

(a) What was Ross's temperature when he was told to stay in bed?

(b) By how much did Ross's temperature rise in the first 24 hours?

(c) What was Ross's highest temperature?

(d) In which 12-hour period did the temperature fall most?

(e) Why do you think there is no record of a temperature at 8 p.m. on Friday?

2 The graph opposite shows the monthly rainfall in (mm) in Cairns, Australia.

(a) How much rain fell in the wettest month?

(b) Which are the driest months?

(c) How much more rain fell in April than in June?

(d) Can you tell how much rain fell on 15 November?

(e) Why do you think it might be a good idea to give an umbrella as a Christmas present?

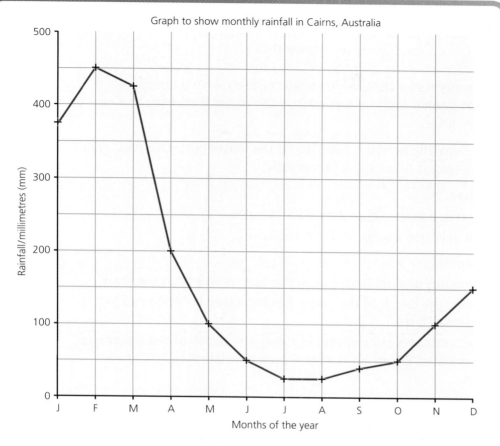

Graph to show monthly rainfall in Cairns, Australia

3 The table shows the average monthly temperature, in °C, in London.

Month	Jan	Feb	Mar	Apr	May	Jun	Jul	Aug	Sept	Oct	Nov	Dec
Temperature (°C)	4	5	7	9	12	16	18	17	15	11	8	5

Draw a graph to show this information. On the temperature axis, use a scale of 1 cm to 2 degrees Celsius.

4 The table shows the height (in metres) of the first high tide of the day for a week at Hastings.

Day	Sun	Mon	Tues	Wed	Thurs	Fri	Sat
Height (m)	6.9	6.5	6.0	5.9	6.2	6.6	7.0

Draw a graph to show this information. Start the height axis at 5.5 and use a scale of 5 cm to 0.5 m.

Some line graphs are continuous straight lines. This happens when a change is **constant**.

Example:

Adam fills his empty water butt, which is 90 cm deep, with a hosepipe connected to the garden tap. He notices that the water level rises at a rate of 20 cm every 5 minutes.

Plot a graph to show the period it takes to fill the water butt. Use your graph to work out how long it takes to fill completely.

First draw the axes.
- On the time axis, use a scale of 2 cm to 5 minutes.
- On the depth axis, use a scale of 2 cm to 20 cm.

Then plot **three** points.
- First plot 0 minutes against 0 cm (the water butt is empty at the start).
- After 5 minutes, the depth of the water has increased by 20 cm, so plot 5 minutes against 20 cm.
- After another 5 minutes (10 minutes in total), the depth of the water has increased by another 20 cm (so is 40 cm deep in total). Plot 10 minutes against 40 cm.

The water level rises at a **constant** rate. This means that you don't have to plot all the points. Instead, you can plot the first three, (0, 0), (5, 20) and (10, 40), and then draw a continuous straight line through them. The line stops at depth = 90 cm because that is how deep the water butt is. After that it will overflow!

Strictly speaking, you need to plot only two points, but it is a good idea to plot three. That way, it will be obvious if you have made a mistake.

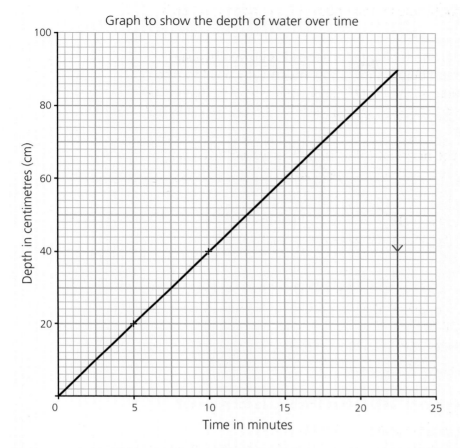

Graph to show the depth of water over time

You can then read down from the end of the line to the time axis, to find how long the butt takes to fill. The answer is halfway between 20 and 25 minutes.

It takes 22.5 minutes to fill the water butt completely.

1 Sally hires a bicycle. She is charged a deposit followed by an hourly rate. The graph below shows how much Sally pays to hire a bicycle for 4 hours.

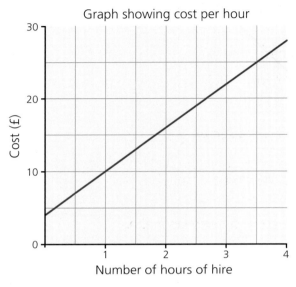

Graph showing cost per hour

(a) How much does it cost Sally to hire the bicycle for 4 hours?

(b) For how long can a bicycle be hired for £16?

(c) How much must Sally pay for the deposit?

(d) How much is the hourly rate that Sally is charged?

2 The table below shows some equivalent sums of pounds (£) and euros (€).

Pounds (£)	0	100	200	300	400
Euros (€)	0	125	250	375	500

(a) Use this information to draw a line graph on graph paper, so that you can convert sums up to £400 to euros. Put pounds on the horizontal axis, using a scale of 2 cm to £100 and euros on the vertical axis, using a scale of 4 cm to €100

(b) Use your graph to answer these questions.

   (i) What is the equivalent of €350 in pounds?

   (ii) What is the equivalent of £125 in euros?

⇨ **Put it into practice**

Exercise 24.4

You have learned about bar charts, pictograms, frequency tables and line graphs. Choose which one you would use to show the data described in each question.

1 The types of pets the class keep at home.

2 The numbers of pets the class keep at home.

3 Converting litres to gallons.

4 The numbers of each newspaper sold at a station each morning.

5 The numbers of viewers watching each television channel at 8 p.m.

6 The colours of the cars that go past the school between 9 a.m. and 10 a.m.

7 The number of people in each car that goes past the school between 9 a.m. and 10 a.m.

8 The heights of the pupils in Year 5 and Year 6.

9 The results of the maths exam.

10 Our favourite sports.

11 Now carry out a survey to collect data on one of the topics above (or another topic agreed with your teacher). Illustrate your data with a suitable table or graph.

 **Time and timetables**

There are:

● 60 **seconds** in one minute

● 60 **minutes** in one hour

● 24 **hours** in one **day**.

There are two types of clock: an analogue clock and a digital clock. It is important to be able to tell the time using both types of clock.

⇨ **Analogue clocks**

An analogue clock is usually round and has an hour hand and a minute hand. It may, or may not, have a second hand.

The hour hand is the shorter hand. It indicates how close you are to the hour.

■ Exactly two o'clock   ■ Nearly two o'clock   ■ Past two o'clock

The longer minute hand tells you exactly how many minutes there are before the next hour, or past the hour. Some clocks also have a second hand, which is normally longer than the minute hand. This shows you how many seconds there are before the next minute, or after the last minute.

■ Exactly two o'clock　　■ Quarter to two　　■ Twenty-five past two

When you tell the time on an analogue clock, you say:

● how long it is to the hour, or

● how long it is past the hour

unless it is exactly on the hour!

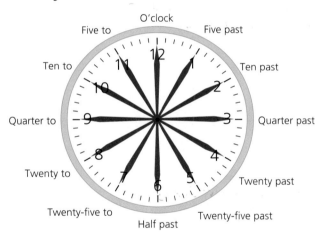

Exercise 25.1

1 Write down the time shown on each of these clocks. 6:45

(a) 5:00

(b)

(c) 10:15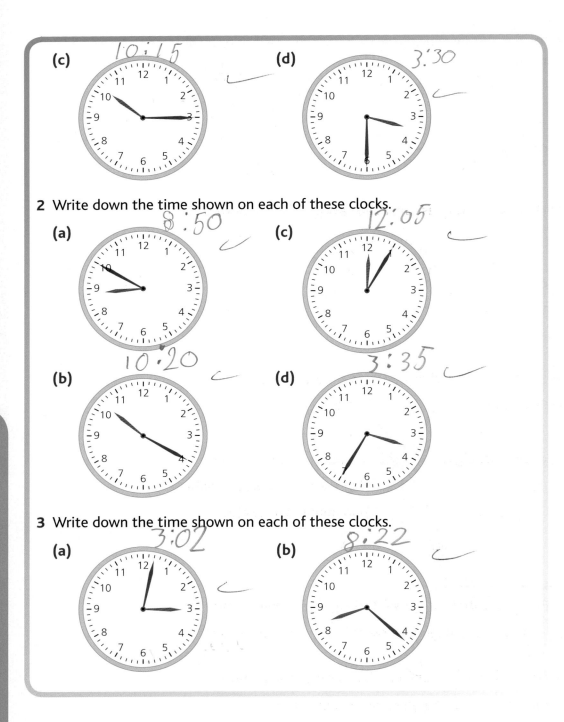

(d) 3:30

2 Write down the time shown on each of these clocks.

(a) 8:50

(c) 12:05

(b) 10·20

(d) 3:35

3 Write down the time shown on each of these clocks.

(a) 3:02

(b) 8:22

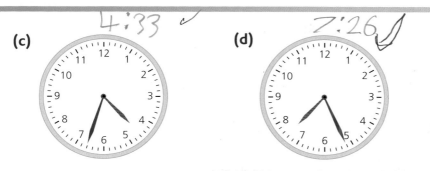

(c) 4:33 ✓

(d) 7:26 ✓

4 For each part of this question, make a copy of this clockface.

Draw hands on the clockface to show these times.

(a) Half past five

(b) Quarter to six

(c) Quarter past eight

(d) Ten past three

(e) Twenty to six

(f) Ten to nine

(g) Five to four

(h) Sixteen minutes to three

(i) Nineteen minutes past eight

(j) Two minutes to twelve

Analogue clock puzzles

The minute hand moves through a full circle (360°) every hour.

The hour hand moves through one-twelfth of the full circle each hour.

The second hand moves through one full circle every minute.

Use these facts to answer the questions in Exercise 25.2

1 Write down the number of degrees turned, in one hour, by:

   (a) the minute hand   **(b)** the hour hand   **(c)** the second hand.

2 (a) Copy and complete these sentences.

     (i) In 20 minutes the minute hand turns through ... degrees.

     (ii) In 20 minutes the hour hand turns through ... degrees.

  (b) What is the angle between the minute and the hour hands at twenty past twelve?

3 (a) Through how many degrees do these hands turn in 15 minutes?

     (i) the minute hand   **(ii)** the hour hand

  (b) What is the angle between the hands at a quarter past twelve?

4 (a) Copy and complete these sentences.

     (i) In 10 minutes the minute hand turns through ... degrees.

     (ii) In 10 minutes the hour hand turns through ... degrees.

  (b) What is the angle between the hands at ten past twelve?

5 What is the angle between the minute and the hour hands at half past twelve?

6 What is the angle between the minute and the hour hands at half past two?

7 What is the angle between the minute and the hour hands at a quarter past three?

8 What is the angle between the minute and the hour hands at twenty to one?

9 What is the angle between the minute and the hour hands at half past six?

10 What is the angle between the minute and the hour hands at a quarter to four?

⇨ Digital clocks

A digital clock records time as numbers like this:

This is twenty-four minutes past ten, or ten twenty-four.

Digital clocks may be set to give the time on a 24-hour clock or a 12-hour clock.

Morning times are a.m. (from the Latin *ante meridiem*, meaning before noon) and afternoon times are p.m. (from the Latin *post meridiem*, meaning after noon.)

For 12 o'clock you can use 12 noon and 12 midnight.

If you need to know a time, for example, when your holiday flight leaves the airport, then it is important to know if the time is in the morning or the afternoon, so most timetables use 24-hour clock times.

Analogue clock	12-hour clock	24-hour clock
5 o'clock (morning)	5.00 a.m.	05:00
Noon	12.00 noon	12:00
Half past two (afternoon)	2.30 p.m.	14:30
Quarter to ten (evening)	9.45 p.m.	21:45
Ten past midnight	0.10 a.m.	00:10
Twenty past midday	12.20 p.m.	12:20

✳ 24-hour clock times always have four digits and there may – or may not – be a colon separating the hours and the minutes.

Exercise 25.3

1 Write each of these 24-hour clock times as:

(i) a 12-hour clock time followed by a.m. or p.m.

(ii) an analogue clock time, using 'past' or 'to'.

(a) 05:00 *5 am* ✓   **(f)** 17:40 *5:40 pm* ✓

(b) 11:30 *11:30 am* ✓   **(g)** 03:25 *3:25 am* ✓

(c) 14:15 *2:15 pm* ✓   **(h)** 11:35 *11:35 am* ✓

(d) 16:45 *4:45 pm* ✓   **(i)** 00:20 *00:20 am* ✓

(e) 19:00 *7:00 pm* ✓   **(j)** 12:40 *12:40 pm* ✓

2 Write each of these 12-hour clock times as:

(i) a 24-hour clock time

(ii) an analogue clock time, using 'past' or 'to'.

(a) 7.00 a.m.   **(f)** 11.40 p.m.

(b) 9.30 a.m.   **(g)** 6.45 a.m.

(c) 1.15 p.m.   **(h)** 7.50 a.m.

(d) 3.45 p.m.   **(i)** 5.24 p.m.

(e) 4.10 p.m.   **(j)** 3.35 p.m.

3 This is part of Jan's diary. Rewrite the times using 24-hour clock.

I woke up at twelve minutes past seven. It was dark. I left the house at twelve minutes to eight and arrived at school at three minutes past eight. We left for swimming after break, at seven minutes to ten. We were late back for lunch, not arriving until thirteen minutes past one. After school, football club ran until a quarter past six and I did not get home until nine minutes to seven. Mum was cross because I was muddy!

4 Sam has a smart new watch and she checks it throughout the day.
These are the times that she noted, but not in the right order.

Copy and complete Sam's daily timetable, using 24-hour clock times.

Event	Time	Event	Time
Got up		Chess club	
Left for school		Got home	
Morning break		Supper	
Lunch		Bedtime	

⇨ Hours, days and minutes

There are:

- 60 seconds in a minute

- 60 minutes in a day

- 24 hours in a day

- 7 days in a week.

When converting from seconds to minutes or from minutes to hours you need to divide by 60. In Chapter 5, you did this by writing 60 as a product of its factors.

$$60 = 6 \times 10 \quad 60 = 5 \times 12$$

To convert from hours to days you need to divide by 24 You can write 24 as a product of its factors in three ways.

$$24 = 2 \times 12 \quad 24 = 3 \times 8 \quad 24 = 4 \times 6$$

Examples:

(i) Change 24 days into weeks and days.

24 days = 24 ÷ 7 weeks   24 ÷ 7 = 3 r3

           = 3 weeks 3 days

(ii) Change 345 minutes into hours and minutes.

345 minutes = 345 ÷ 60 hours

              = 345 ÷ 5 ÷ 12 hours   as 60 = 5 × 12

                                        5 is a factor of 345, so divide by 5 first

              = 69 ÷ 12 hours   69 ÷ 12 = 5 r9

              = 5 hours 45 minutes

Exercise 25.4

1 Change these to weeks and days.

  (a) 28 days   **(b)** 60 days   **(c)** 40 days   **(d)** 100 days

2 Write these times in days and hours.

  (a) 72 hours   **(b)** 120 hours   **(c)** 200 hours   **(d)** 150 hours

3 Write these times in hours and minutes.

  (a) 240 minutes   **(c)** 500 minutes

  (b) 280 minutes   **(d)** 760 minutes

4 Write these times in minutes and seconds.

(a) 600 seconds *10 minutes* (c) 350 seconds *5 minutes 50 seconds* ✓

(b) 200 seconds *3 minutes 20 seconds* (d) 920 seconds *15 minutes 20 seconds* ✓

5 Calculate the times of these train journeys, in hours and minutes.

(a) London to Bristol: 113 minutes *1 hour 53 minutes* ✓

(b) York to Cardiff: 350 minutes *5 hours 50 minutes* ✓

(c) Birmingham to Penzance: 403 minutes *6 hours 43 minutes* ✓

6 (a) The average life of an old type of light bulb is 2000 hours.

Write this time in *3 days 20 hours*

(i) days and hours　　(ii) weeks, hours and days.

(b) The average life of a new type of light bulb is 10 000 hours.

Write this time in:

(i) days and hours　　(ii) weeks, hours and days.

7 The Orient Express takes 1872 minutes to travel from Paris to Venice.

Write this time in:

(a) hours and minutes　　(b) days, hours and minutes.

8 The Trans-Siberian Railway takes 133 hours to travel from Moscow to Beijing. Write this time in days and hours.

⇨ How long?

Elapsed time is the time between the start of an event and the end of it. You have to be careful when calculating with time as you cannot add and subtract in the same way that you do with normal numbers because there are 60 seconds in a minute and 60 minutes in an hour.

Example:

I leave for school at 7.45 a.m. and arrive at school at 8.17 a.m.

How long does my journey take?

Method 1: The timeline

Use a time line to break the journey into parts.

From 7.45 to 8.00 is 15 minutes.

From 8.00 to 8.17 is 17 minutes.

Total time is 15 + 17 = 32 minutes.

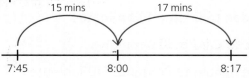

Method 2: Subtraction

	h			m	
	$^7\cancel{8}$		$^7\cancel{1}$	7	
	7		4	5	
			3	2	

You cannot take 45 from 17 so you must take 60 minutes from the hours column to make 77

77 − 45 = 32

The journey time is 32 minutes.

> ✳ It is very easy to forget that there are 60 minutes in an hour when you set up your subtraction frame and many people find the time line easier.

Example:

My flight to New York takes 7 hours and 35 minutes. If the flight takes off at 11:45, at what time will I arrive?

Method 1: The timeline

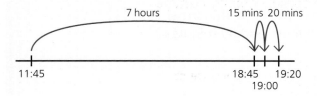

The journey is broken into 7 hours, 15 minutes and 20 minutes.

The arrival time is 19:20

Method 2: Addition

	h			m	
1	1		4	5	
	7		3	5	
1	9		2	0	
	1				

$45 + 35 = 80$

80 minutes = 1 hour 20 minutes

Write down 20 and carry the 1 hour.

The arrival time is 19:20

Exercise 25.5

1 I leave home at 07:35 and arrive at school at 08:10 *35 minutes*

How long did it take me to walk to school?

2 I cycle for 2 hours and 12 minutes and reach home at 11:27 *9:15 AM*

At what time did I set off?

3 The ferry takes 2 hours and 40 minutes to get from England to France. If we left England at 13:50 French time, at what time *4:30 pm* do we arrive in France?

4 Freddie won the cross-country race in 1 hour 43 minutes. The race started at 13:45 *3:28 PM*

At what time did he finish?

5 School starts at 08:35 and finishes at 15:55

How long is the school day? *7 hours 20 minutes*

6 We leave home at 08:35 and reach our seaside holiday cottage at 12:12 *3 hours* *37 minutes*

How long did our our journey take?

7 It takes 1 hour 25 minutes to reach the airport and we must be there by 11.15 *9:50 am*

What is the latest time that we can leave home?

8 The train takes 143 minutes to travel from London to Manchester. If I catch the train at 12:55, at what time will I arrive in Manchester? *3:18*

9 My flight leaves Heathrow at 13:45 and arrives in Sydney at 11:10 (English time) the next morning. How long is the flight time? *22 hours 25 minutes*

10 *Apollo 11* left Kennedy space station at 09:32 on 16 July 1969 and landed on the Moon 4 days, 6 hours and 45 minutes later. At what time and on what date did *Apollo 11* land on the Moon?

⇨ Timetables

Timetables help you to organise your time. This is a school timetable.

Time	Mon	Tues	Wed	Thur	Fri
	5A TIMETABLE				
8.15 : 8.45	Registration and Assembly				
8.45 : 9.25	English	Maths	English	Maths	Maths
9.25 : 10.05	English	Maths	English	Maths	DT
10.05 : 10.45	PE	English	French	English	DT
10.45 : 11.05	Break				
11.05 : 11.45	Maths	History	Maths	Science	English
11.45 : 12.25	Maths	Geography	RE	Science	English
12.25 : 13.25	Lunch and play				
13.25 : 13.35	Registration				
13.35 : 14.15	Science	French	Games	Geography	Games
14.15 : 14.55	Science	Art	Games	History	Games
14.55 : 15.35	PSHE	Art	Games	French	Games
15.35 : 15.45	Form Time then Home				

There are other sorts of timetable, too. How many can you think of?

Exercise 25.6

1 Use the timetable for 5A to answer these questions.

   (a) How long is the English lesson on Monday? *1 hour 20 minutes*

   (b) How long is the Games lesson on Friday? *2 hours 15 minutes*

   (c) How many hours and minutes of Maths lessons do 5A have each week? *5 hours 20 minutes*

   (d) How many hours and minutes of Science lessons do 5A have each week? *2 hours 40 minutes*

2 Here is Year 1's timetable for Monday. Write out the timetable, using 12-hour clock times.

9:00 am   10:15 am   10:45 am   12:00 pm   1:10 pm   1:50 pm   3:30 pm

Time							
Monday	Literacy	Break	Numeracy	Lunch	Science	Games	Home

3 This is part of a Sunday evening's television schedule.

	Channel 1		Channel 2
4.55	Songs of Praise	4.55	Film: *Snow White*
5.35	News	7.25	Mum's Army
6.00	Jubilee Street	7.55	West Enders
6.50	Antiques Roadshow	8.50	News
7.45	Film: *Sailors of the Caribbean*	9.20	Film: *Robin Hood*
10.00	Weather	10.55	Weather

   (a) How long is Songs of Praise? *40 minutes*

   (b) Which channel has the longer news programme? *channel 2*

   (c) How long is it from the start of Mum's Army to the end of the Channel 2 News? *1 hour 55 minutes*

   (d) Which is the longest film? *Snow white*

4 This timetable shows different ways of travelling into Newtown from Amchester via Barford and Hampton.

	Amchester	Barford	Hampton	Newtown
Yellow Bus	8.00	8.15	8.20	8.30
Greenline	8.12	8.17	8.22	8.27
Black's Taxis	8.15	8.18	8.22	8.25
Blue Coaches	7.55	8.05	8.15	8.35

(a) How long does the Yellow Bus take to travel from Amchester to Newtown? *30 minutes*

(b) Greenline and Black's Taxis both claim to be the fastest. Which company is correct? *Black's Taxis*

(c) Where is the Blue Coach at 8.10? *in the middle of Barford and Hampton*

(d) Which company arrives at twenty-five past eight? *Black's Taxi*

(e) Which company is fastest from Barford to Hampton? *Black's Taxi*

5 Here is the local bus timetable for the early morning.

Clapham	0748	0755	0802	0817	0832	0857	0921	0951
Battersea	0757	0805	0812	0827	0842	0906	0930	1000
Palace Gate	0829	0837	0844	0859	0913	0934	0956	1026
Addison Road	0837	0845	0852	0908	0922	0943	1005	1035
White City	0849	0857	0904	0919	0933	0954	1016	1046

(a) How long does it take to travel from Battersea to Addison Road, if I catch the bus before 0815? *40 minutes*

(b) How long does it take to travel from Clapham to Palace Gate, if I catch the bus between 0750 and 0830? *42 minutes*

(c) My mum is going to the shopping centre at White City. She is meeting her friend there at 0930. What is the latest time she can leave home? *It depends where she lives if she lives in clapham 8:17, if Battersea 8:?? if palace gate 8:59, and finally if addison road 9:08.*

Travel timetables often leave out the colon, so the times are given just as four digits.

6 Here is a London bus timetable.

	Bus A	Bus B	Bus C
Acton Green	1448	1454	1459
Askew Road	1455	1501	1506
Shepherd's Bush	1503	1509	1511
Notting Hill	1509	1515	1516
Marble Arch	1525	1531	1530
Piccadilly Circus	1546	1552	1551

Bus A leaves Acton Green at 1448 and arrives at Piccadilly Circus at 1546. Bus C leaves Action Green at 1459 and does not stop at Penn Road or Lancaster Gate. It reaches Piccadilly Circus at 1551

(a) Which bus is at Marble Arch at half past three?

(b) Which bus is at Notting Hill at a quarter past three?

(c) How long does the journey take from Acton Green to Askew Road?

(d) What is the difference in the journey time from Askew Road to Shepherd's Bush if I take Bus C rather than Bus A?

(e) Calculate the total journey time from Acton Green to Piccadilly Circus for Bus A, Bus B and Bus C.

7 Here is the local bus timetable. Each column shows the times for a different bus. The travel time between adjacent stops is the same for every bus but I have spilt water on my timetable and some of the times are missing. Copy the timetable and fill in the missing times.

	Bus 1	Bus 2	Bus 3	Bus 4
Village Church	0745	0805	0830	
Green Field	0755			0905
Farmer's Cross		0827	0852	0917
Gate House	0822		0907	
Market	0830	0850		0840

8 Use the bus timetable you completed in question 7 to answer these questions.

(a) Which bus reaches the Market at ten to nine?

(b) Which bus arrives at Green Field at a five to eight?

(c) Which bus leaves the Village Church at five to nine?

(d) What is the total journey time from Village Church to the Market?

9 Here are the timetables between Portsmouth/Havant and Waterloo.

Morning: Portsmouth to Waterloo					Evening: Waterloo to Portsmouth				
Portsmouth	0640	0713	0745	0815	Waterloo	1730	1800	1815	1830
Havant	0657	0730	0803	0832	Woking	1754	--	--	1857
Haslemere	0731	--	0830	--	Guildford	1806	1832	1850	1906
Guildford	0750	0813	0846	0915	Haslemere	--	1851	--	1925
Woking	--	0826	--	0927	Havant	1850	1915	1940	1950
Waterloo	0830	0855	0931	0955	Portsmouth	1910	1936	--	2010

(a) How long is the journey time from Portsmouth to Waterloo if you leave at:

(i) 0640   (ii) 0815   (iii) 0713?

(b) How long is the journey from Waterloo to Havant if you leave at:

(i) 1730   (ii) 1800   (iii) 1815?

(c) (i) Mr Brown lives in Havant and has to be at Waterloo by 0900. At what time should he catch the train?

(ii) He has to be back in Havant by 1930. What train should he catch from Waterloo?

(d) (i) Miss Green lives in Haslemere and has to be at Waterloo by 0930. At what time should she catch the train?

(ii) She has to be home in Haslemere by 1920. What train should she catch from Waterloo?

10 We are going on a school trip to the theatre at Mudford. The performance starts at half past one and lasts for three and a quarter hours.

We shall be travelling by train. The train takes forty-five minutes from the local station at Puddleton to get to Mudford and it takes us twenty minutes to walk from school to Puddleton station. Mudford station is across the road from the theatre. Trains run from Puddleton to Mudford every hour, leaving at 12 minutes past each hour. Trains run from Mudford to Puddleton every hour leaving Mudford at 25 minutes to each hour.

Work out a sensible timetable showing when we should leave school and when we should arrive back.

Glossary

Acute angle An angle that is between 0 and 90°.

Area The amount of space inside a plane (2D) shape such as a rectangle or circle. It is measured in square units, such as square centimetres (cm²).

Axis x and y reference lines in a co-ordinate grid. (Plural is axes.)

Composite number A number that is not a prime number (but not 1).

Co-ordinates The horizontal and vertical distances from the origin (0, 0), used to plot a point on a grid; for example, the point with co-ordinates (3, 5) is 3 units along the horizontal axis and 5 units up the vertical axis, counting from 0 on each axis.

Consecutive Numbers that follow each other, such as 3, 4 and 5

Cube number The result of the number multiplied by itself twice; for example, $3 \times 3 \times 3 = 27$, so 27 is a cubed number.

Data A piece of information, for example, the highest daily temperature.

Decimal fraction A number less than one, written after a decimal point.

Denominator The bottom number on a fraction. It tells you how many parts one whole has been divided into.

Diagonal A line joining non-adjacent corners on a plane shape.

Difference The result of subtracting one number from another. How much one number differs from another. For example, the difference between 5 and 11 is 6 ($11 - 5 = 6$).

Digit Any numeral from 0 to 9

Equilateral triangle A triangle that has three equal sides and three angles of 60°.

Factor A number that divides exactly into another number.

Factor pair A pair of factors that, when multiplied together, give the number of which they are both factors. For example, 1, 2, 3 and 6 are factors of 6 and $6 = 2 \times 3 = 1 \times 6$, so 1 and 6, 2 and 3 are factor pairs of 6

Fraction A number less than one, written like this: $\frac{3}{4}$

Function A rule connecting two sets of numbers.

Imperial units Non-metric units in common usage in Britain and America.

16 **ounces** (oz) = 1 pound (lb)	
14 **pounds** (lb) = 1 **stone** (st)	1 **ton** (t) = 2240 pounds (lb)
12 **inches** (ins) = 1 foot (ft)	3 **feet** (ft) = 1 yard (yd)
1760 **yards** (yds) = 1 **mile** (m)	
2 **pints** (pts) = 1 **quart** (qt)	8 pints (pts) = 1 **gallon** (gal)

Improper fraction A fraction in which the numerator (top number) is larger than the denominator (bottom number), for example, $\frac{7}{4}$

Inverse The opposite. For example, the inverse of addition is subtraction.

Isosceles triangle A triangle that has two equal sides and two equal angles.

Metric units Units of mass (weight), length and volume that are in use in Britain and in Europe, as well as many other countries.

1000 **milligrams** (mg) = 1 gram (g)

1000 **grams** (g) = 1 kilogram (kg)

1000 **kilograms** (kg) = 1 **metric tonne** (t)

10 **millimetres** (mm) = 1 centimetre (cm)

100 **centimetres** (cm) = 1 metre (m)

1000 millimetres (mm) = 1 metre (m)

1000 **metres** (m) = 1 **kilometre** (km)

1000 **millitres** (ml) = 1 **litre** (l)

Mixed number A combination of a whole number and a fraction, for example, $2\frac{3}{4}$

Multiple A number that is a product (multiplication) of a factor. For example, 6 is a multiple of 2, because $6 = 2 \times 3$.

Negative number A number that is less than zero, such as $^{-}4$

Numerator The top number on a fraction. It tells you how many parts there are.

Obtuse angle An angle between 90° and 180°.

Obtuse-angled triangle A triangle in which one angle is an obtuse angle.

Parallel Lines that are the same distance apart and will never meet, however long they are.

Perimeter The line around the outside of a plane (2D) shape.

Polygon A plane shape with sides that are straight lines.

3 sides – a triangle	4 sides – a quadrilateral
5 sides – a pentagon	6 sides – a hexagon
7 sides – a heptagon	8 sides – an octagon
9 sides – a nonagon	10 sides – a decagon
12 sides – a dodecagon	20 sides – an icosagon

Power of 10 The numbers that are ten multiplied by itself several times: 10, 100, 1000, 10 000, 100 000, 1 000 000

Prime number A prime number can be divided evenly only by 1, or itself. It must be a whole number greater than 1. For example, 7 can only be divided evenly by 7 or 1, so it is a prime number.

Prime factor   A factor that is a prime number. For example, 2 and 3 are prime factors of 6 because they are prime numbers.

Product   The answer to a multiplication. For example, the product of 3 and 4 is 12

Proper fraction   A fraction where the numerator (top number) is smaller than the denominator (bottom number), for example $\frac{3}{4}$

Protractor   A transparent circular or semi-circular scale, used to measure angles.

Quotient   The whole-number part of an answer to a division calculation. For example, in $25 \div 2 = 12$ remainder 1, 12 is the quotient.

Reflection   How a shape would look if it were seen in a mirror. The resulting shape is its image.

Reflex angle   An angle that is between 180° and 360°.

Remainder   The 'left over' part of a division calculation. For example, $25 \div 2 = 12$ remainder 1

Right angle   An angle that is equal to 90°.

Right-angled triangle   A triangle in which one of the angles is 90°.

Round   Write a number so that it is not exact but is a close approximation. A number can be rounded to the nearest whole number, ten, hundred thousand, etc. or to one, two, three or more decimal places. For example, 239 is 240 to the nearest ten; 3.2546 is 3.3, correct to one decimal place.

Round down   Round a number to an approximation that is smaller than the number.

Round up   Round a number to an approximation that is larger than the number.

Scalene triangle   A triangle with three sides of different lengths and three angles of different sizes.

Square number   The result of multiplying a number by itself. For example, $4 \times 4 = 16$ so 16 is a square number.

Square root   A factor of a number that can be multiplied by itself to give the number. For example, $16 = 4 \times 4$, so 4 is the square root of 16.

Sum   The answer to an addition calculation. For example, the sum of 3 and 4 is 7.

Translation   The description of how an object is moved, first along and then up or down, to make an image.

Index

One aspect of architecture that raises an ethical dilemma is that of sheer scale and therefore the environmental impact of the materials and energy required to create and use buildings. Construction of buildings and their use account for around half of all greenhouse gas emissions and energy consumed in the US each year. Waste from the construction industry in the UK is three times that of waste from all domestic use and many building materials are considered hazardous and require specialist waste treatments.

As the people who create the early stage designs for buildings before construction takes place, architects are well placed to realise buildings that operate with less energy and use less materials. This can be accomplished through a great number of approaches; from proper siting, material selection or day-lighting strategies. But how much responsibility should an architect have for the impacts of buildings when they work alongside town planners, housing developers or building regulators? Is it up to these people to request and plan for more sustainable architecture or should architects have the influence and inclination to change to the way we live?

The mid-nineteenth century saw the rise in state-supported treatment of the mentally ill in the US and consequently, there was a rise in the building of public 'lunatic asylums'. Dr Thomas Story Kirkbride was a founding member of the Association of Medical Superintendents of American Institutions for the Insane (AMSAII). He promoted a standardised method of asylum construction and mental health treatment, known as the 'Kirkbride Plan'. The first asylum opened in New Jersey in 1847.

The building itself was meant to have a curative effect and was considered 'a special apparatus for the care of lunacy'. Each building followed the same basic floor plan described as a 'shallow V', where central administration buildings were flanked by two wings of tiered wards. Wards were to be short enough that a breeze of fresh air could be carried through them and have spacious windows to let in light. Wards for the most difficult patients had single corridors, which made surveillance easier and security better. At a time when few private homes had central heating, gas or toilets, Kirkbride Buildings incorporated gas lamps in each room, central water tanks above the administration centre, and boilers in the basements that heated air to be pumped into wards.

Your specifications
What are the impacts of your materials?

In relatively recent times, we are learning that many natural materials are in short supply. At the same time, we are increasingly aware that some man-made materials can have harmful, long-term effects on people or the planet. How much do you know about the materials that you use? Do you know where they come from, how far they travel and under what conditions they are obtained? When your creation is no longer needed, will it be easy and safe to recycle? Will it disappear without a trace? Are these considerations your responsibility or are they out of your hands?

Using the scale, mark how ethical your material choices are.

Your creation
What is the purpose of your work?

Between you, your colleagues and an agreed brief, what will your creation achieve? What purpose will it have in society and will it make a positive contribution? Should your work result in more than commercial success or industry awards? Might your creation help save lives, educate, protect or inspire? Form and function are two established aspects of judging a creation, but there is little consensus on the obligations of visual artists and communicators toward society, or the role they might have in solving social or environmental problems. If you want recognition for being the creator, how responsible are you for what you create and where might that responsibility end?

Using the scale, mark how ethical the purpose of your work is.

01 02 03 04 05 06 07 08 09 10

01 02 03 04 05 06 07 08 09 10

You
What are your ethical beliefs?

Central to everything you do will be your attitude to people and issues around you. For some people, their ethics are an active part of the decisions they make every day as a consumer, a voter or a working professional. Others may think about ethics very little and yet this does not automatically make them unethical. Personal beliefs, lifestyle, politics, nationality, religion, gender, class or education can all influence your ethical viewpoint.

Using the scale, where would you place yourself? What do you take into account to make your decision? Compare results with your friends or colleagues.

Your client
What are your terms?

Working relationships are central to whether ethics can be embedded into a project, and your conduct on a day-to-day basis is a demonstration of your professional ethics. The decision with the biggest impact is whom you choose to work with in the first place. Cigarette companies or arms traders are often-cited examples when talking about where a line might be drawn, but rarely are real situations so extreme. At what point might you turn down a project on ethical grounds and how much does the reality of having to earn a living affect your ability to choose?

Using the scale, where would you place a project? How does this compare to your personal ethical level?

01 02 03 04 05 06 07 08 09 10

01 02 03 04 05 06 07 08 09 10

Some ethical considerations are already enshrined in government laws and regulations or in professional codes of conduct. For example, plagiarism and breaches of confidentiality can be punishable offences. Legislation in various nations makes it unlawful to exclude people with disabilities from accessing information or spaces. The trade of ivory as a material has been banned in many countries. In these cases, a clear line has been drawn under what is unacceptable.

But most ethical matters remain open to debate, among experts and lay-people alike, and in the end we have to make our own choices on the basis of our own guiding principles or values. Is it more ethical to work for a charity than for a commercial company? Is it unethical to create something that others find ugly or offensive?

Specific questions such as these may lead to other questions that are more abstract. For example, is it only effects on humans (and what they care about) that are important, or might effects on the natural world require attention too?

Is promoting ethical consequences justified even when it requires ethical sacrifices along the way? Must there be a single unifying theory of ethics (such as the Utilitarian thesis that the right course of action is always the one that leads to the greatest happiness of the greatest number), or might there always be many different ethical values that pull a person in various directions?

As we enter into ethical debate and engage with these dilemmas on a personal and professional level, we may change our views or change our view of others. The real test though is whether, as we reflect on these matters, we change the way we act as well as the way we think. Socrates, the 'father' of philosophy, proposed that people will naturally do 'good' if they know what is right. But this point might only lead us to yet another question: *how do we know what is right?*